EIGHT-LANE RUNAWAYS

HENRY McCAUSLAND

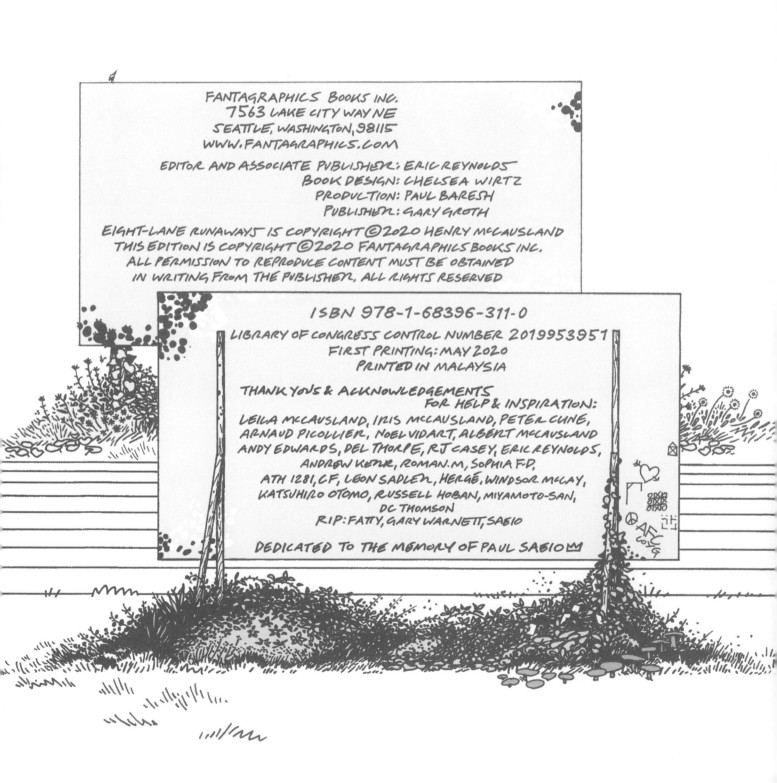

FANTAGRAPHICS BOOKS INC.
7563 LAKE CITY WAY NE
SEATTLE, WASHINGTON, 98115
WWW.FANTAGRAPHICS.COM
EDITOR AND ASSOCIATE PUBLISHER: ERIC REYNOLDS
BOOK DESIGN: CHELSEA WIRTZ
PRODUCTION: PAUL BARESH
PUBLISHER: GARY GROTH
EIGHT-LANE RUNAWAYS IS COPYRIGHT © 2020 HENRY McCAUSLAND
THIS EDITION IS COPYRIGHT © 2020 FANTAGRAPHICS BOOKS INC.
ALL PERMISSION TO REPRODUCE CONTENT MUST BE OBTAINED
IN WRITING FROM THE PUBLISHER. ALL RIGHTS RESERVED
ISBN 978-1-68396-311-0
LIBRARY OF CONGRESS CONTROL NUMBER 2019953951
FIRST PRINTING: MAY 2020
PRINTED IN MALAYSIA
THANK YOUS & ACKNOWLEDGEMENTS
FOR HELP & INSPIRATION:
LEILA McCAUSLAND, IRIS McCAUSLAND, PETER CUNE,
ARNAUD PICOLLIER, NOEL VIDART, ALBERT McCAUSLAND
ANDY EDWARDS, DEL THORPE, RJ CASEY, ERIC REYNOLDS,
ANDREW KEHR, ROMAN.M, SOPHIA F-D,
ATH 1281, CF, LEON SADLER, HERGÉ, WINDSOR McCAY,
KATSUHIRO OTOMO, RUSSELL HOBAN, MIYAMOTO-SAN,
DC THOMSON
RIP: FATTY, GARY WARNETT, SABIO
DEDICATED TO THE MEMORY OF PAUL SABIO

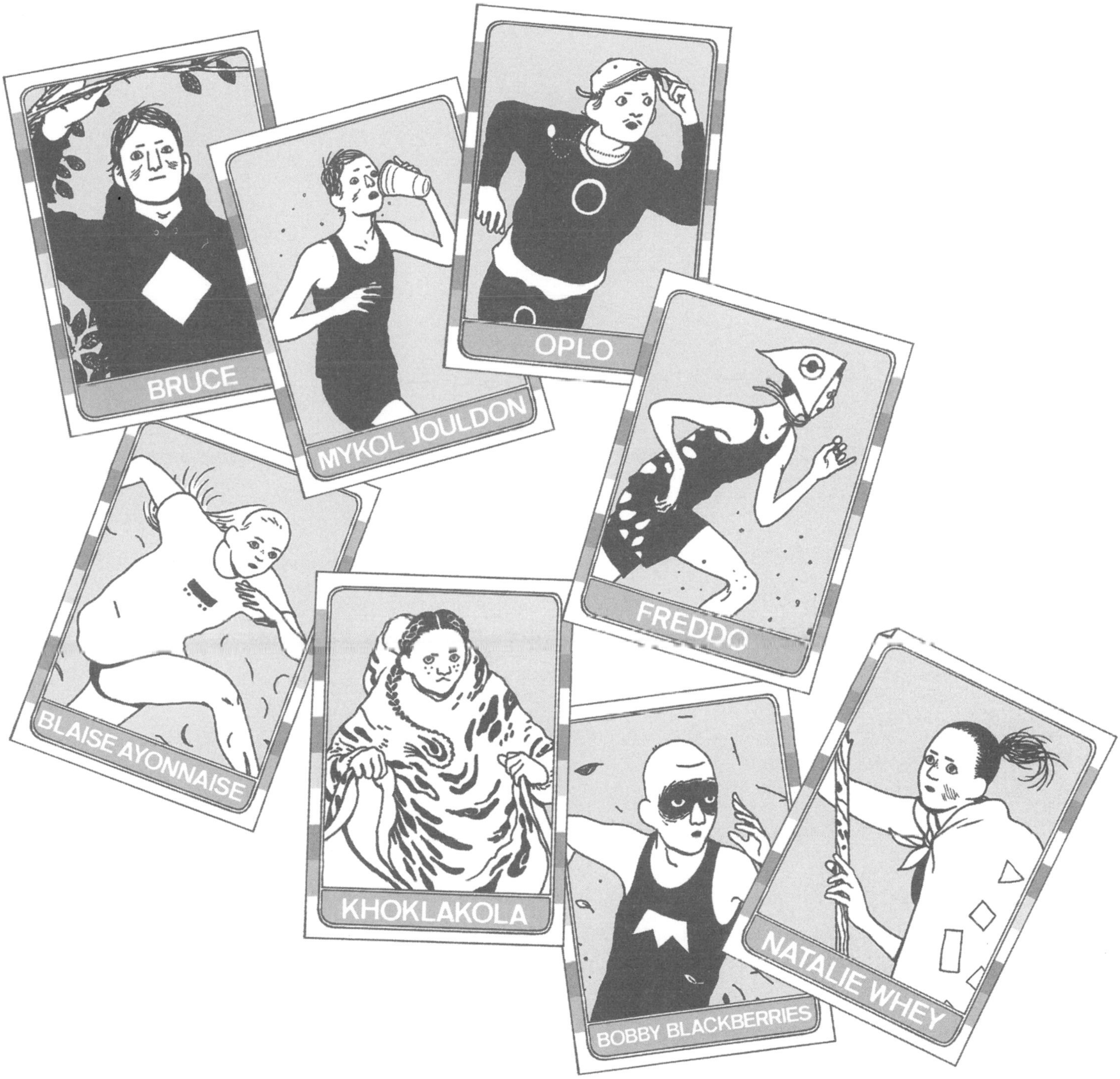
BRUCE
MYKOL JOULDON
OPLO
FREDDO
BLAISE AYONNAISE
KHOKLAKOLA
BOBBY BLACKBERRIES
NATALIE WHEY

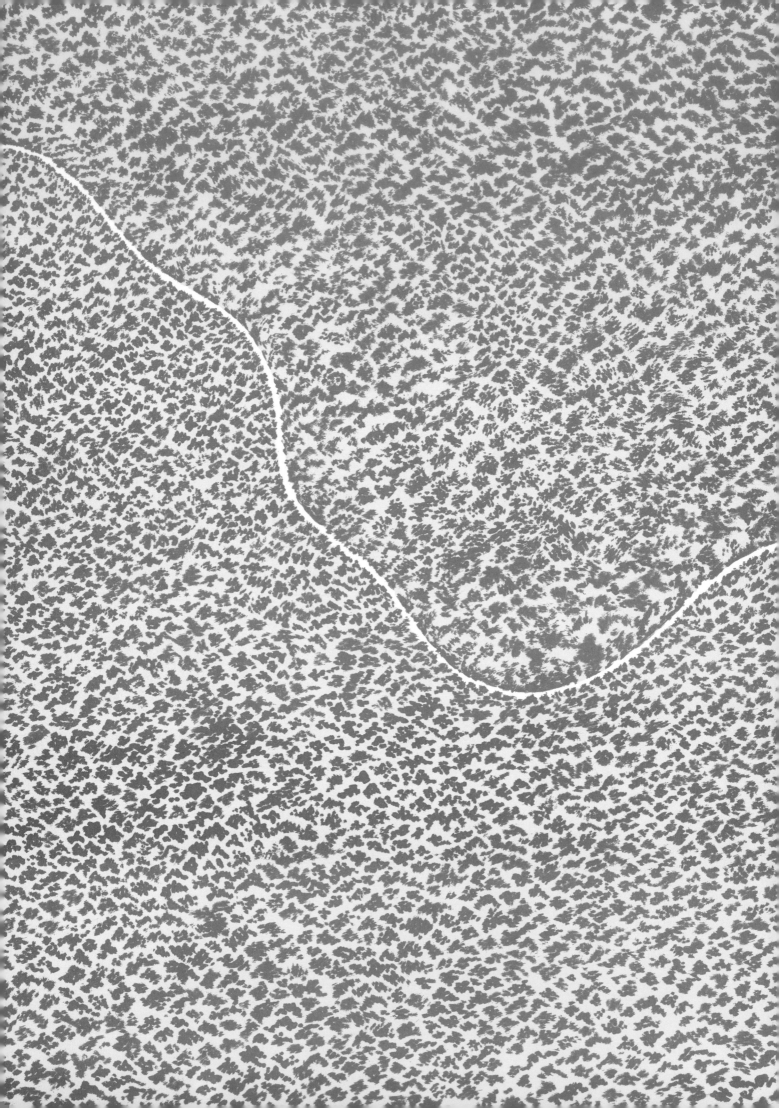

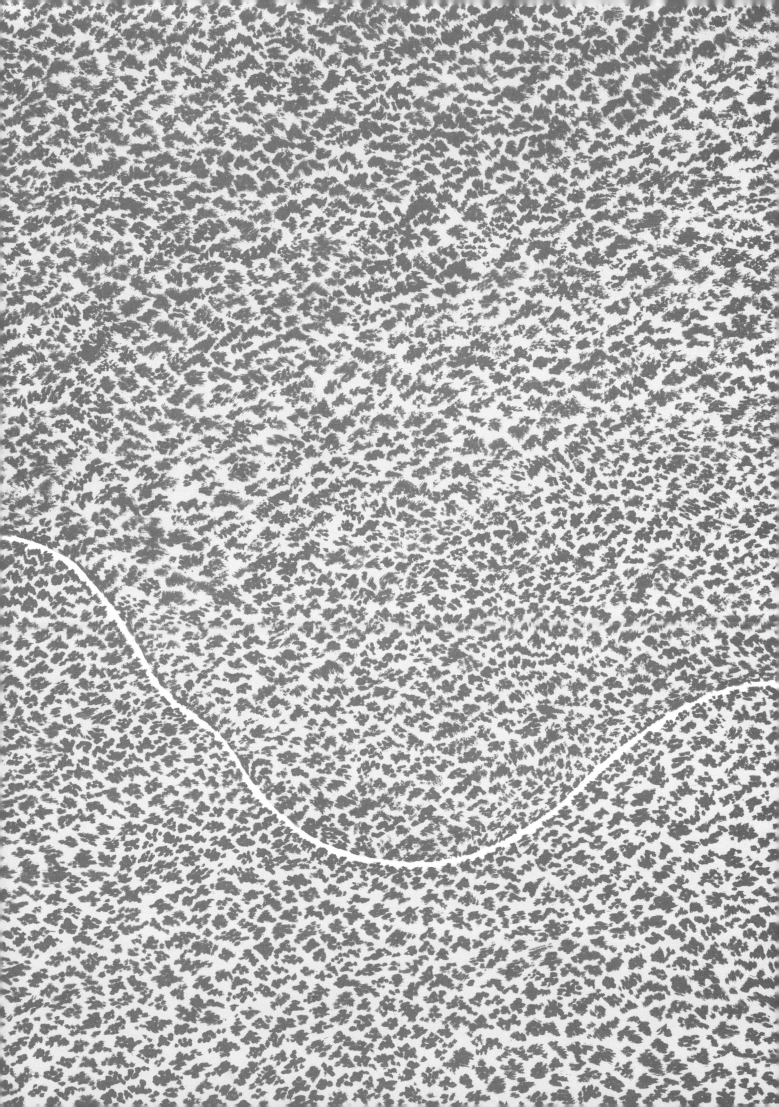

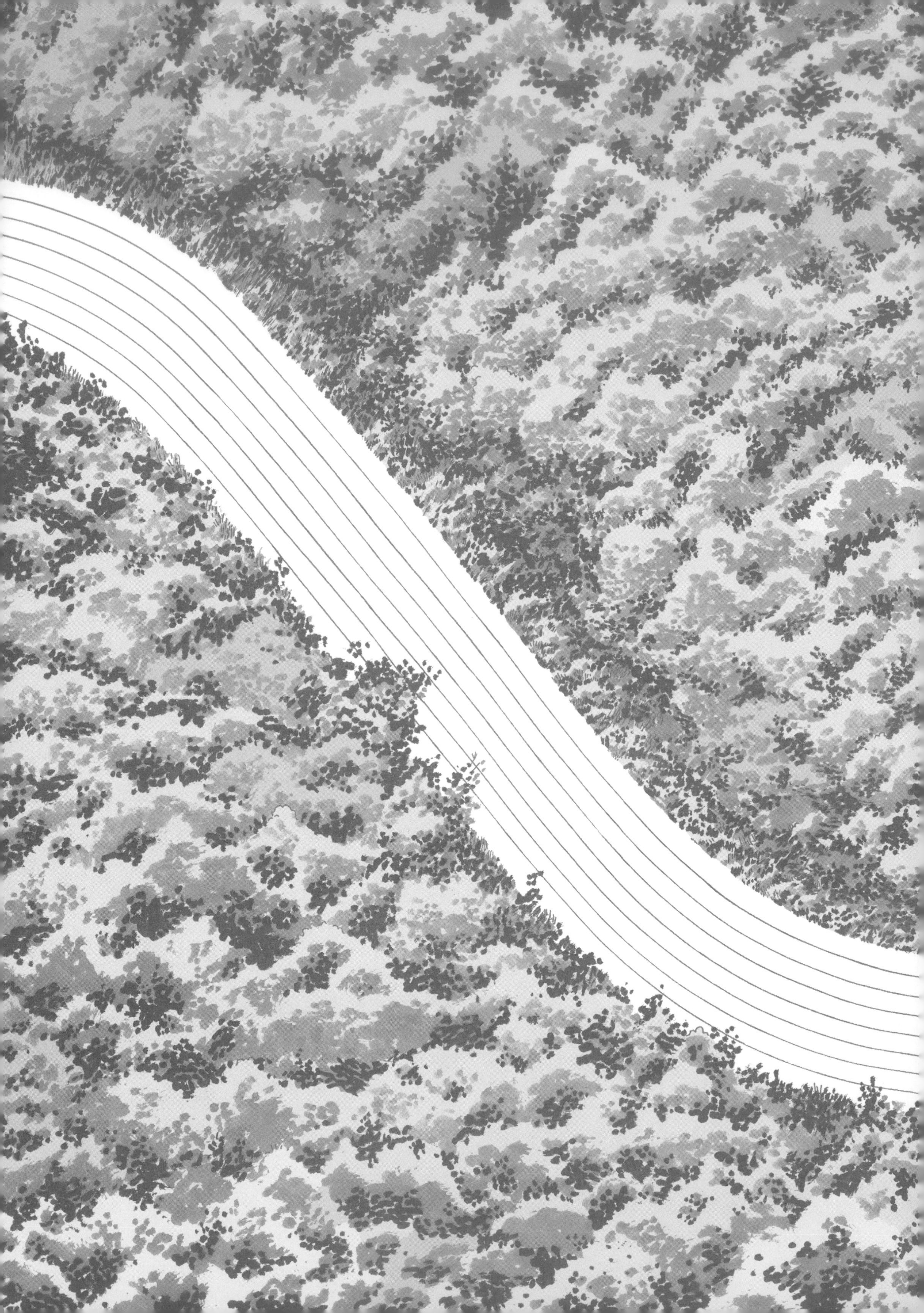

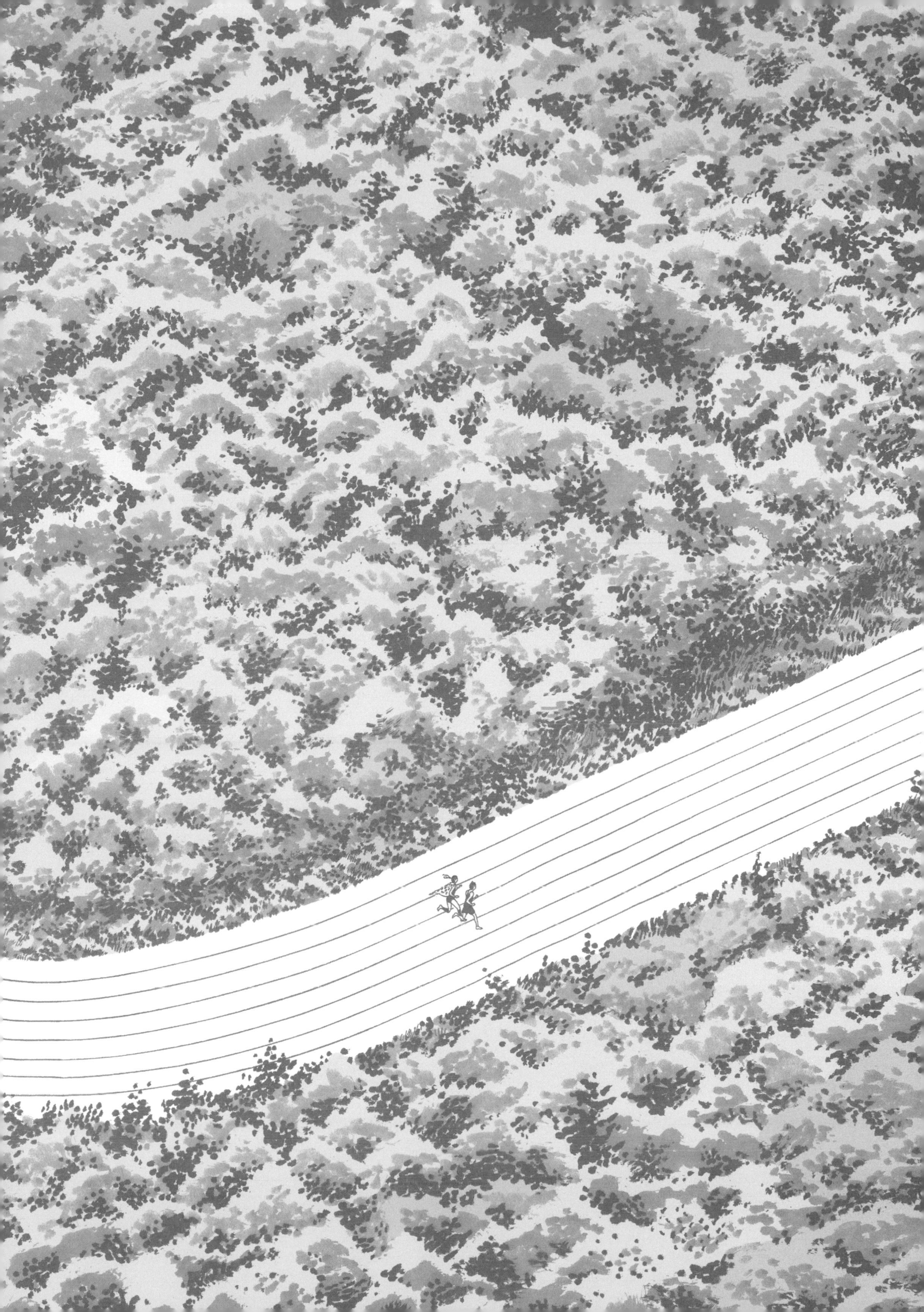

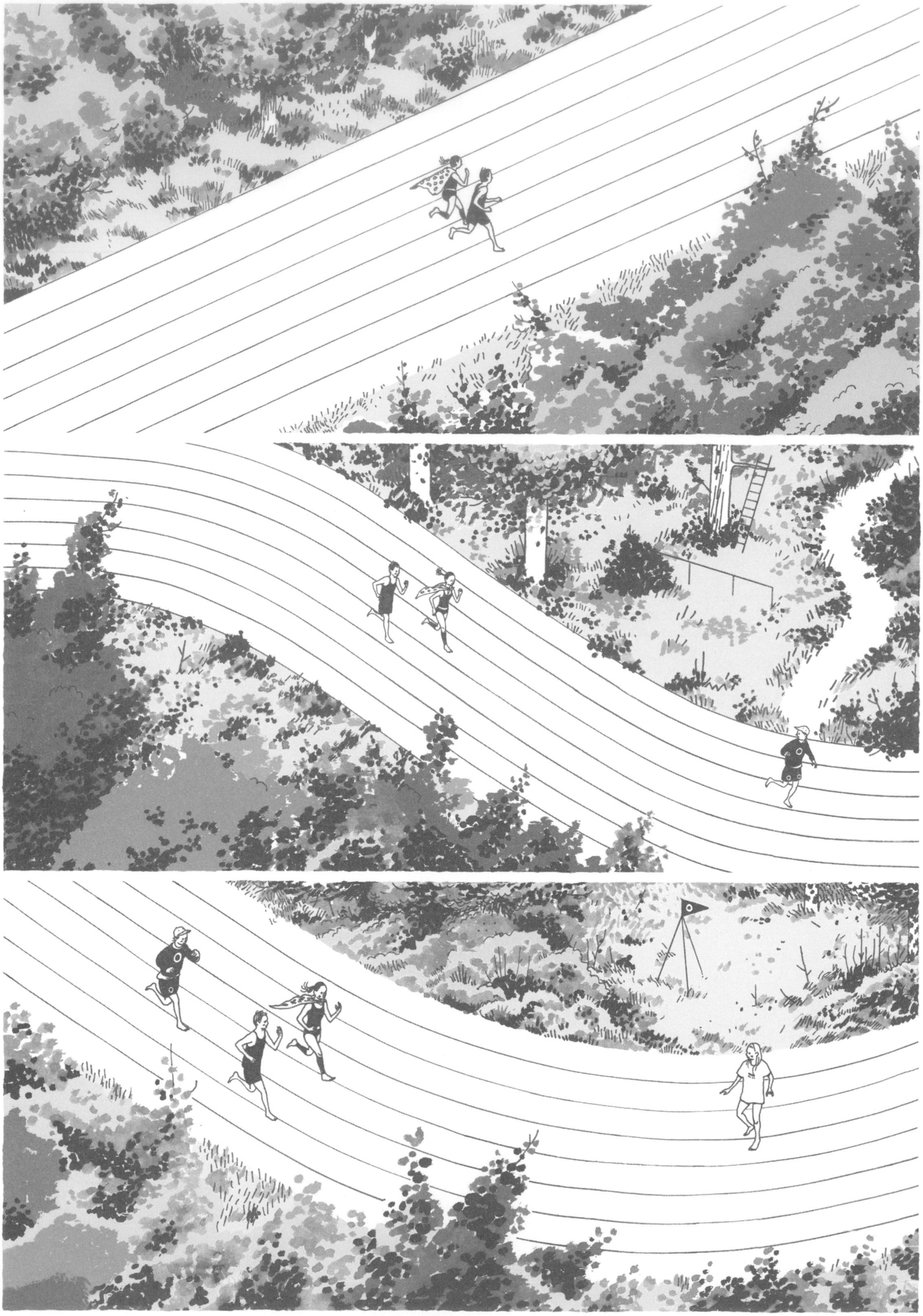

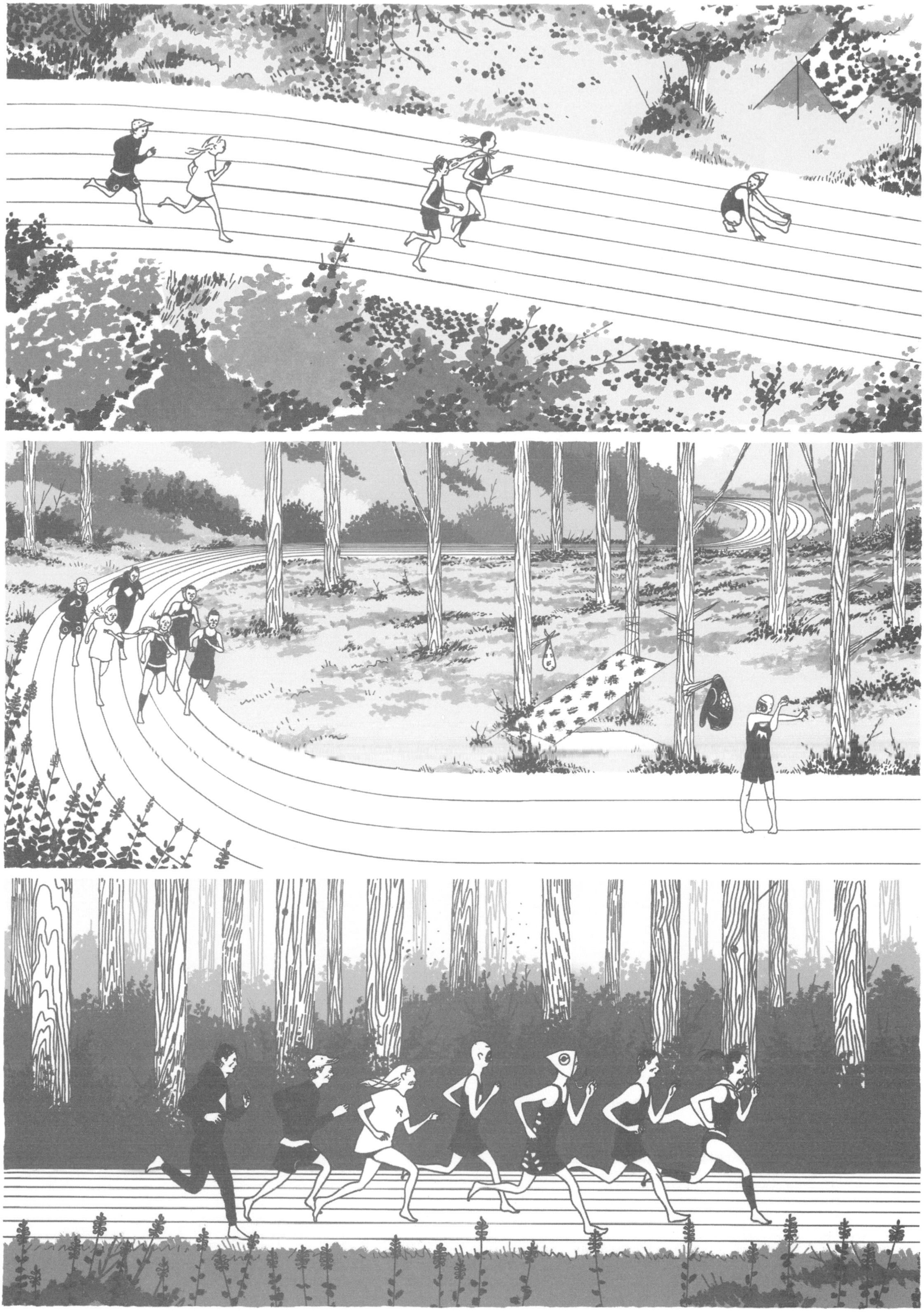

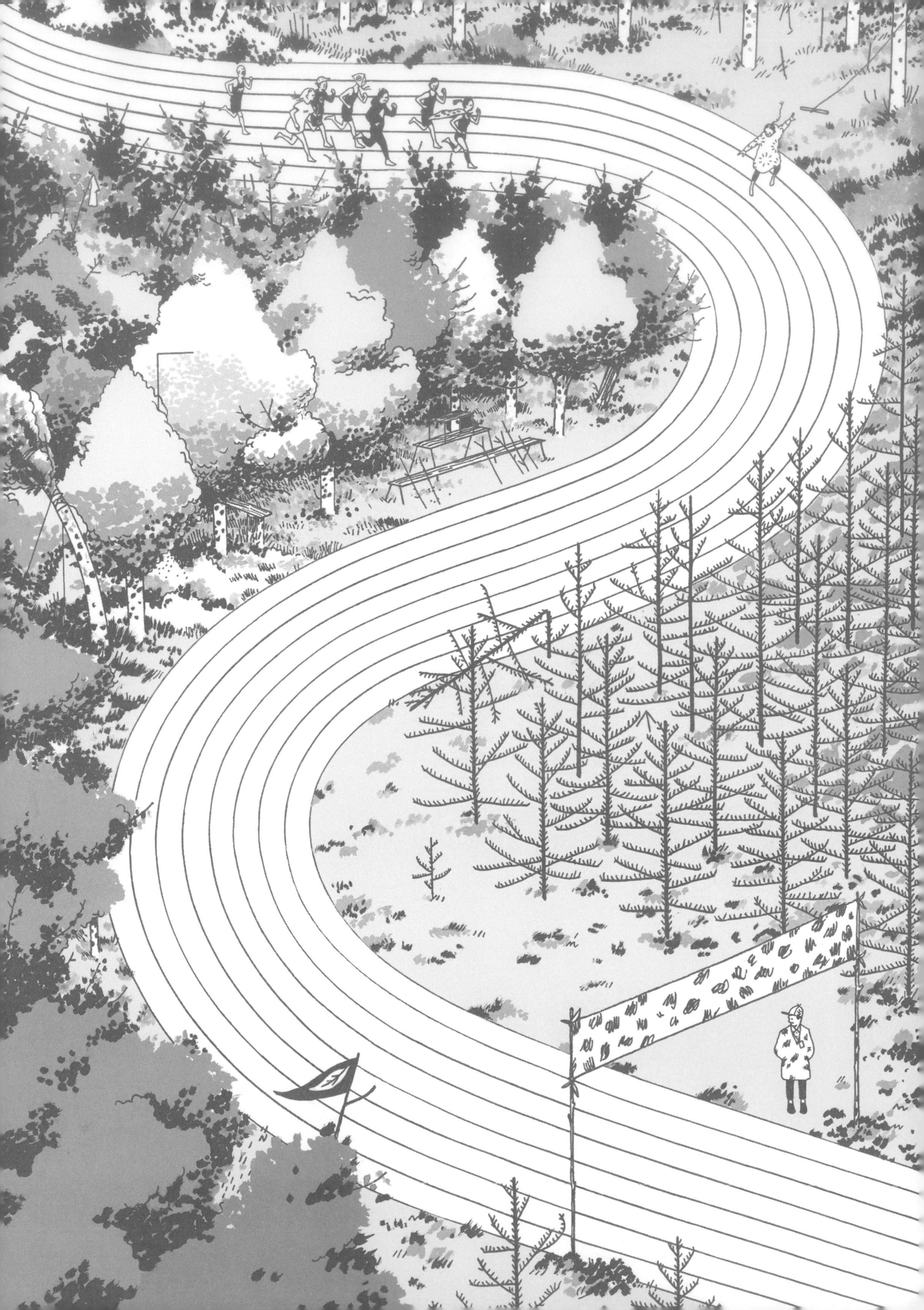

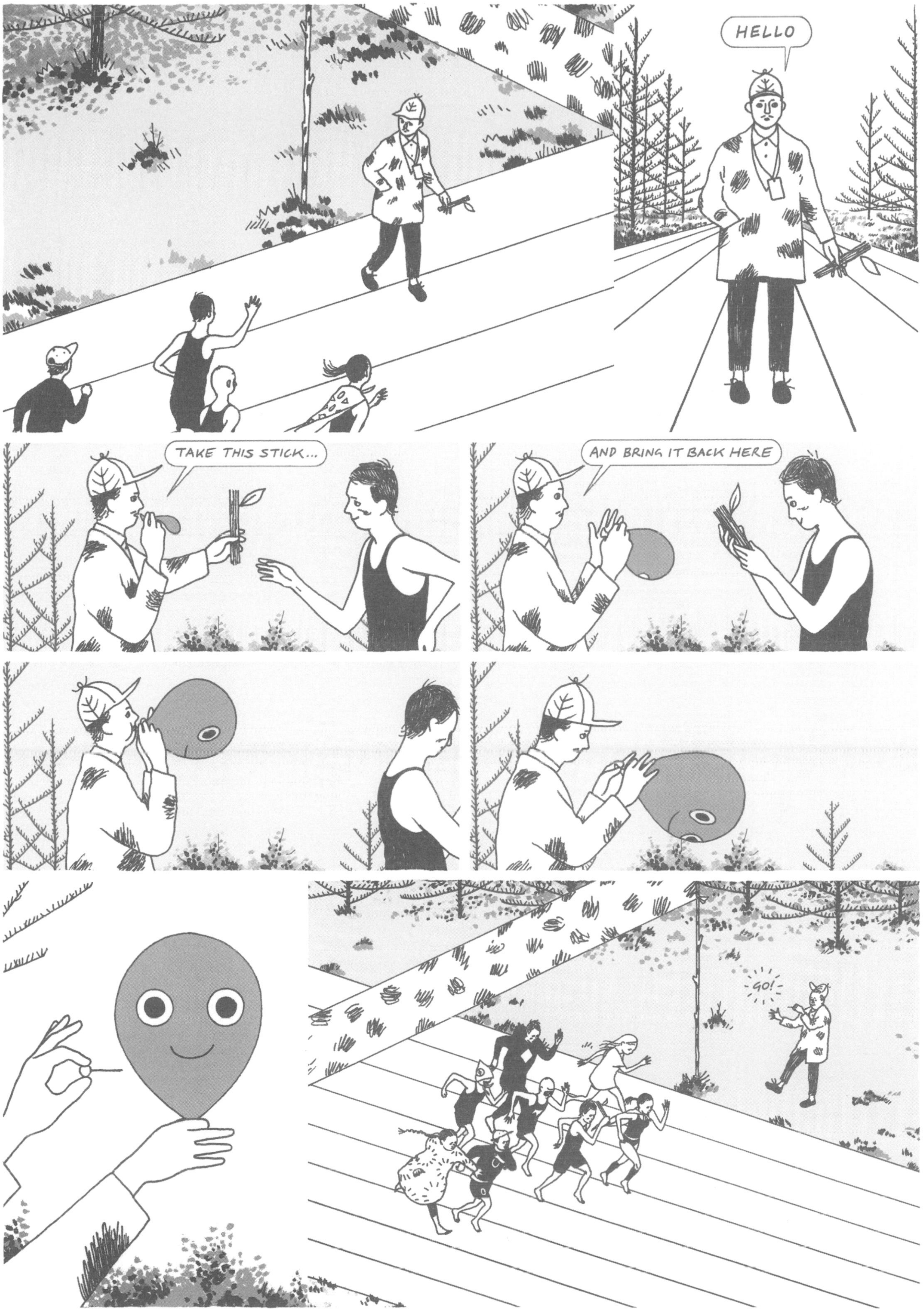
HELLO
TAKE THIS STICK...
AND BRING IT BACK HERE
GO!

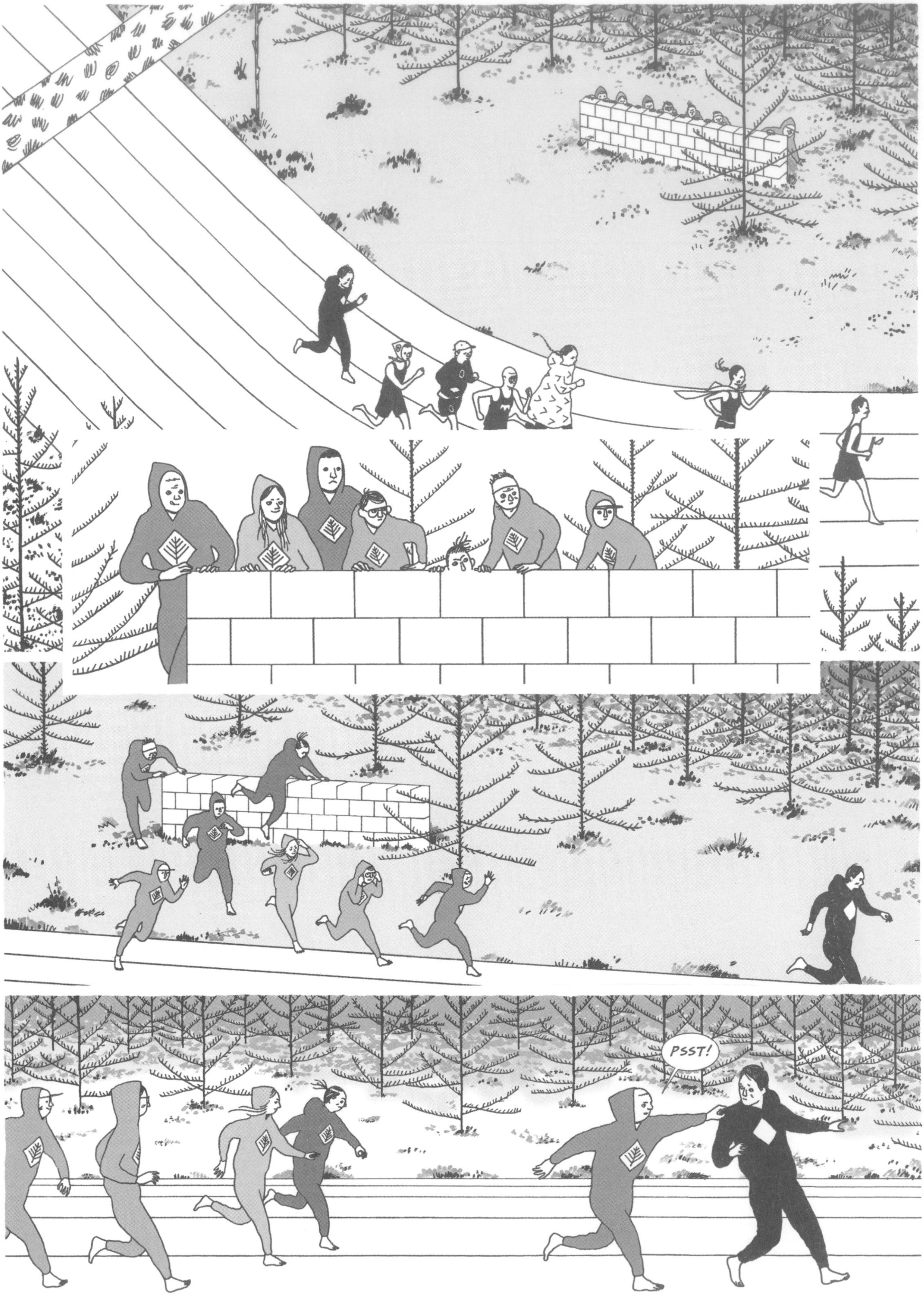
PSST!

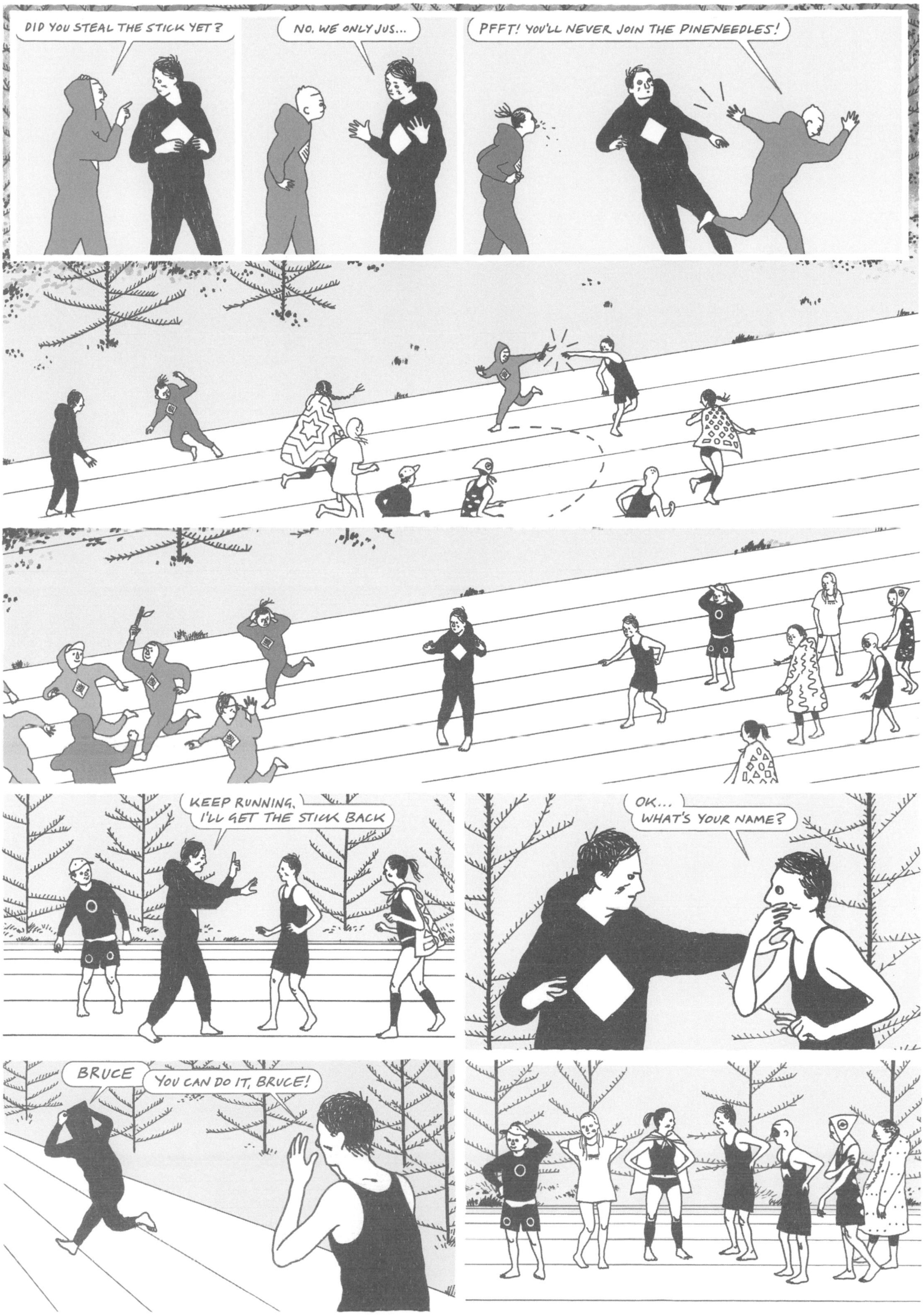
DID YOU STEAL THE STICK YET?
NO. WE ONLY JUS...
PFFT! YOU'LL NEVER JOIN THE PINENEEDLES!
KEEP RUNNING. I'LL GET THE STICK BACK
OK... WHAT'S YOUR NAME?
BRUCE
YOU CAN DO IT, BRUCE!

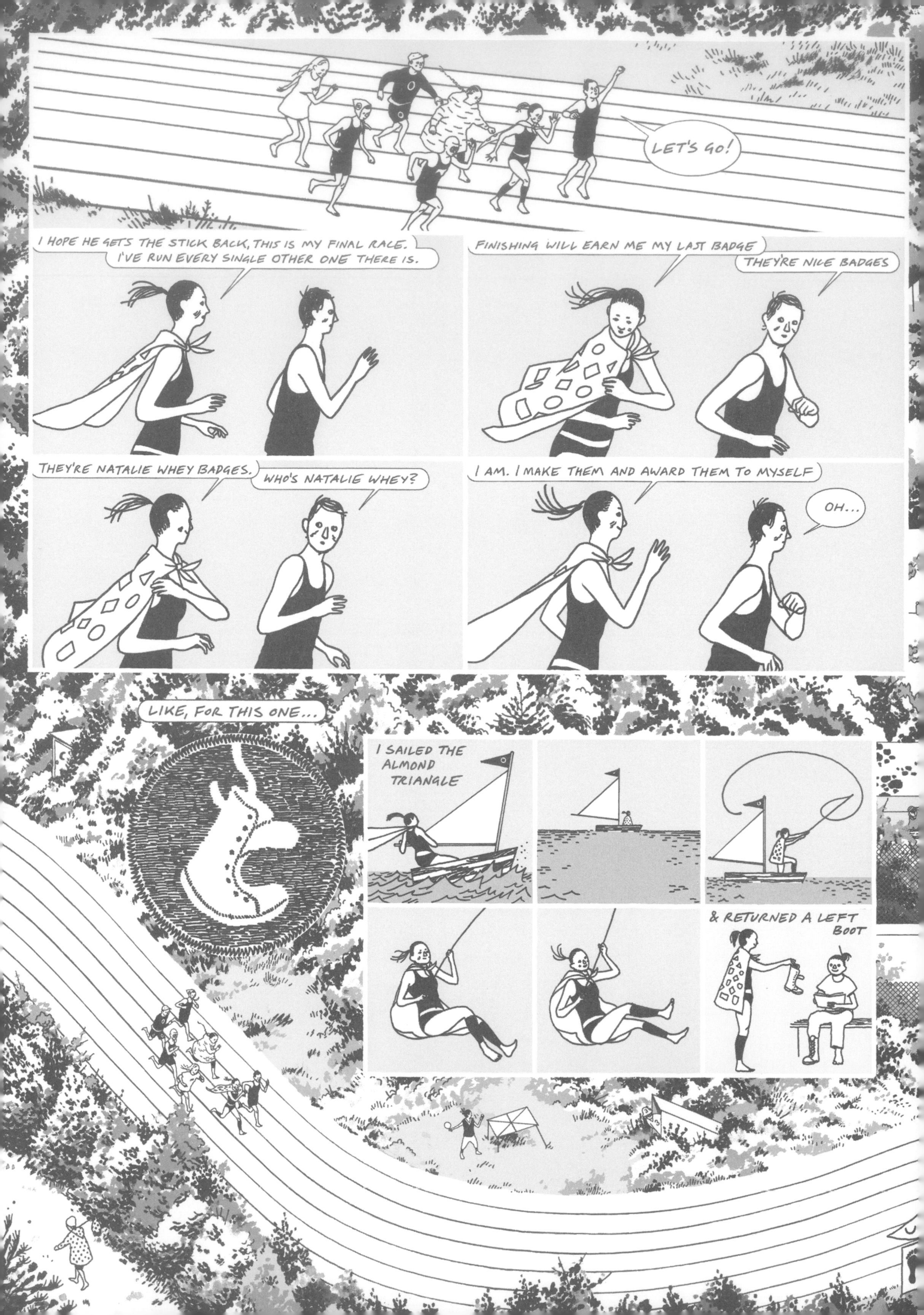
LET'S GO!
I HOPE HE GETS THE STICK BACK, THIS IS MY FINAL RACE.
I'VE RUN EVERY SINGLE OTHER ONE THERE IS.
FINISHING WILL EARN ME MY LAST BADGE
THEY'RE NICE BADGES
THEY'RE NATALIE WHEY BADGES.
WHO'S NATALIE WHEY?
I AM. I MAKE THEM AND AWARD THEM TO MYSELF
OH...
LIKE, FOR THIS ONE...
I SAILED THE ALMOND TRIANGLE
& RETURNED A LEFT BOOT

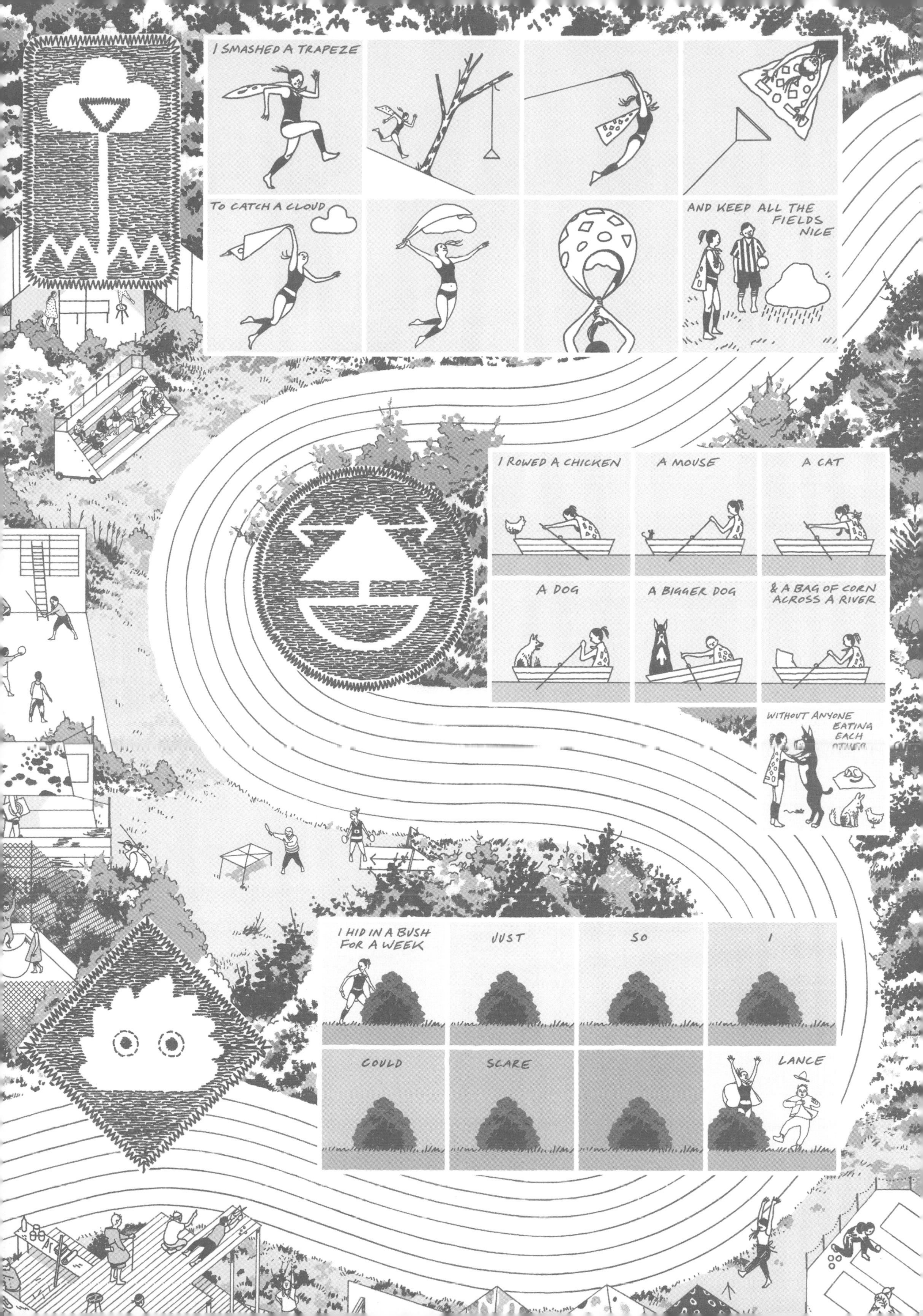
I SMASHED A TRAPEZE
TO CATCH A CLOUD
AND KEEP ALL THE FIELDS NICE
I ROWED A CHICKEN
A MOUSE
A CAT
A DOG
A BIGGER DOG
& A BAG OF CORN ACROSS A RIVER
WITHOUT ANYONE EATING EACH OTHER
I HID IN A BUSH FOR A WEEK
JUST
SO
I
COULD
SCARE
LANCE

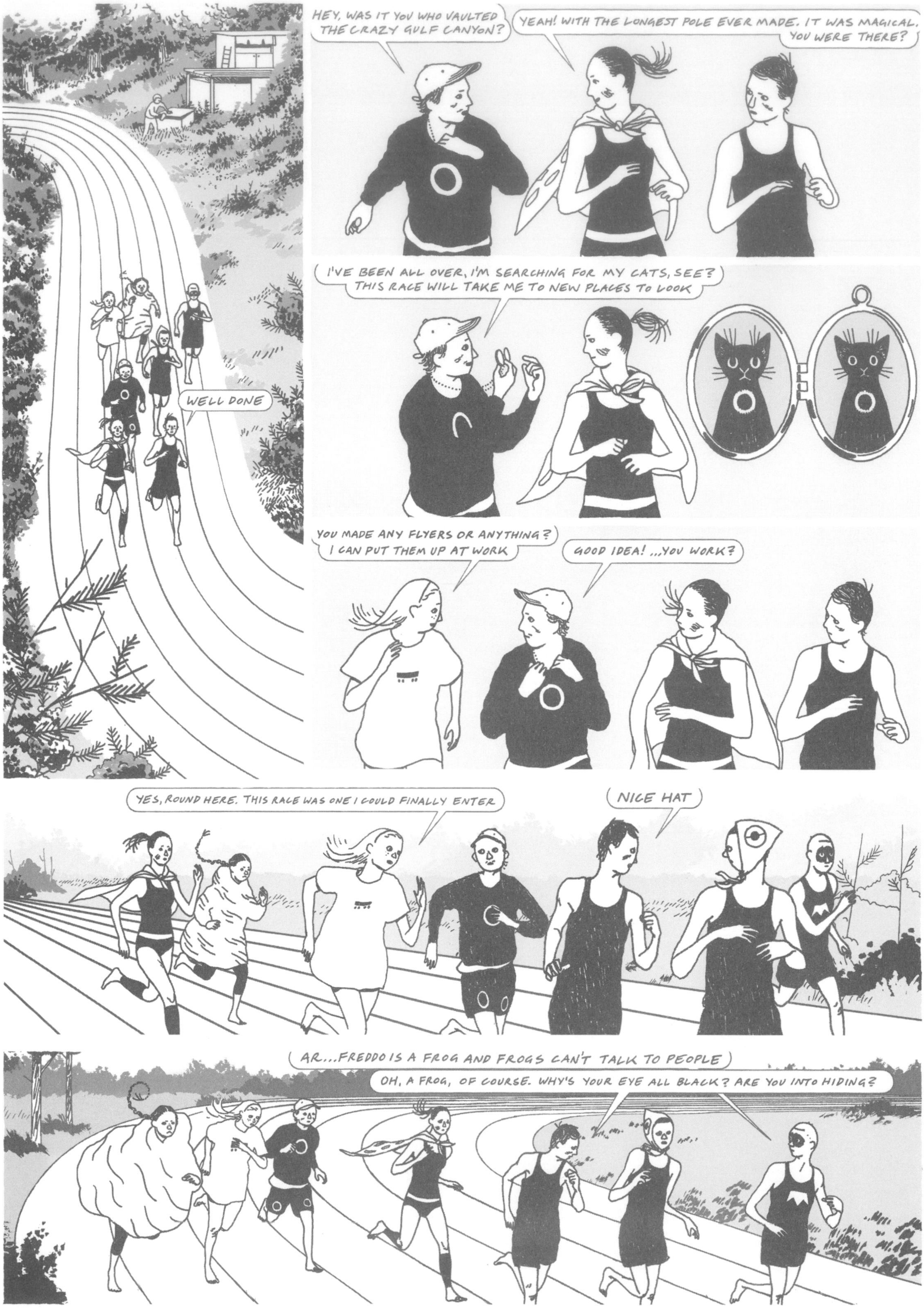
WELL DONE
HEY, WAS IT YOU WHO VAULTED THE CRAZY GULF CANYON?
YEAH! WITH THE LONGEST POLE EVER MADE. IT WAS MAGICAL. YOU WERE THERE?
I'VE BEEN ALL OVER, I'M SEARCHING FOR MY CATS, SEE? THIS RACE WILL TAKE ME TO NEW PLACES TO LOOK
YOU MADE ANY FLYERS OR ANYTHING? I CAN PUT THEM UP AT WORK
GOOD IDEA! ...YOU WORK?
YES, ROUND HERE. THIS RACE WAS ONE I COULD FINALLY ENTER
NICE HAT
AR...FREDDO IS A FROG AND FROGS CAN'T TALK TO PEOPLE
OH, A FROG, OF COURSE. WHY'S YOUR EYE ALL BLACK? ARE YOU INTO HIDING?

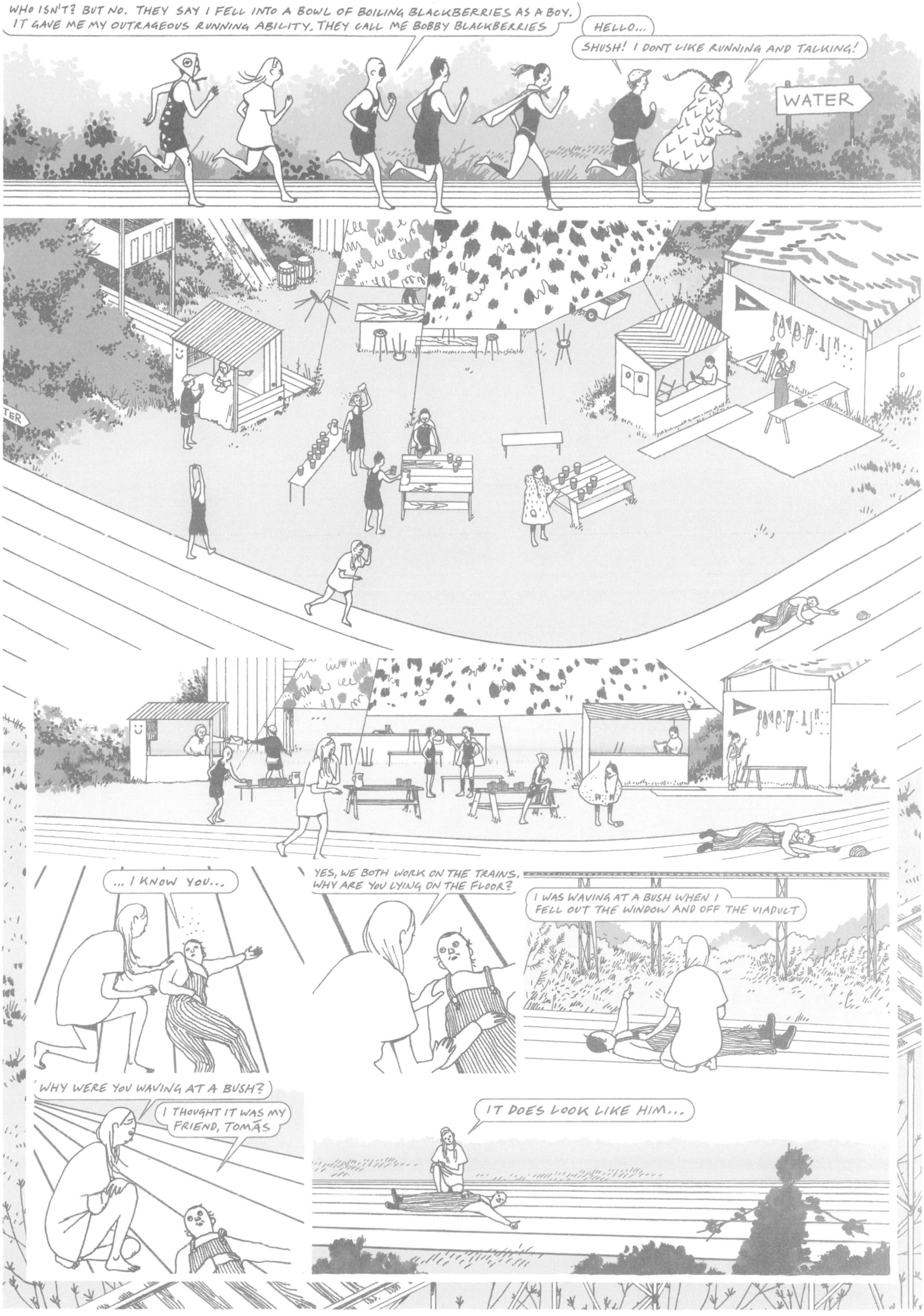
WHO ISN'T? BUT NO. THEY SAY I FELL INTO A BOWL OF BOILING BLACKBERRIES AS A BOY. IT GAVE ME MY OUTRAGEOUS RUNNING ABILITY. THEY CALL ME BOBBY BLACKBERRIES
HELLO...
SHUSH! I DONT LIKE RUNNING AND TALKING!
WATER
...I KNOW YOU...
YES, WE BOTH WORK ON THE TRAINS. WHY ARE YOU LYING ON THE FLOOR?
I WAS WAVING AT A BUSH WHEN I FELL OUT THE WINDOW AND OFF THE VIADUCT
WHY WERE YOU WAVING AT A BUSH?
I THOUGHT IT WAS MY FRIEND, TOMÁS
IT DOES LOOK LIKE HIM...

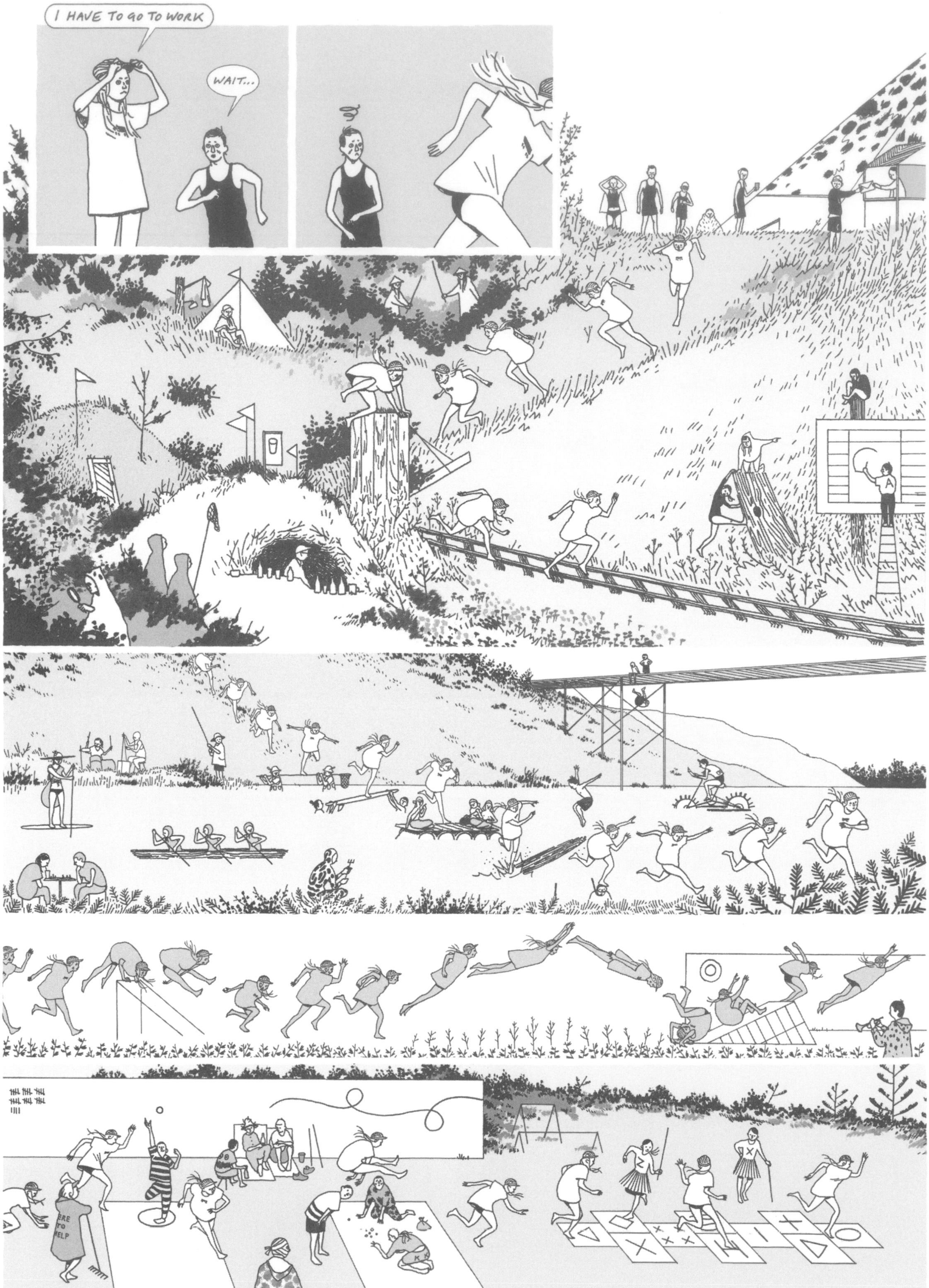
I HAVE TO GO TO WORK
WAIT...

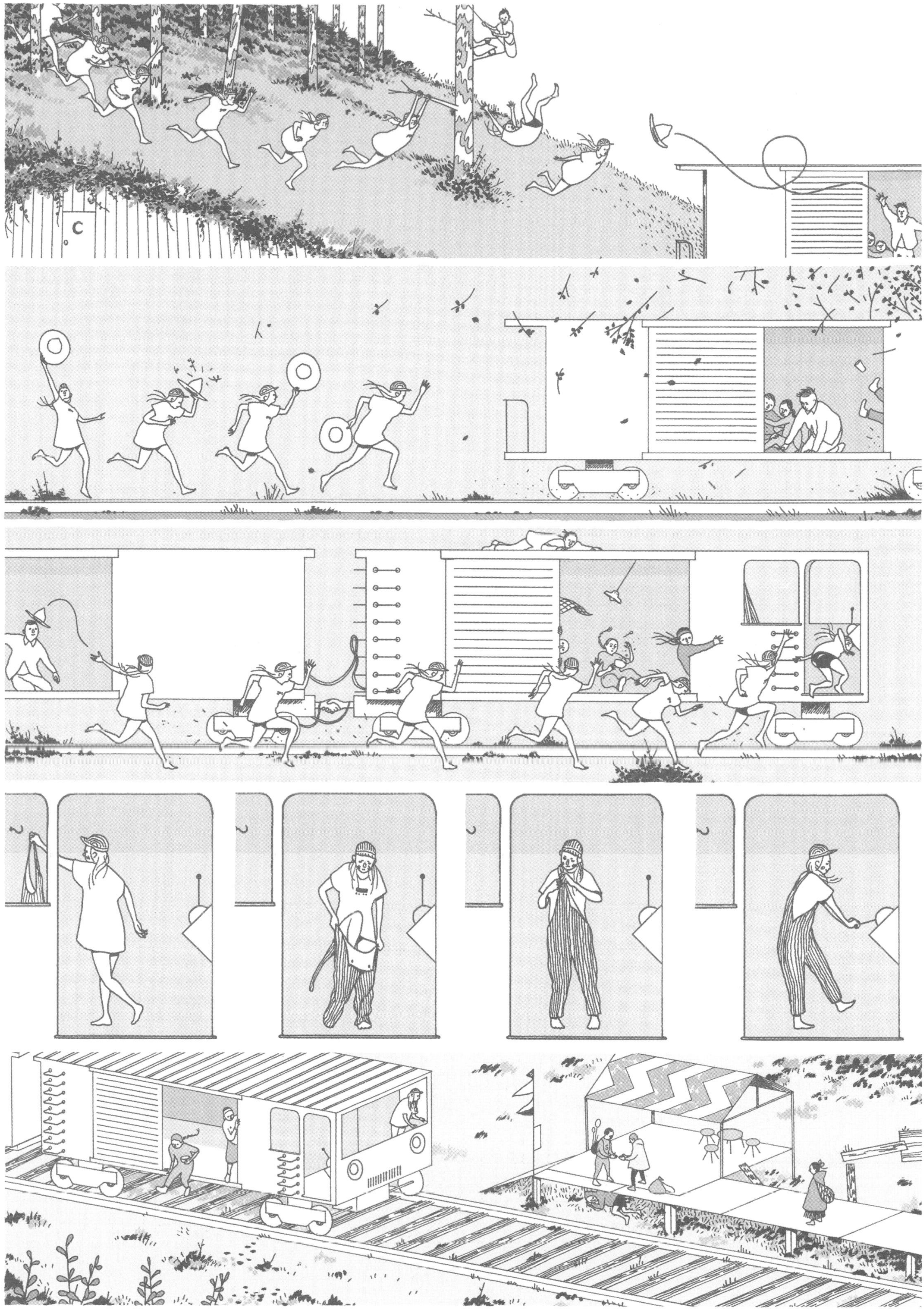
C

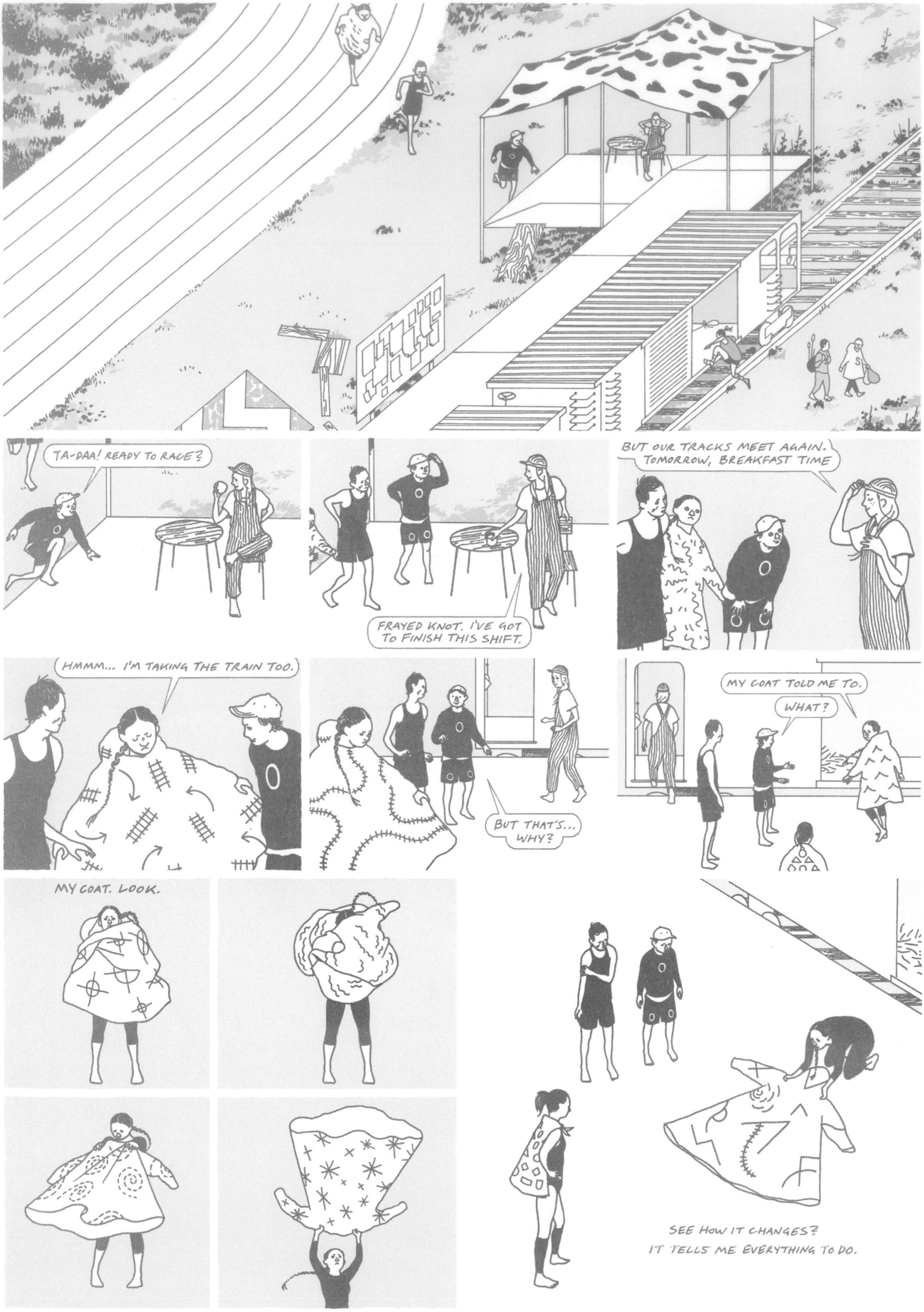
TA-DAA! READY TO RACE?
FRAYED KNOT. I'VE GOT TO FINISH THIS SHIFT.
BUT OUR TRACKS MEET AGAIN. TOMORROW, BREAKFAST TIME
HMMM... I'M TAKING THE TRAIN TOO.
BUT THAT'S... WHY?
MY COAT TOLD ME TO.
WHAT?
MY COAT. LOOK.
SEE HOW IT CHANGES?
IT TELLS ME EVERYTHING TO DO.

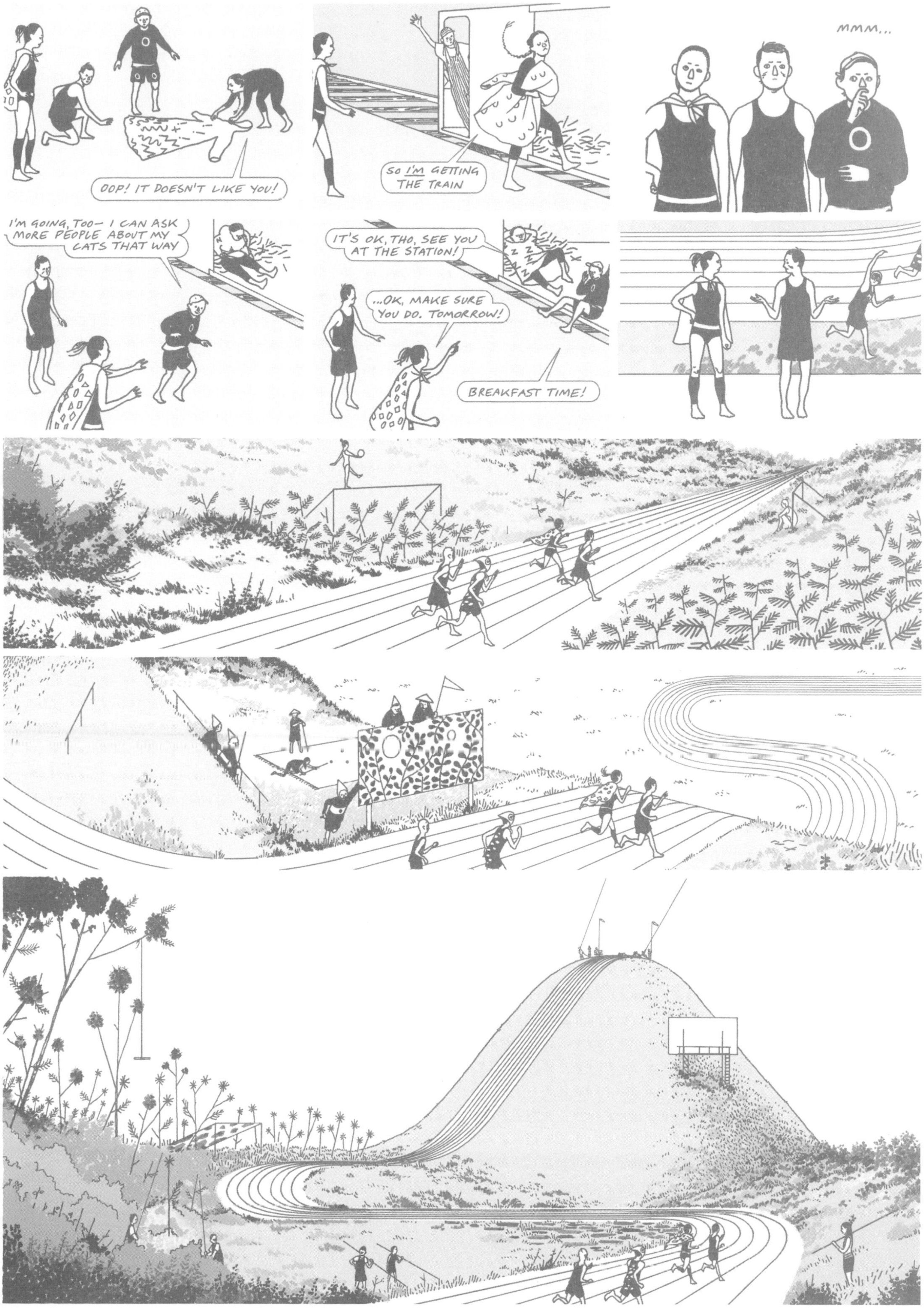
OOP! IT DOESN'T LIKE YOU!
SO I'M GETTING THE TRAIN
MMM...
I'M GOING, TOO— I CAN ASK MORE PEOPLE ABOUT MY CATS THAT WAY
IT'S OK, THO, SEE YOU AT THE STATION!
...OK, MAKE SURE YOU DO. TOMORROW!
BREAKFAST TIME!

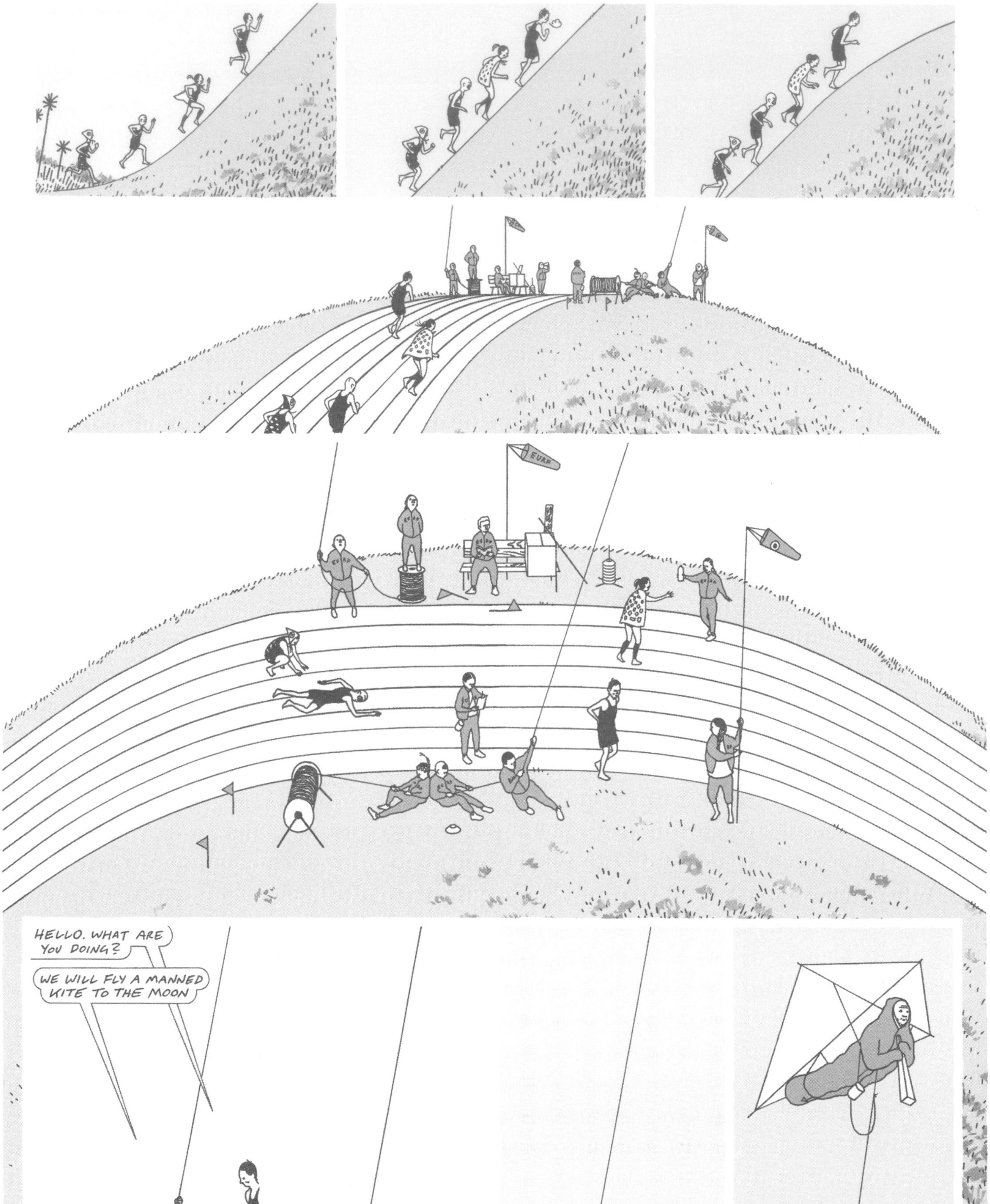
HELLO. WHAT ARE YOU DOING?
WE WILL FLY A MANNED KITE TO THE MOON

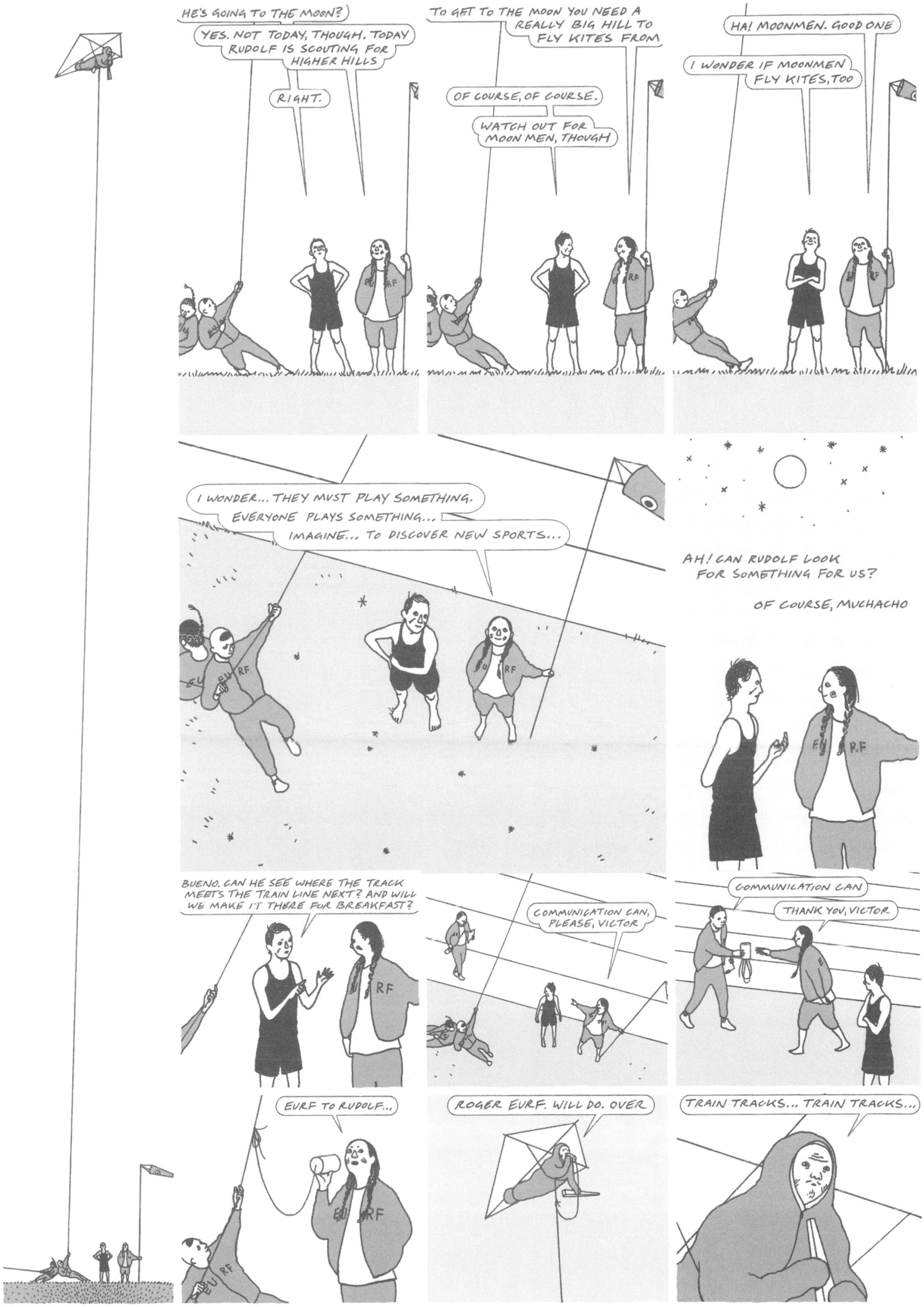

HE'S GOING TO THE MOON?
YES. NOT TODAY, THOUGH. TODAY RUDOLF IS SCOUTING FOR HIGHER HILLS
RIGHT.
TO GET TO THE MOON YOU NEED A REALLY BIG HILL TO FLY KITES FROM
OF COURSE, OF COURSE.
WATCH OUT FOR MOON MEN, THOUGH
HA! MOONMEN. GOOD ONE
I WONDER IF MOONMEN FLY KITES, TOO
I WONDER... THEY MUST PLAY SOMETHING.
EVERYONE PLAYS SOMETHING...
IMAGINE... TO DISCOVER NEW SPORTS...
AH! CAN RUDOLF LOOK FOR SOMETHING FOR US?
OF COURSE, MUCHACHO
BUENO. CAN HE SEE WHERE THE TRACK MEETS THE TRAIN LINE NEXT? AND WILL WE MAKE IT THERE FOR BREAKFAST?
COMMUNICATION CAN, PLEASE, VICTOR
COMMUNICATION CAN
THANK YOU, VICTOR
EURF TO RUDOLF...
ROGER EURF. WILL DO. OVER
TRAIN TRACKS... TRAIN TRACKS...

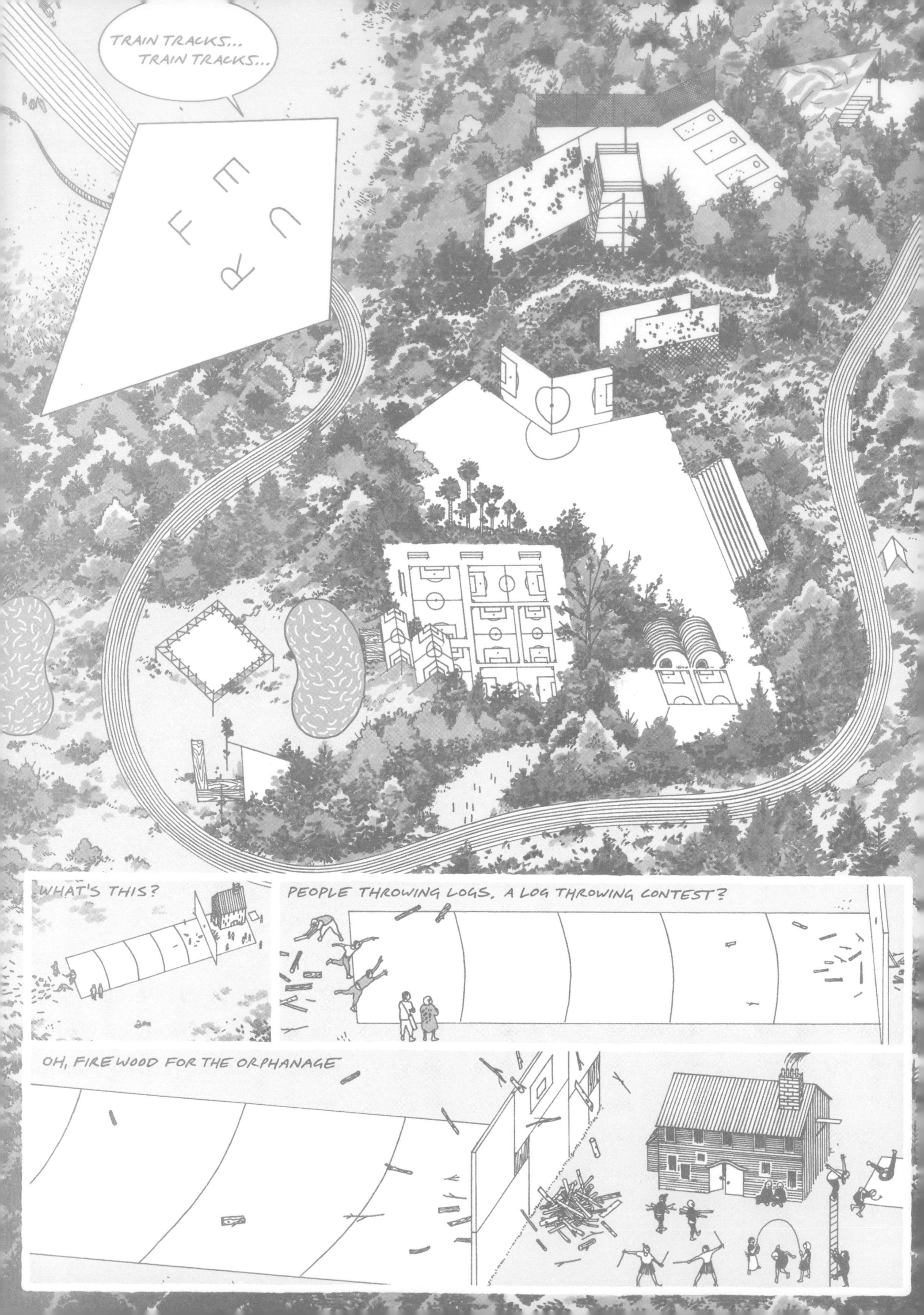
TRAIN TRACKS...
TRAIN TRACKS...
WHAT'S THIS?
PEOPLE THROWING LOGS. A LOG THROWING CONTEST?
OH, FIREWOOD FOR THE ORPHANAGE

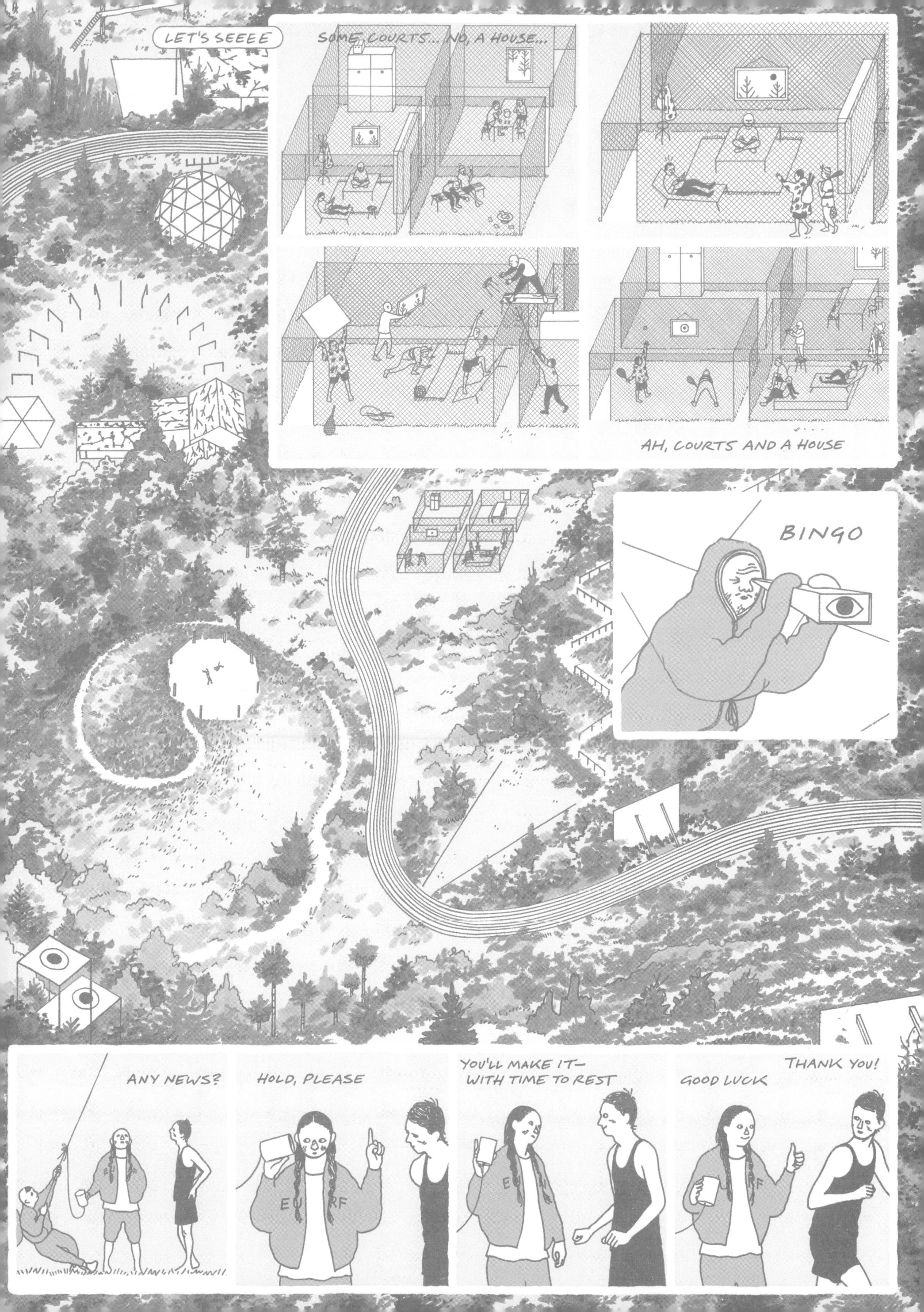
LET'S SEEEE
SOME COURTS... NO, A HOUSE...
AH, COURTS AND A HOUSE
BINGO
ANY NEWS?
HOLD, PLEASE
YOU'LL MAKE IT—
WITH TIME TO REST
GOOD LUCK
THANK YOU!

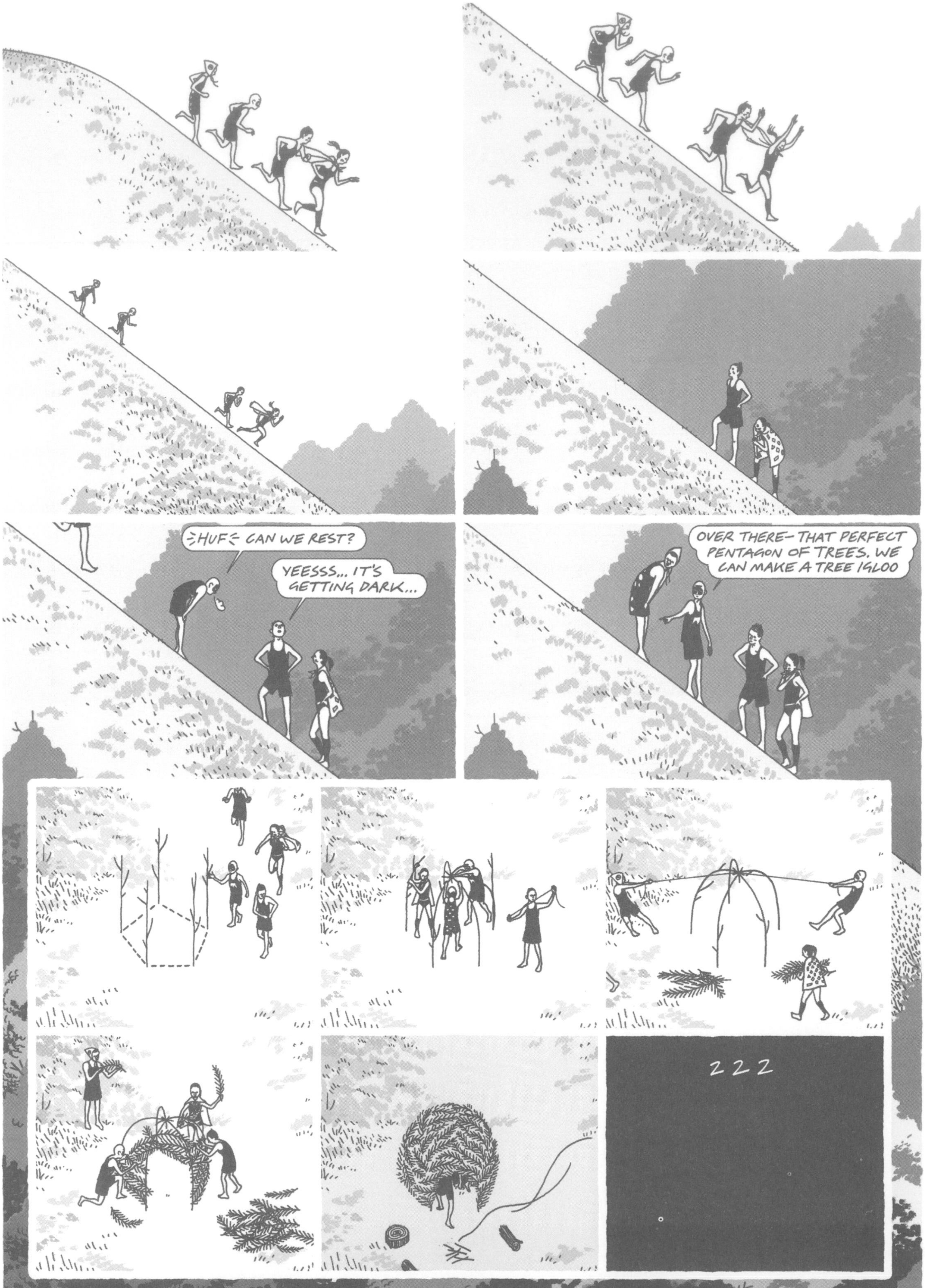
HUF CAN WE REST?
YEESSS... IT'S GETTING DARK...
OVER THERE— THAT PERFECT PENTAGON OF TREES. WE CAN MAKE A TREE IGLOO
Z Z Z

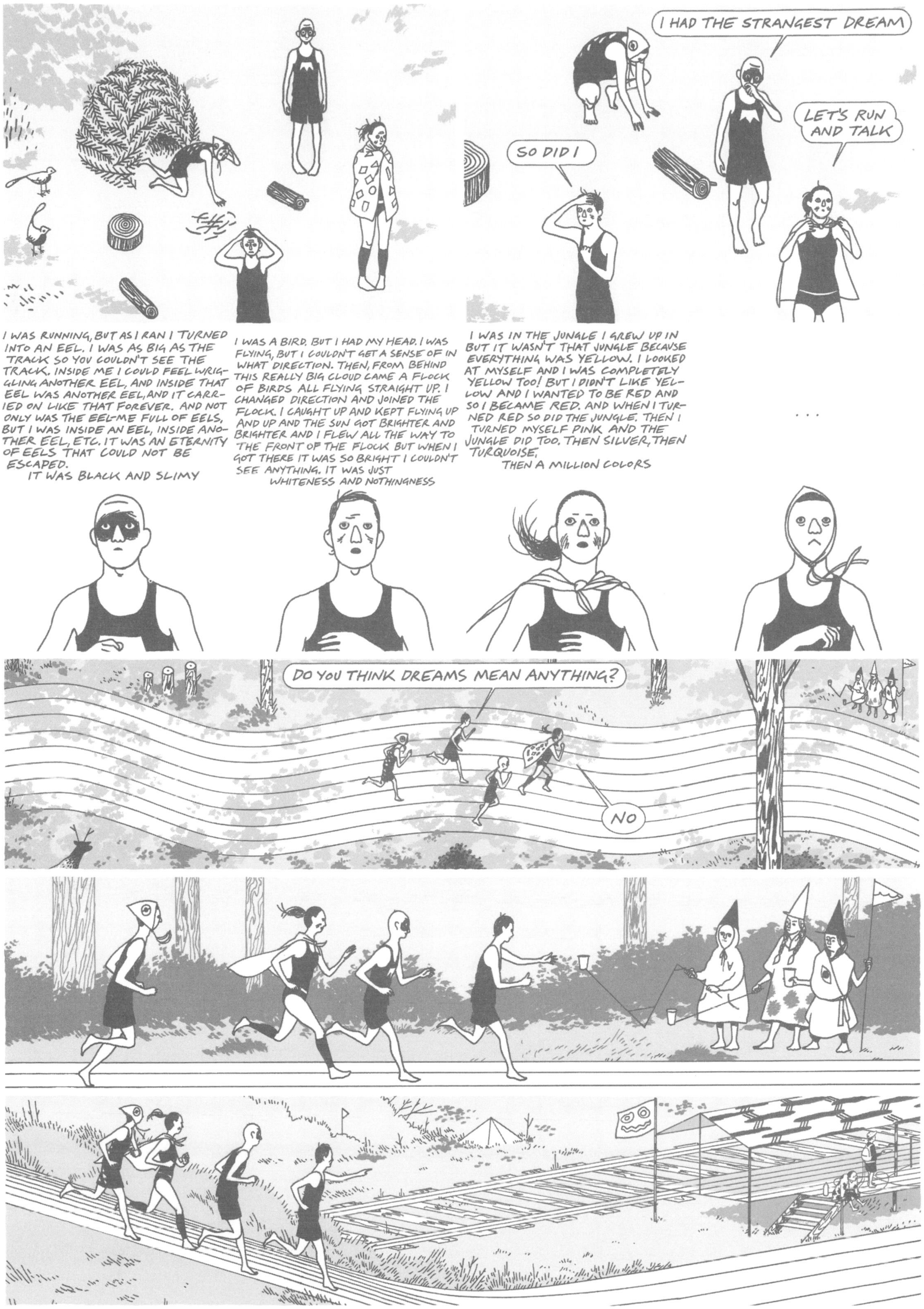
I HAD THE STRANGEST DREAM
SO DID I
LET'S RUN AND TALK
I WAS RUNNING, BUT AS I RAN I TURNED INTO AN EEL. I WAS AS BIG AS THE TRACK SO YOU COULDN'T SEE THE TRACK. INSIDE ME I COULD FEEL WRIGGLING ANOTHER EEL, AND INSIDE THAT EEL WAS ANOTHER EEL, AND IT CARRIED ON LIKE THAT FOREVER. AND NOT ONLY WAS THE EEL-ME FULL OF EELS, BUT I WAS INSIDE AN EEL, INSIDE ANOTHER EEL, ETC. IT WAS AN ETERNITY OF EELS THAT COULD NOT BE ESCAPED.
IT WAS BLACK AND SLIMY
I WAS A BIRD. BUT I HAD MY HEAD. I WAS FLYING, BUT I COULDN'T GET A SENSE OF IN WHAT DIRECTION. THEN, FROM BEHIND THIS REALLY BIG CLOUD CAME A FLOCK OF BIRDS ALL FLYING STRAIGHT UP. I CHANGED DIRECTION AND JOINED THE FLOCK. I CAUGHT UP AND KEPT FLYING UP AND UP AND THE SUN GOT BRIGHTER AND BRIGHTER AND I FLEW ALL THE WAY TO THE FRONT OF THE FLOCK BUT WHEN I GOT THERE IT WAS SO BRIGHT I COULDN'T SEE ANYTHING. IT WAS JUST
WHITENESS AND NOTHINGNESS
I WAS IN THE JUNGLE I GREW UP IN BUT IT WASN'T THAT JUNGLE BECAUSE EVERYTHING WAS YELLOW. I LOOKED AT MYSELF AND I WAS COMPLETELY YELLOW TOO! BUT I DIDN'T LIKE YELLOW AND I WANTED TO BE RED AND SO I BECAME RED. AND WHEN I TURNED RED SO DID THE JUNGLE. THEN I TURNED MYSELF PINK AND THE JUNGLE DID TOO. THEN SILVER, THEN TURQUOISE,
THEN A MILLION COLORS
. . .
DO YOU THINK DREAMS MEAN ANYTHING?
NO

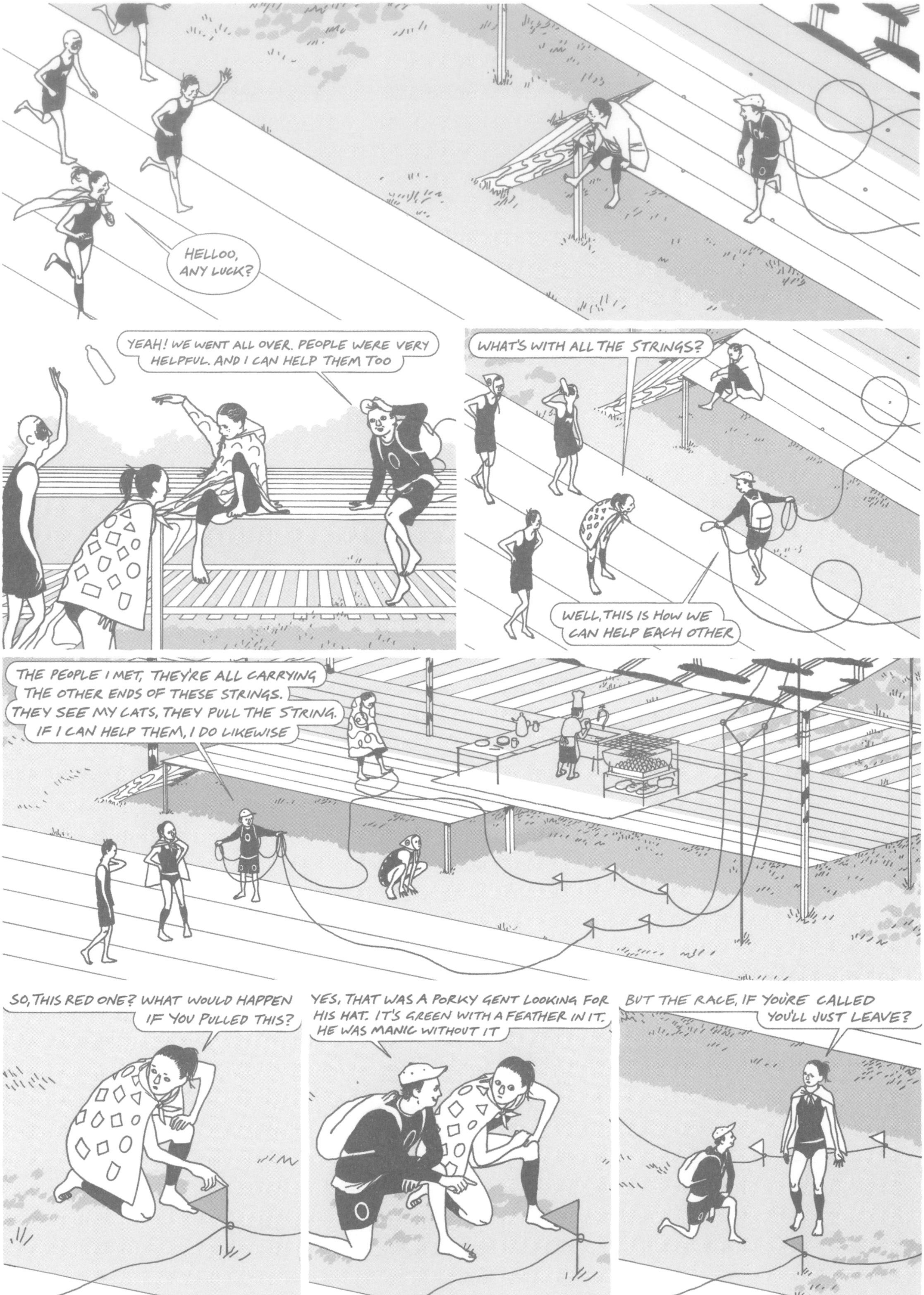
HELLOO, ANY LUCK?
YEAH! WE WENT ALL OVER. PEOPLE WERE VERY HELPFUL. AND I CAN HELP THEM TOO
WHAT'S WITH ALL THE STRINGS?
WELL, THIS IS HOW WE CAN HELP EACH OTHER
THE PEOPLE I MET, THEY'RE ALL CARRYING THE OTHER ENDS OF THESE STRINGS. THEY SEE MY CATS, THEY PULL THE STRING. IF I CAN HELP THEM, I DO LIKEWISE
SO, THIS RED ONE? WHAT WOULD HAPPEN IF YOU PULLED THIS?
YES, THAT WAS A PORKY GENT LOOKING FOR HIS HAT. IT'S GREEN WITH A FEATHER IN IT. HE WAS MANIC WITHOUT IT
BUT THE RACE, IF YOU'RE CALLED YOU'LL JUST LEAVE?

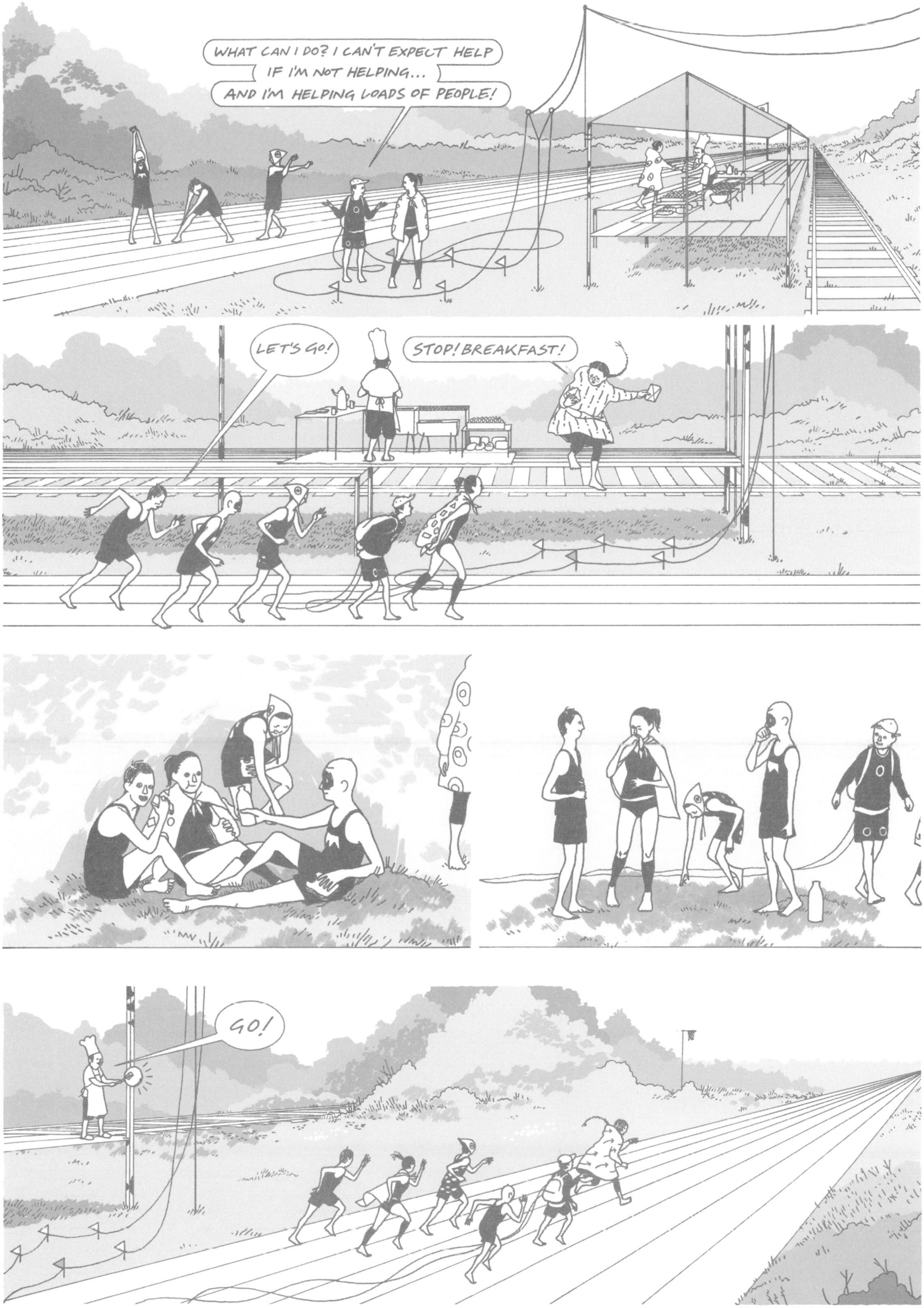
WHAT CAN I DO? I CAN'T EXPECT HELP
IF I'M NOT HELPING...
AND I'M HELPING LOADS OF PEOPLE!
LET'S GO!
STOP! BREAKFAST!
GO!

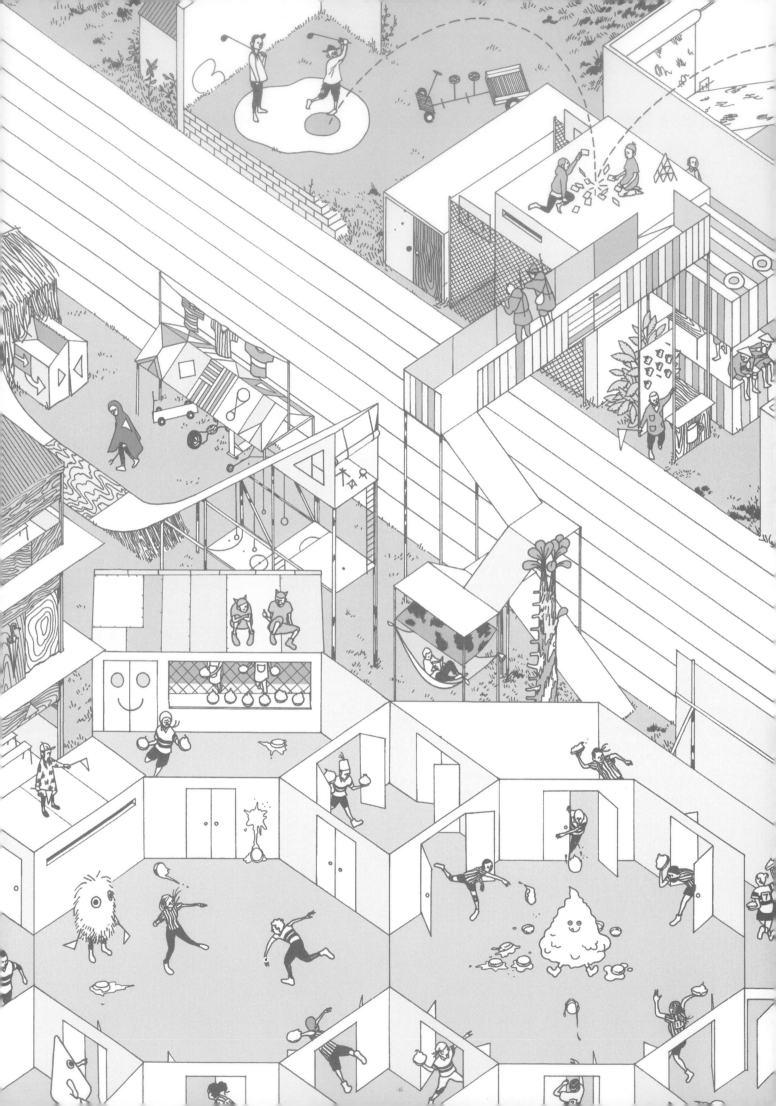

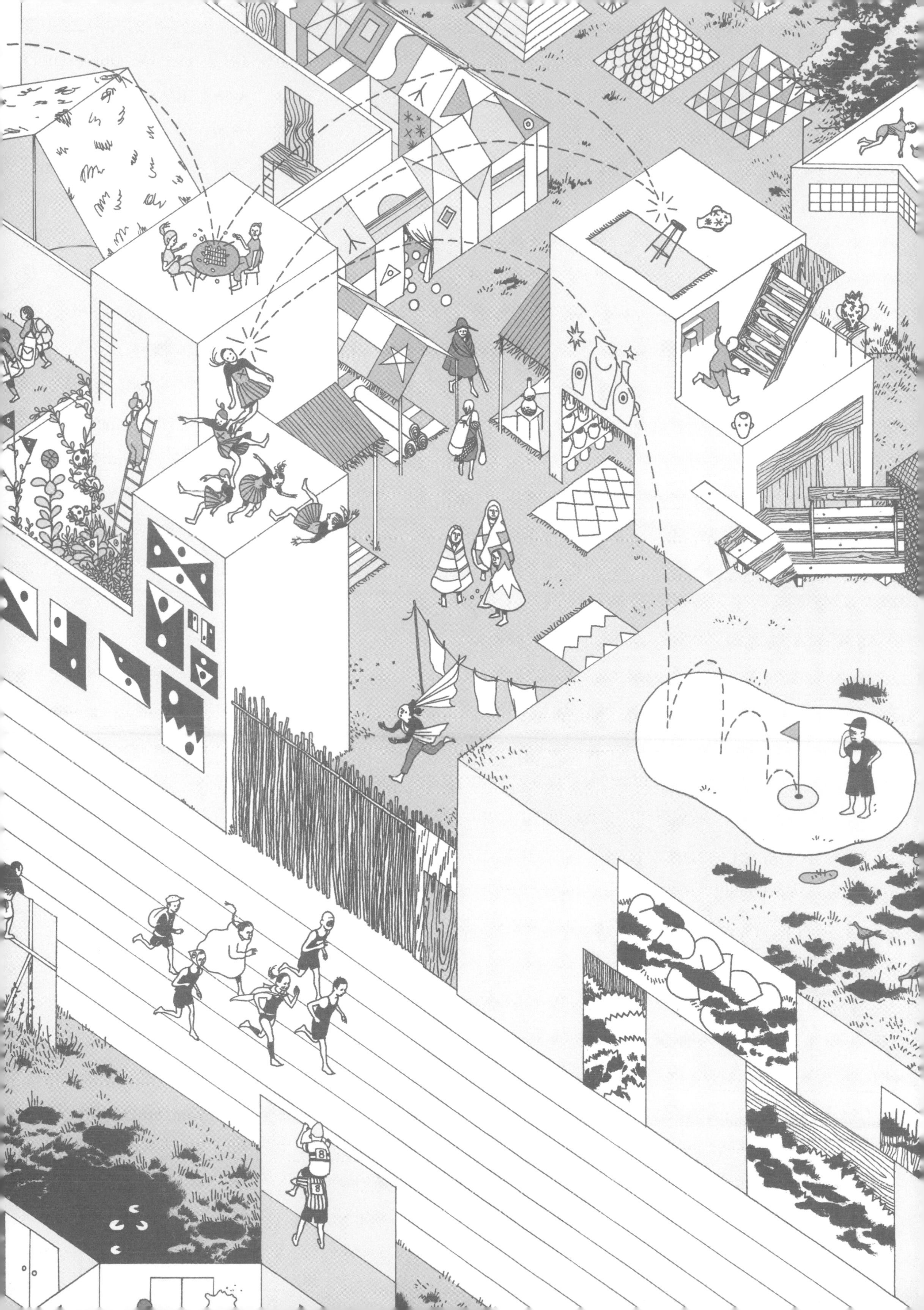

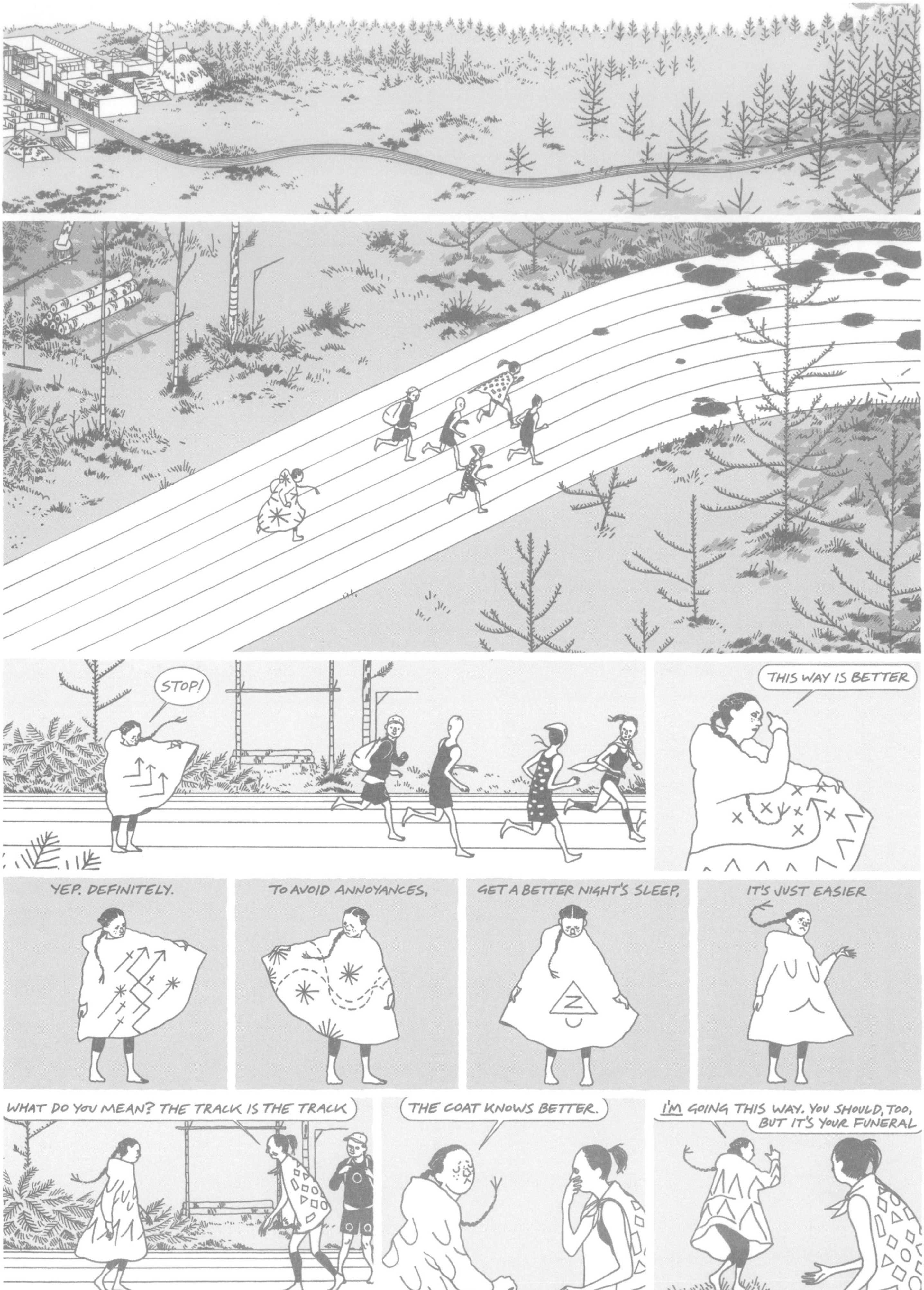
STOP!
THIS WAY IS BETTER
YEP. DEFINITELY.
TO AVOID ANNOYANCES,
GET A BETTER NIGHT'S SLEEP,
IT'S JUST EASIER
WHAT DO YOU MEAN? THE TRACK IS THE TRACK
THE COAT KNOWS BETTER.
I'M GOING THIS WAY. YOU SHOULD, TOO, BUT IT'S YOUR FUNERAL

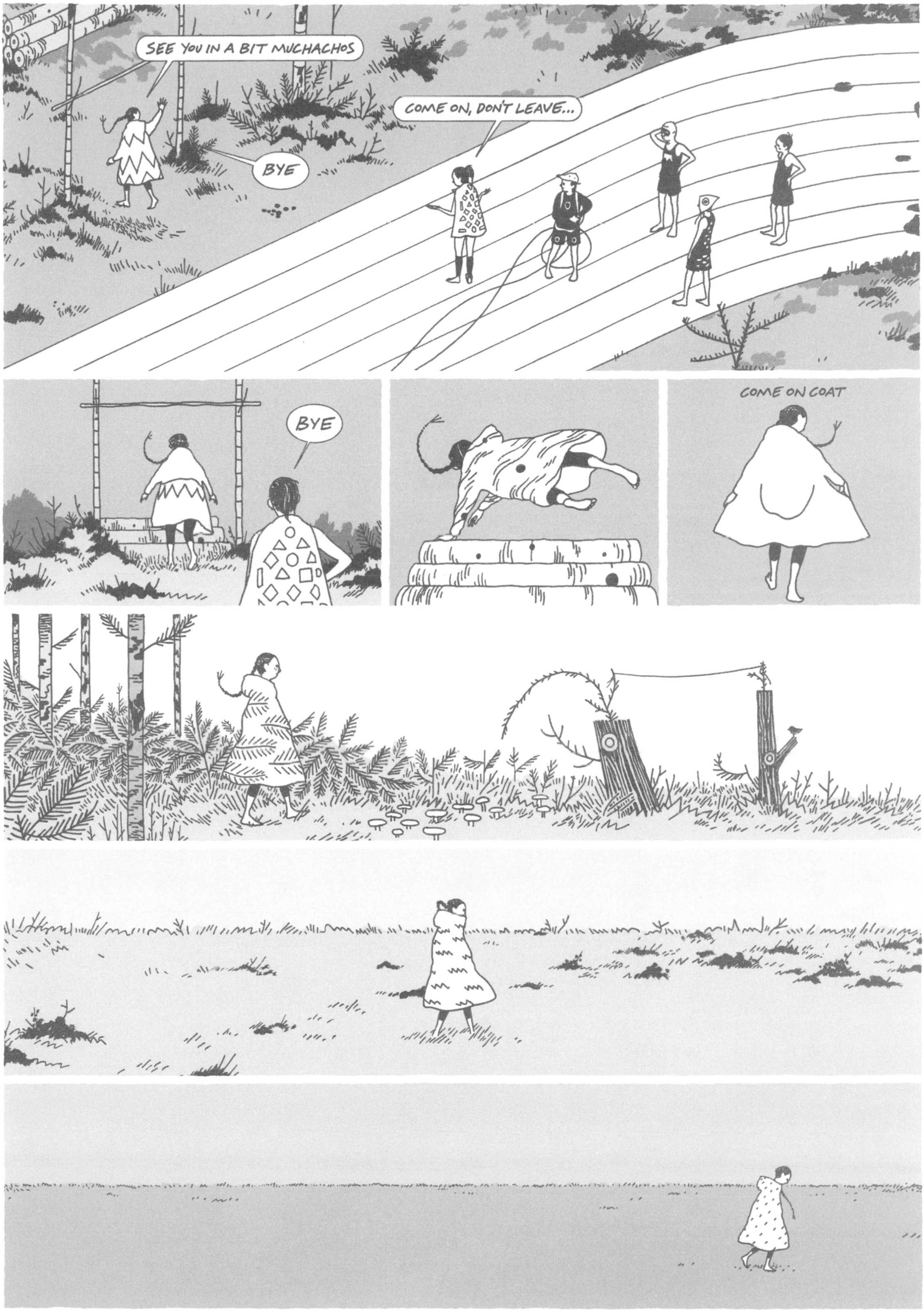
SEE YOU IN A BIT MUCHACHOS
BYE
COME ON, DON'T LEAVE...
BYE
COME ON COAT

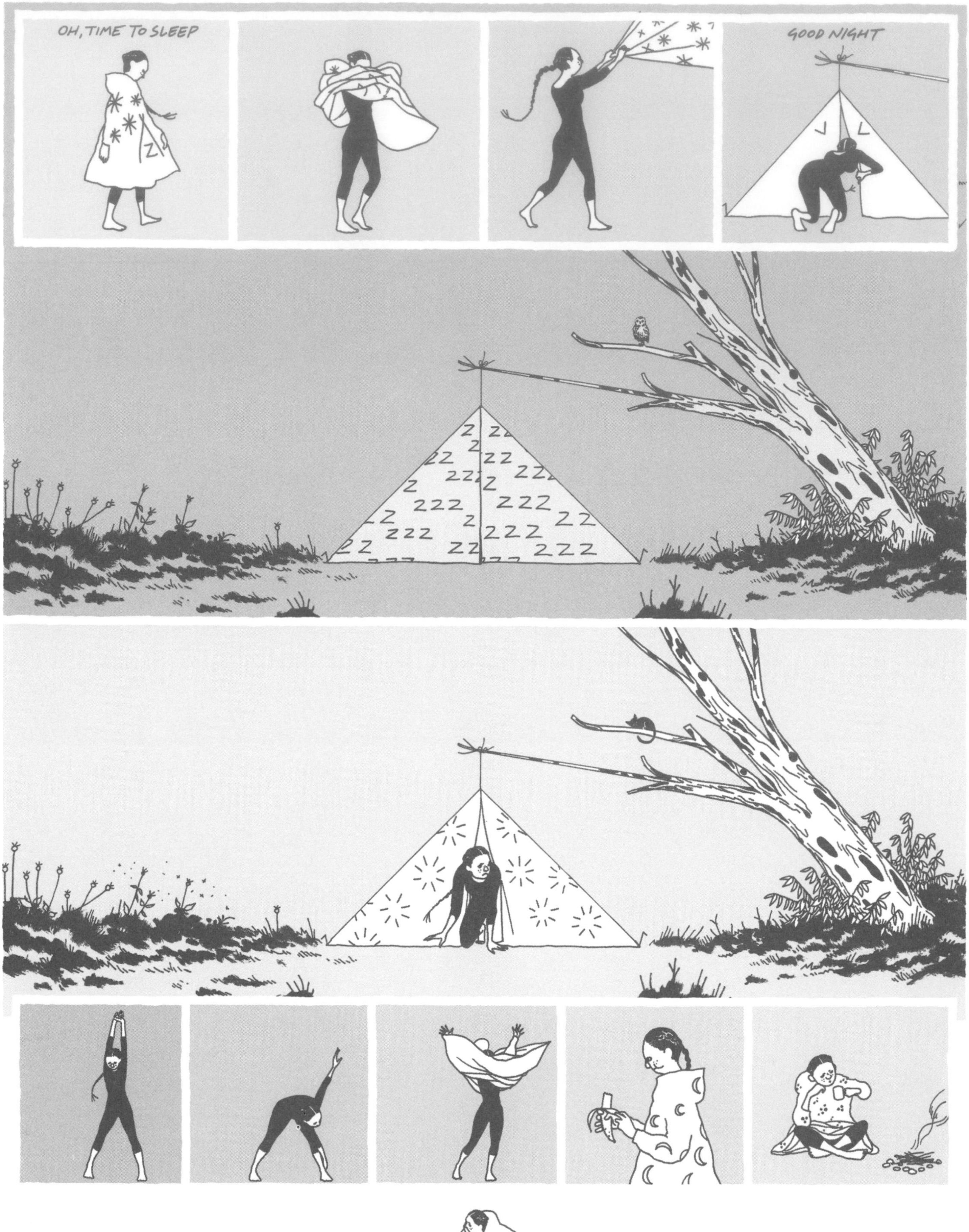
OH, TIME TO SLEEP
GOOD NIGHT

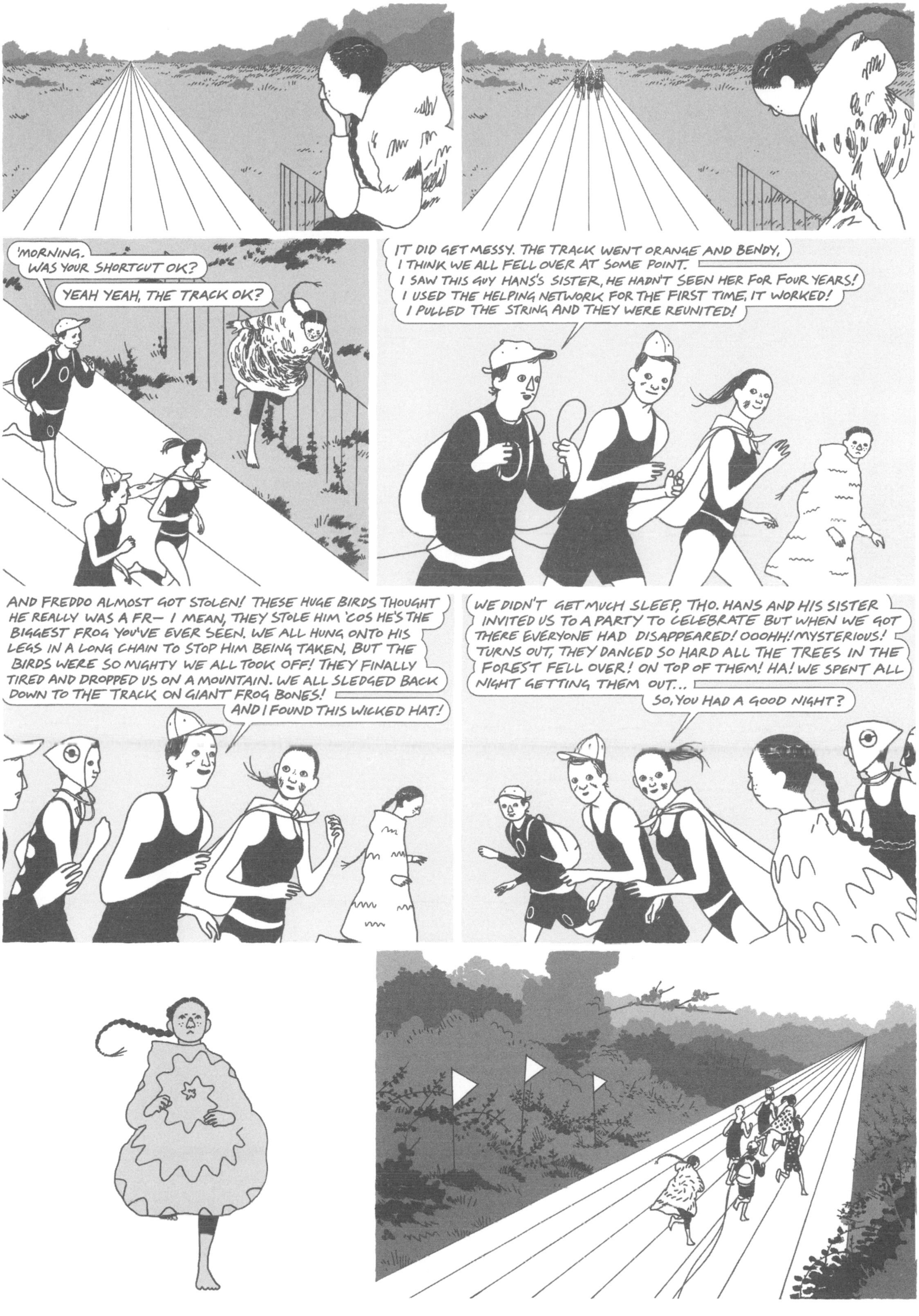

'MORNING. WAS YOUR SHORTCUT OK?
YEAH YEAH, THE TRACK OK?
IT DID GET MESSY. THE TRACK WENT ORANGE AND BENDY, I THINK WE ALL FELL OVER AT SOME POINT. I SAW THIS GUY HANS'S SISTER, HE HADN'T SEEN HER FOR FOUR YEARS! I USED THE HELPING NETWORK FOR THE FIRST TIME, IT WORKED! I PULLED THE STRING AND THEY WERE REUNITED!
AND FREDDO ALMOST GOT STOLEN! THESE HUGE BIRDS THOUGHT HE REALLY WAS A FR– I MEAN, THEY STOLE HIM 'COS HE'S THE BIGGEST FROG YOU'VE EVER SEEN. WE ALL HUNG ONTO HIS LEGS IN A LONG CHAIN TO STOP HIM BEING TAKEN, BUT THE BIRDS WERE SO MIGHTY WE ALL TOOK OFF! THEY FINALLY TIRED AND DROPPED US ON A MOUNTAIN. WE ALL SLEDGED BACK DOWN TO THE TRACK ON GIANT FROG BONES!
AND I FOUND THIS WICKED HAT!
WE DIDN'T GET MUCH SLEEP, THO. HANS AND HIS SISTER INVITED US TO A PARTY TO CELEBRATE BUT WHEN WE GOT THERE EVERYONE HAD DISAPPEARED! OOOHH! MYSTERIOUS! TURNS OUT, THEY DANCED SO HARD ALL THE TREES IN THE FOREST FELL OVER! ON TOP OF THEM! HA! WE SPENT ALL NIGHT GETTING THEM OUT...
SO, YOU HAD A GOOD NIGHT?

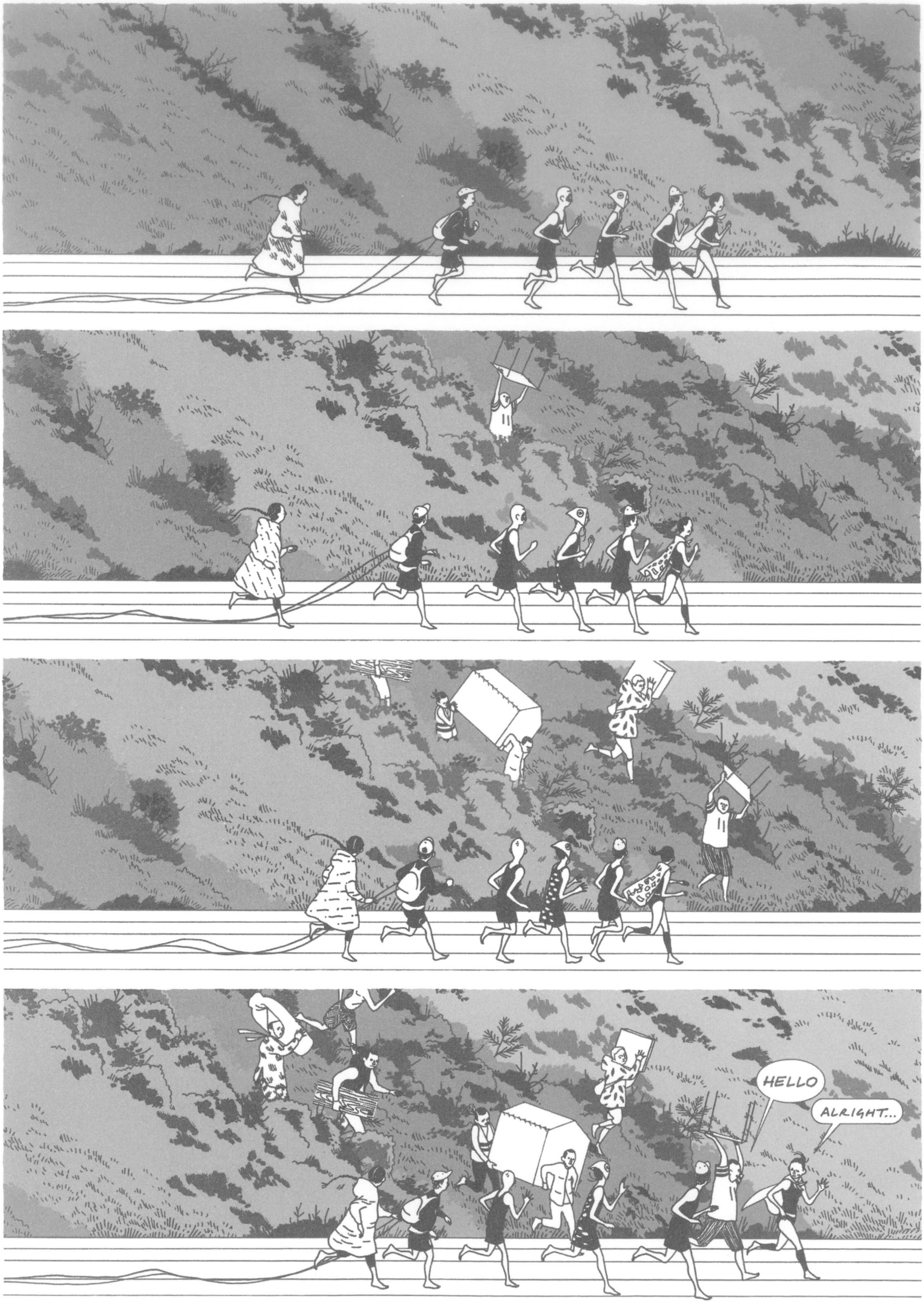
HELLO
ALRIGHT...

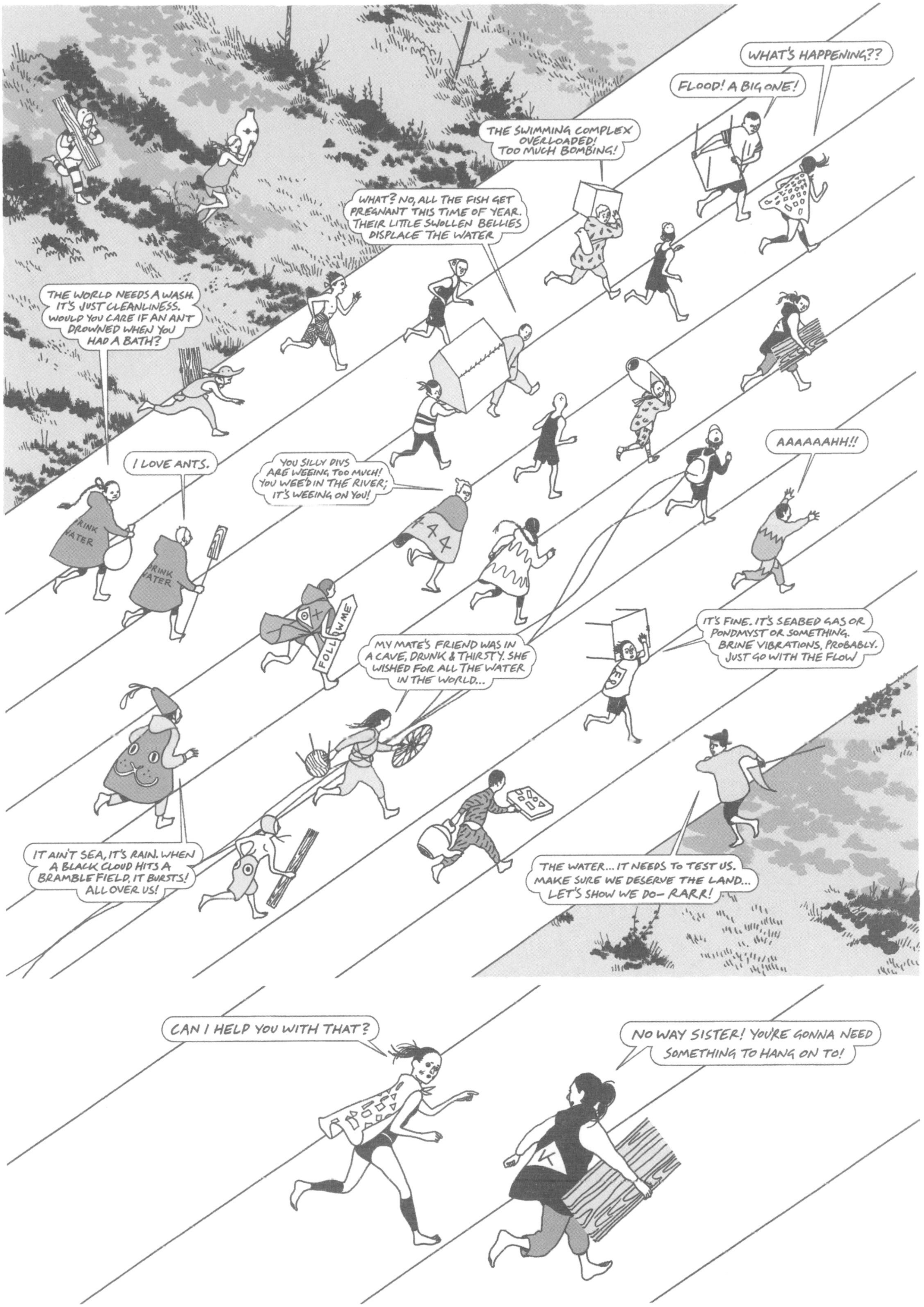
WHAT'S HAPPENING??
FLOOD! A BIG ONE!
THE SWIMMING COMPLEX OVERLOADED! TOO MUCH BOMBING!
WHAT? NO, ALL THE FISH GET PREGNANT THIS TIME OF YEAR. THEIR LITTLE SWOLLEN BELLIES DISPLACE THE WATER
THE WORLD NEEDS A WASH. IT'S JUST CLEANLINESS. WOULD YOU CARE IF AN ANT DROWNED WHEN YOU HAD A BATH?
I LOVE ANTS.
DRINK WATER
DRINK WATER
YOU SILLY DIVS ARE WEEING TOO MUCH! YOU WEE'D IN THE RIVER; IT'S WEEING ON YOU!
AAAAAAHH!!
FOLLOW ME
MY MATE'S FRIEND WAS IN A CAVE, DRUNK & THIRSTY. SHE WISHED FOR ALL THE WATER IN THE WORLD...
IT'S FINE. IT'S SEABED GAS OR PONDMYST OR SOMETHING. BRINE VIBRATIONS, PROBABLY. JUST GO WITH THE FLOW
IT AIN'T SEA, IT'S RAIN. WHEN A BLACK CLOUD HITS A BRAMBLE FIELD, IT BURSTS! ALL OVER US!
THE WATER... IT NEEDS TO TEST US. MAKE SURE WE DESERVE THE LAND... LET'S SHOW WE DO- RARR!
CAN I HELP YOU WITH THAT?
NO WAY SISTER! YOU'RE GONNA NEED SOMETHING TO HANG ON TO!

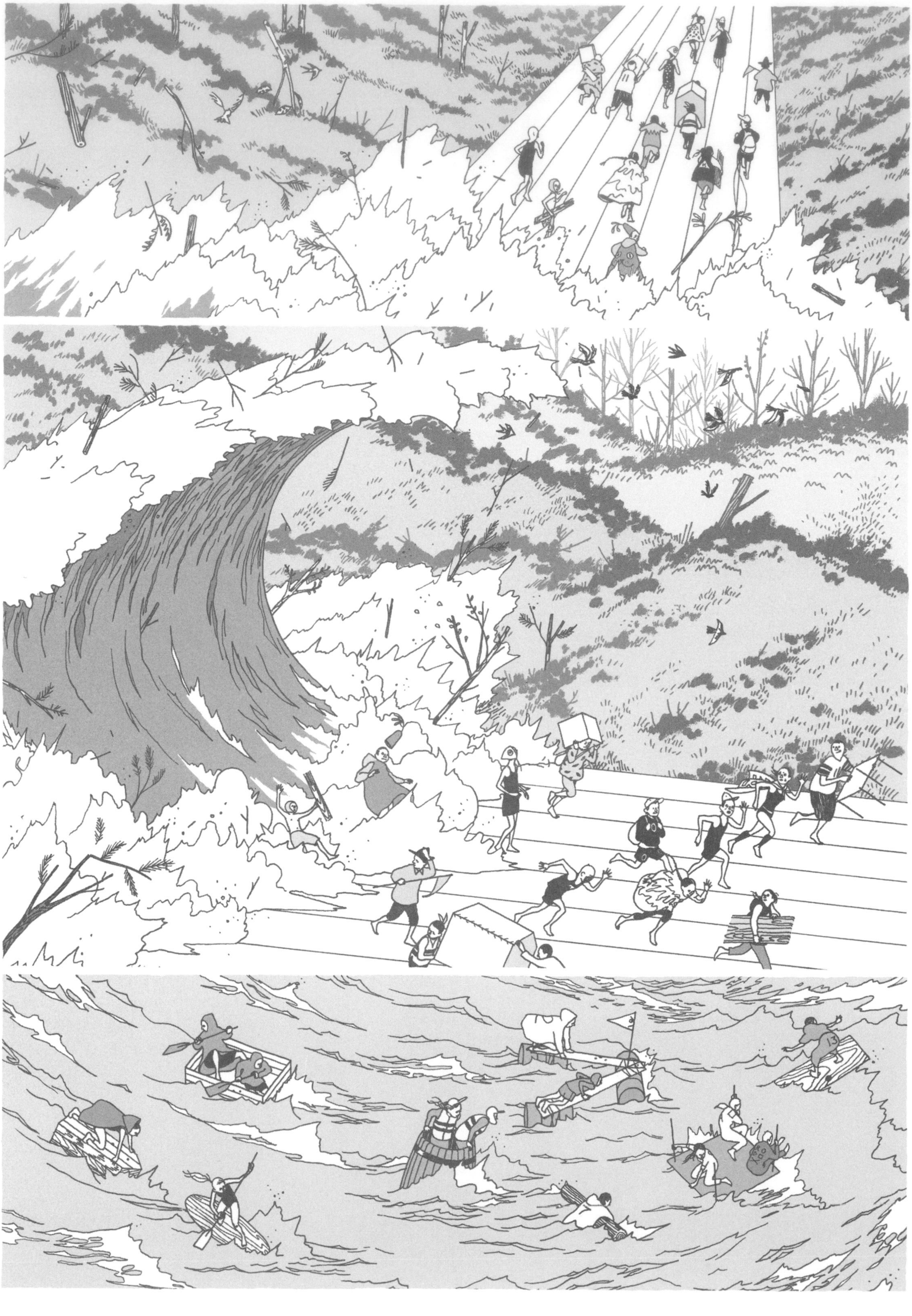
13

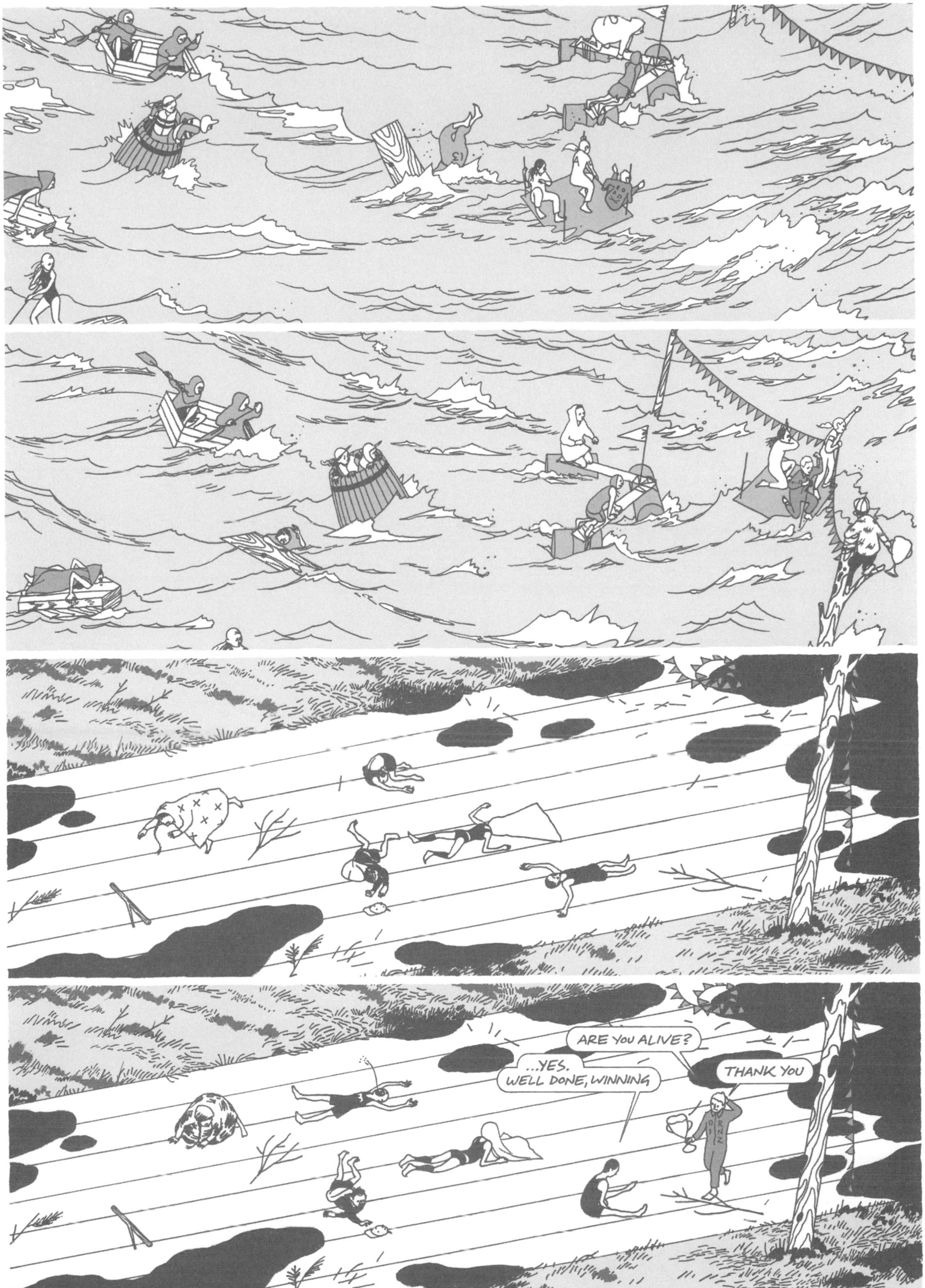
ARE YOU ALIVE?
...YES. WELL DONE, WINNING
THANK YOU

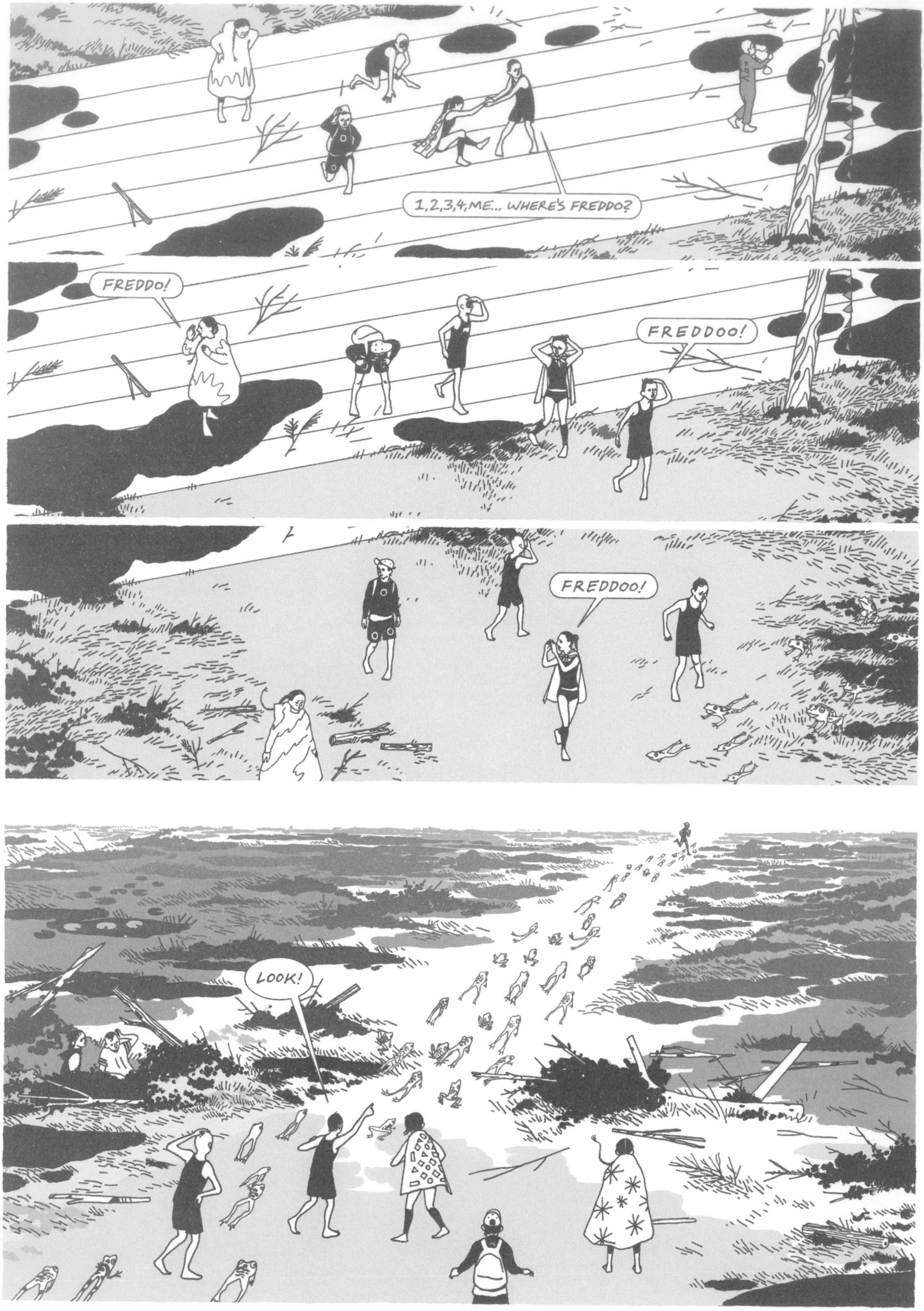
1,2,3,4,ME... WHERE'S FREDDO?
FREDDO!
FREDDOO!
FREDDOO!
LOOK!

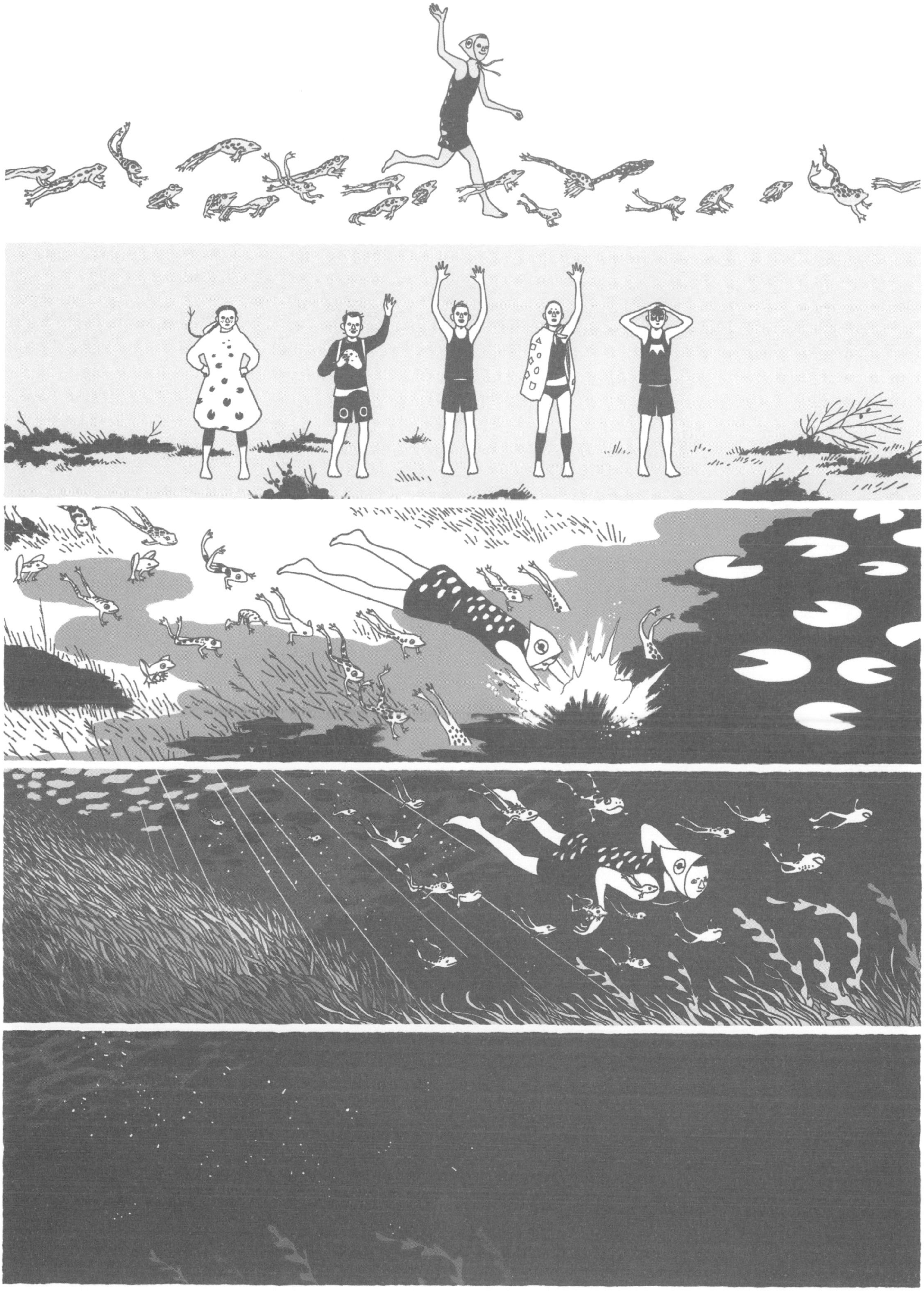

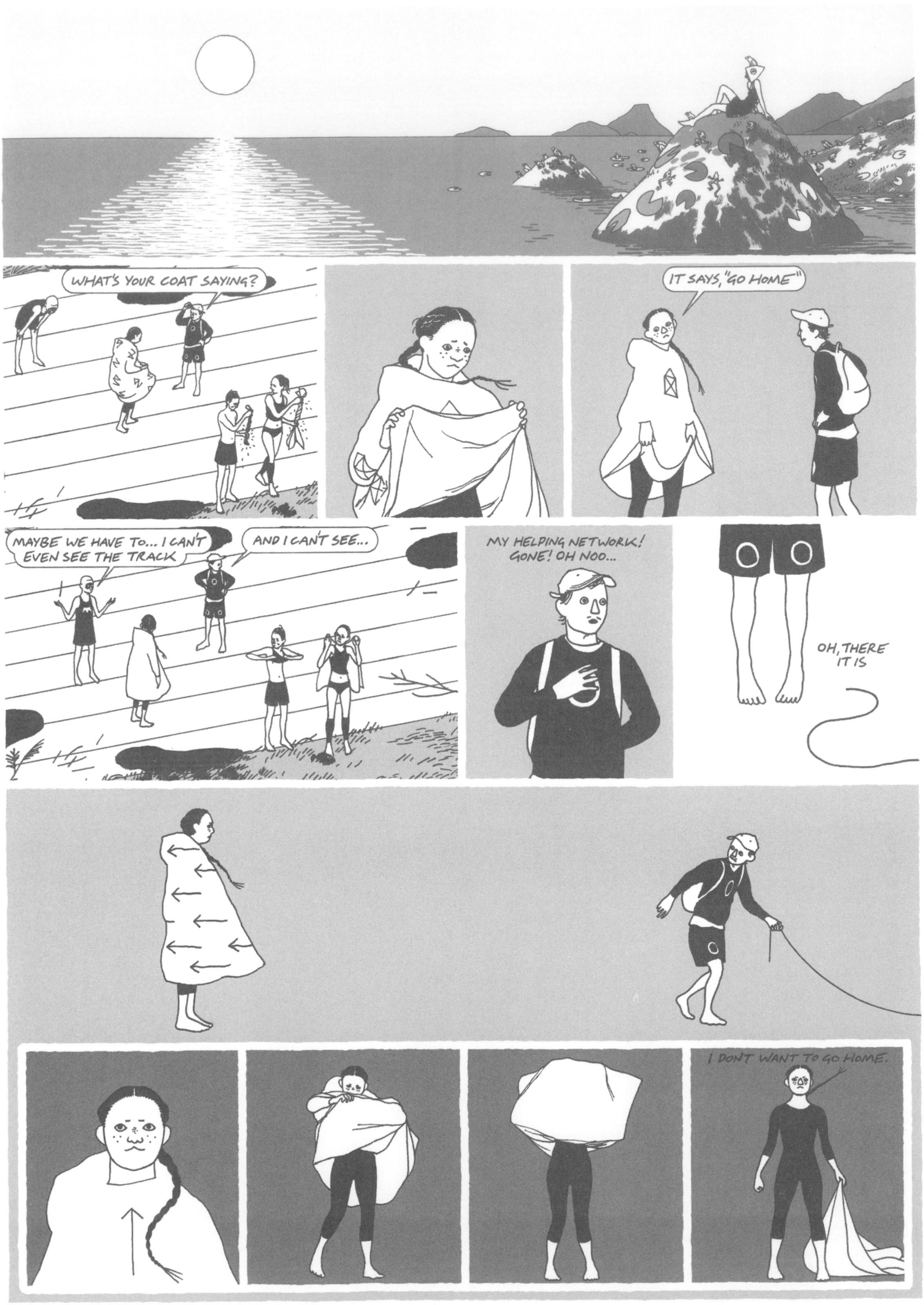
WHAT'S YOUR COAT SAYING?
IT SAYS, "GO HOME"
MAYBE WE HAVE TO... I CAN'T EVEN SEE THE TRACK
AND I CAN'T SEE...
MY HELPING NETWORK! GONE! OH NOO...
OH, THERE IT IS
I DON'T WANT TO GO HOME.

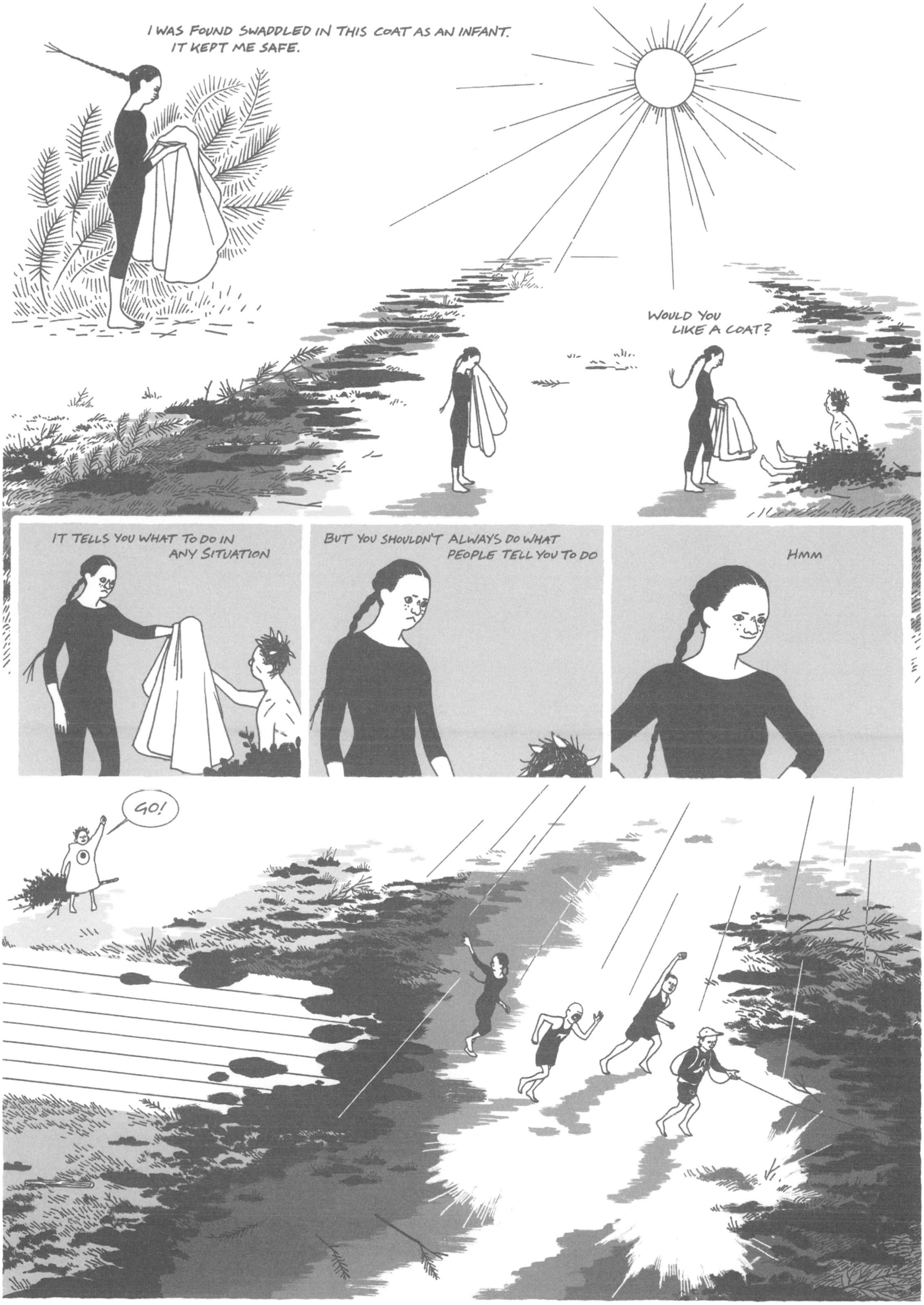
I WAS FOUND SWADDLED IN THIS COAT AS AN INFANT. IT KEPT ME SAFE.
WOULD YOU LIKE A COAT?
IT TELLS YOU WHAT TO DO IN ANY SITUATION
BUT YOU SHOULDN'T ALWAYS DO WHAT PEOPLE TELL YOU TO DO
HMM
GO!

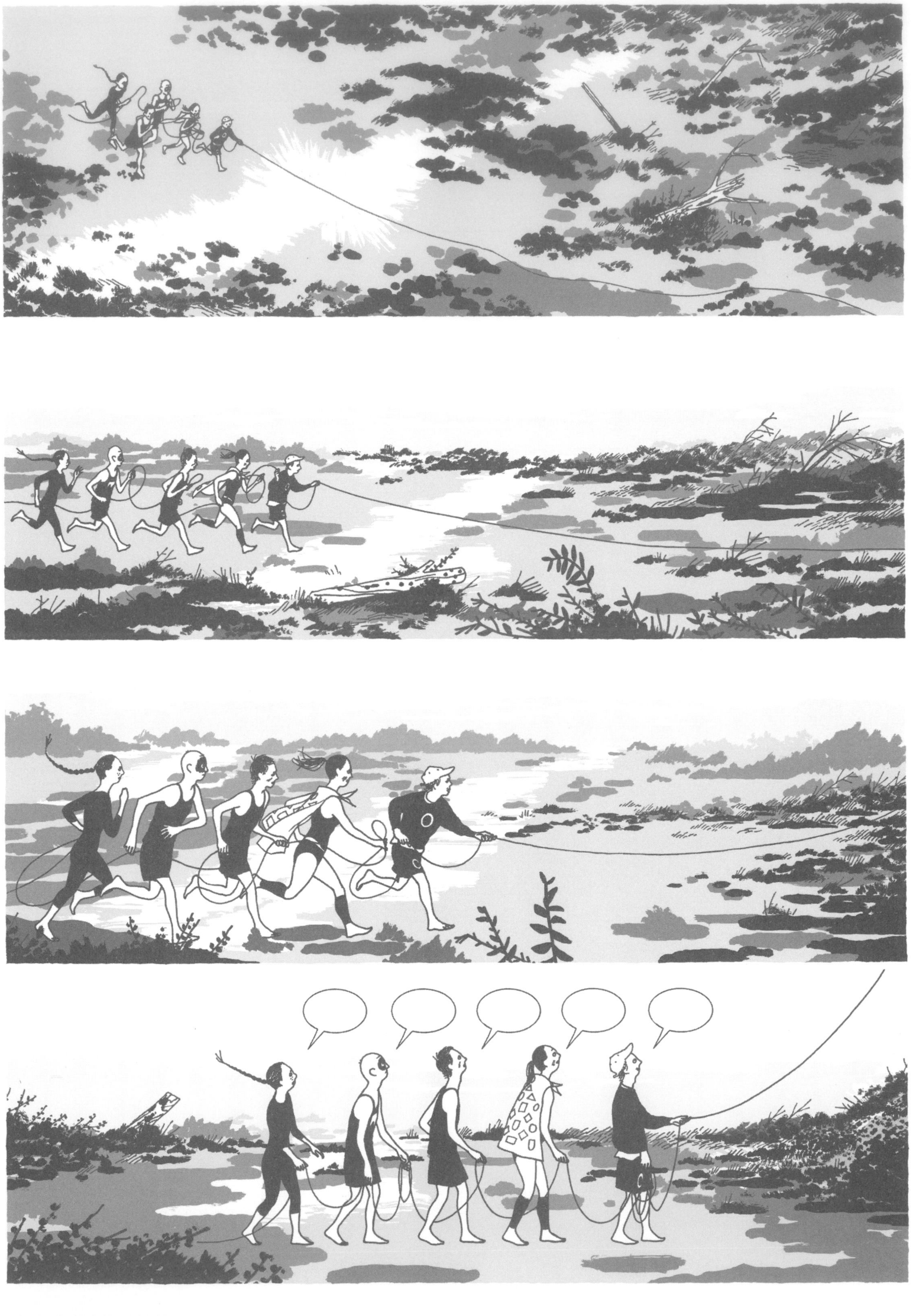

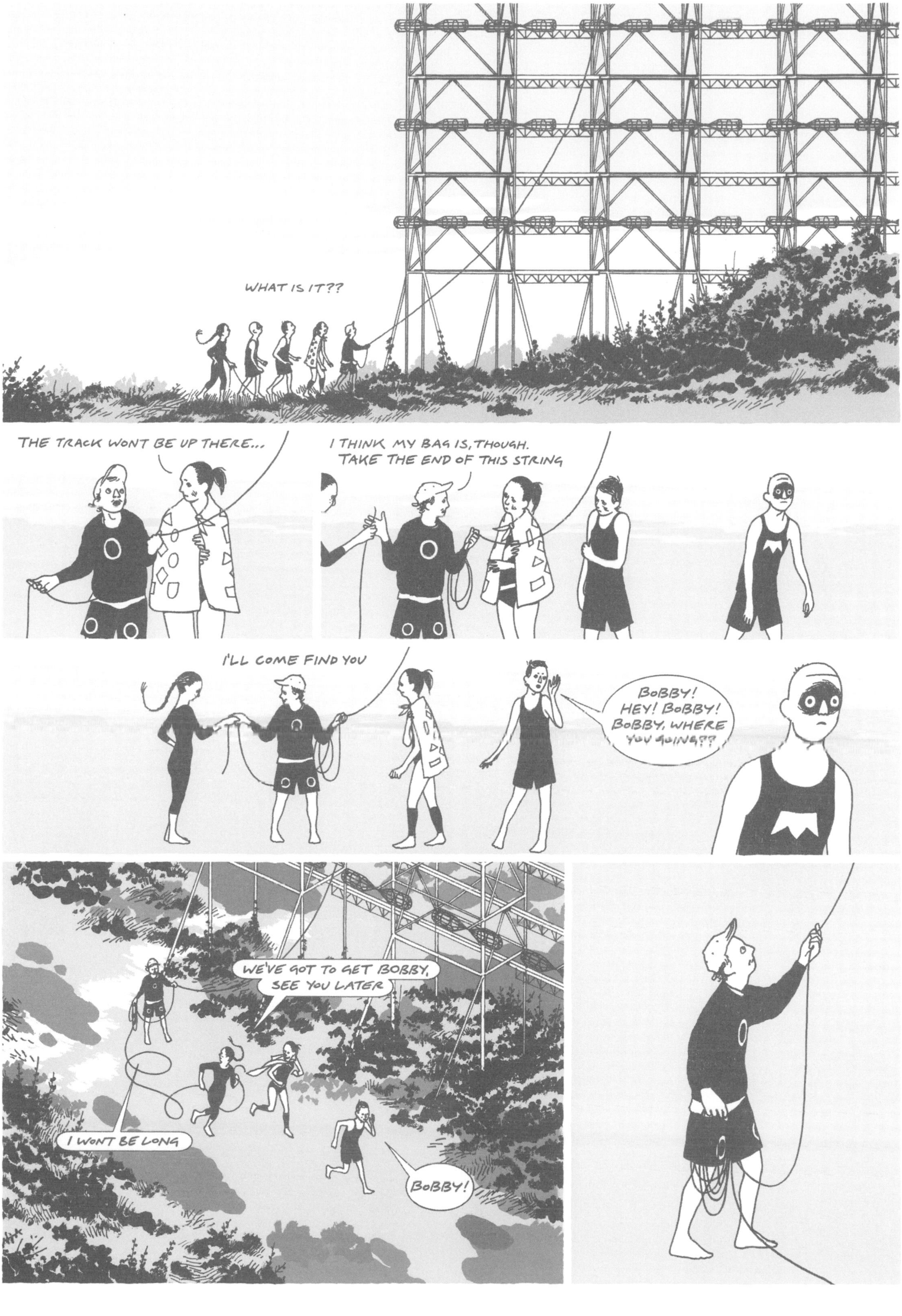

WHAT IS IT??
THE TRACK WONT BE UP THERE...
I THINK MY BAG IS, THOUGH.
TAKE THE END OF THIS STRING
I'LL COME FIND YOU
BOBBY!
HEY! BOBBY!
BOBBY, WHERE
YOU GOING??
WE'VE GOT TO GET BOBBY,
SEE YOU LATER
I WONT BE LONG
BOBBY!

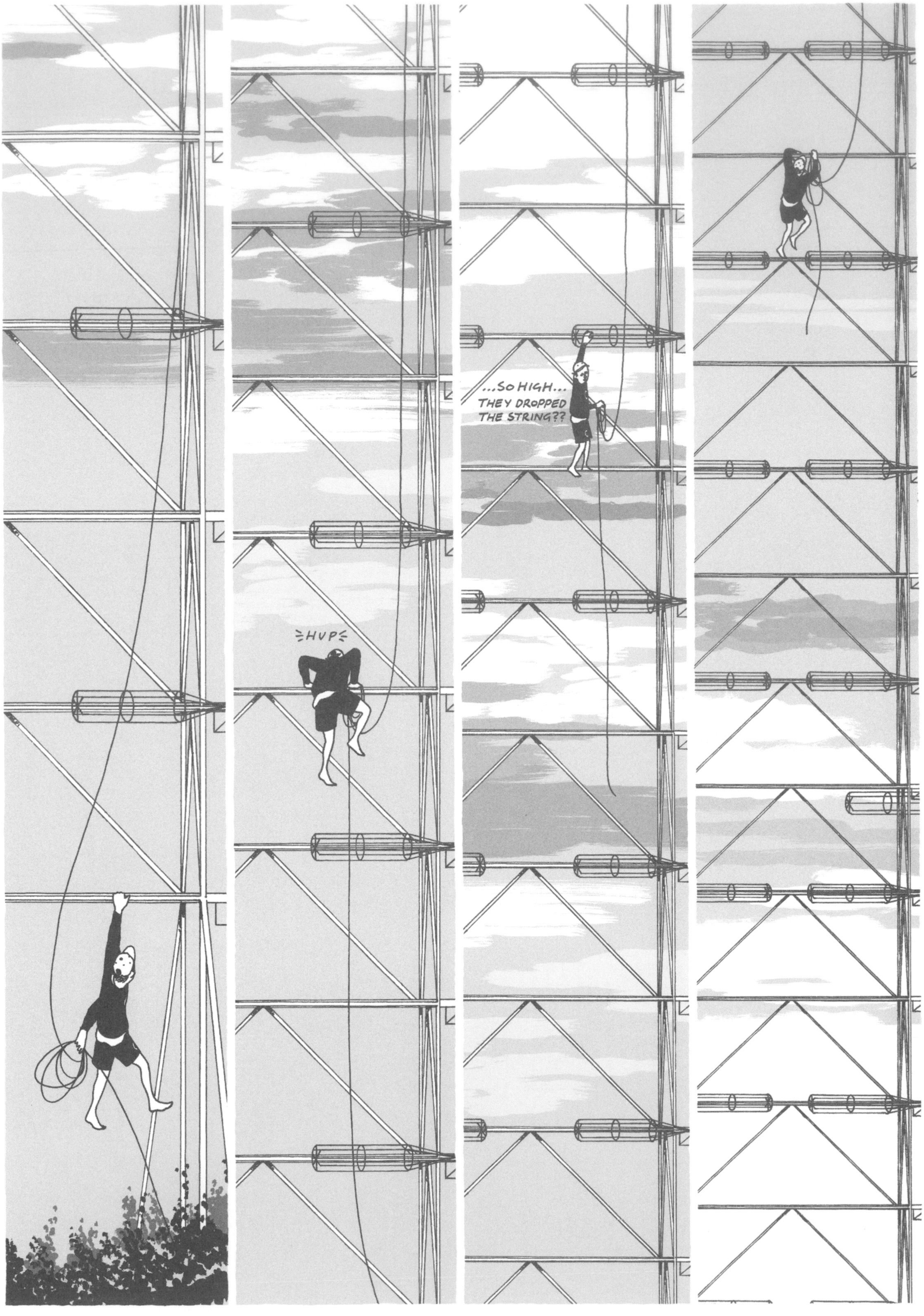
HUP
...SO HIGH...
THEY DROPPED THE STRING??

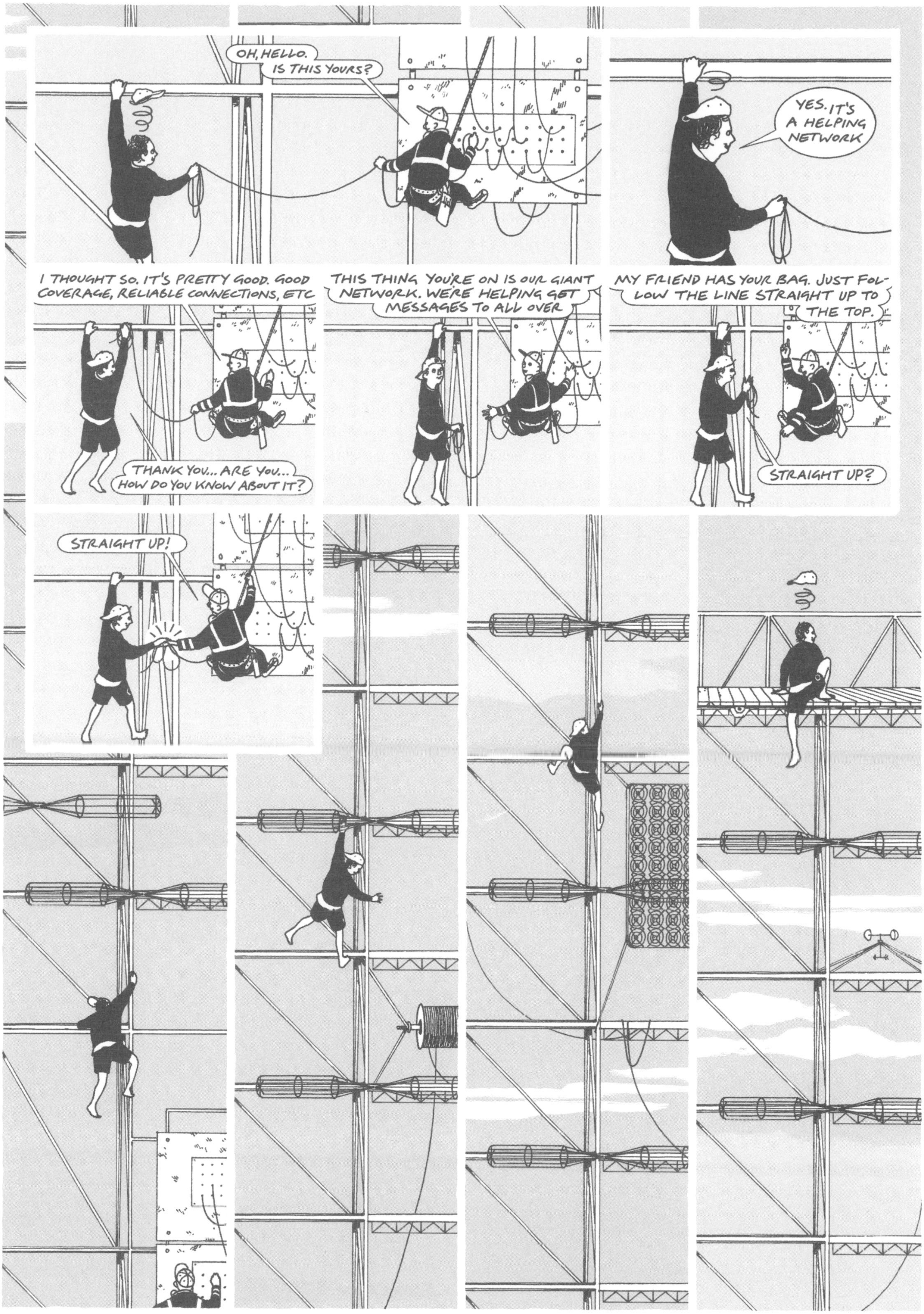
OH, HELLO.
IS THIS YOURS?
YES. IT'S A HELPING NETWORK
I THOUGHT SO. IT'S PRETTY GOOD. GOOD COVERAGE, RELIABLE CONNECTIONS, ETC
THANK YOU... ARE YOU... HOW DO YOU KNOW ABOUT IT?
THIS THING YOU'RE ON IS OUR GIANT NETWORK. WE'RE HELPING GET MESSAGES TO ALL OVER
MY FRIEND HAS YOUR BAG. JUST FOLLOW THE LINE STRAIGHT UP TO THE TOP.
STRAIGHT UP?
STRAIGHT UP!

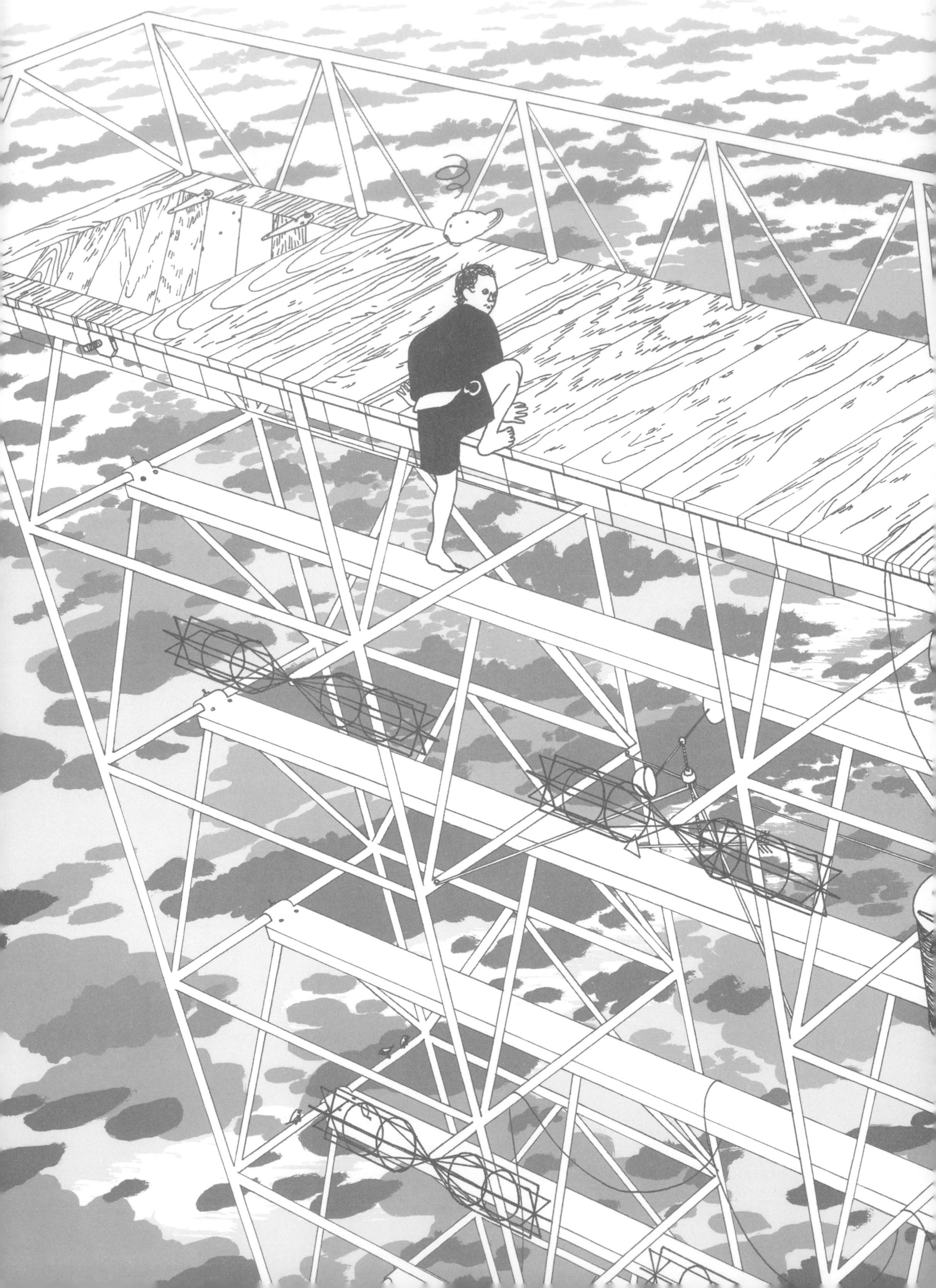

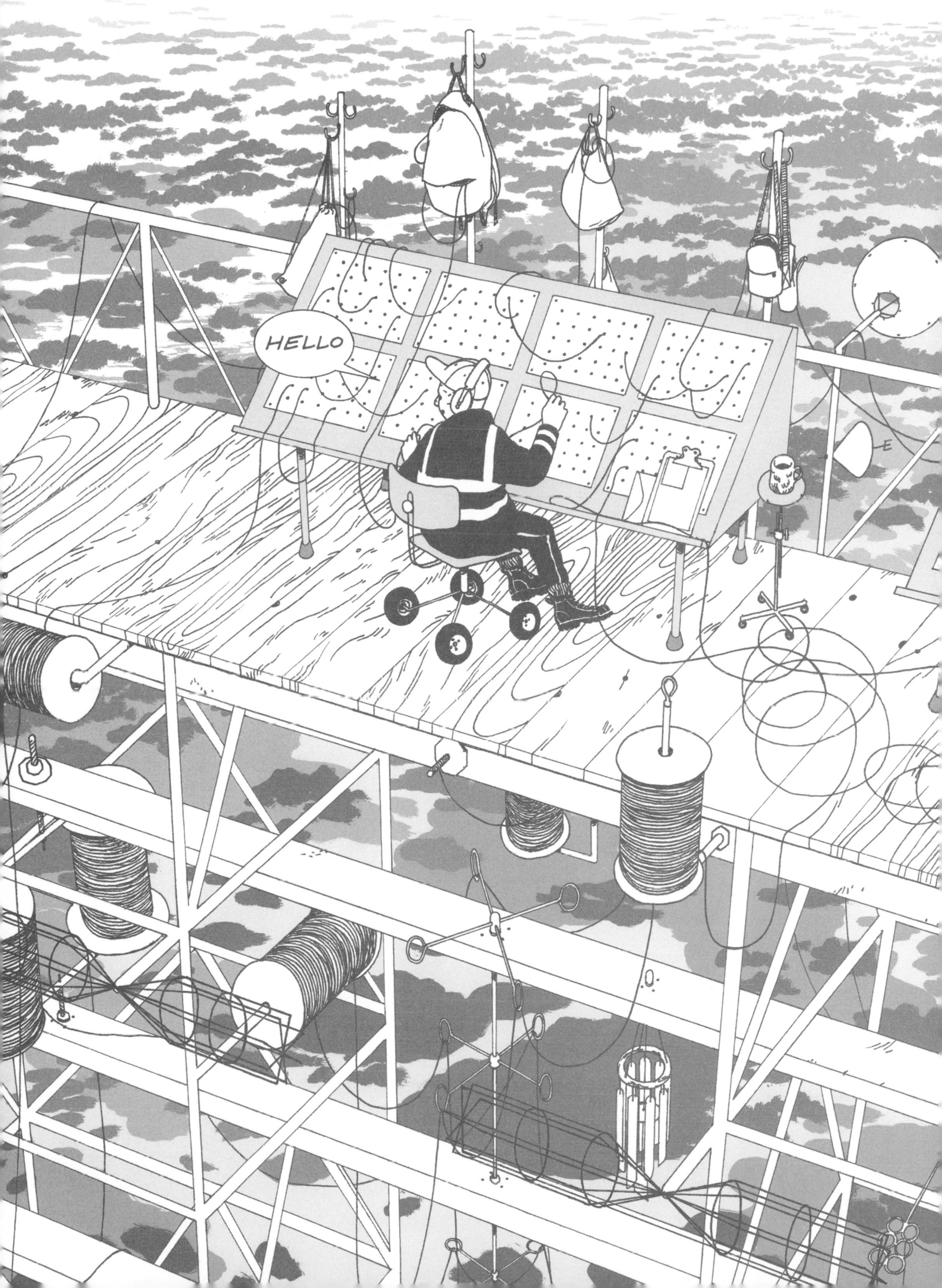
HELLO

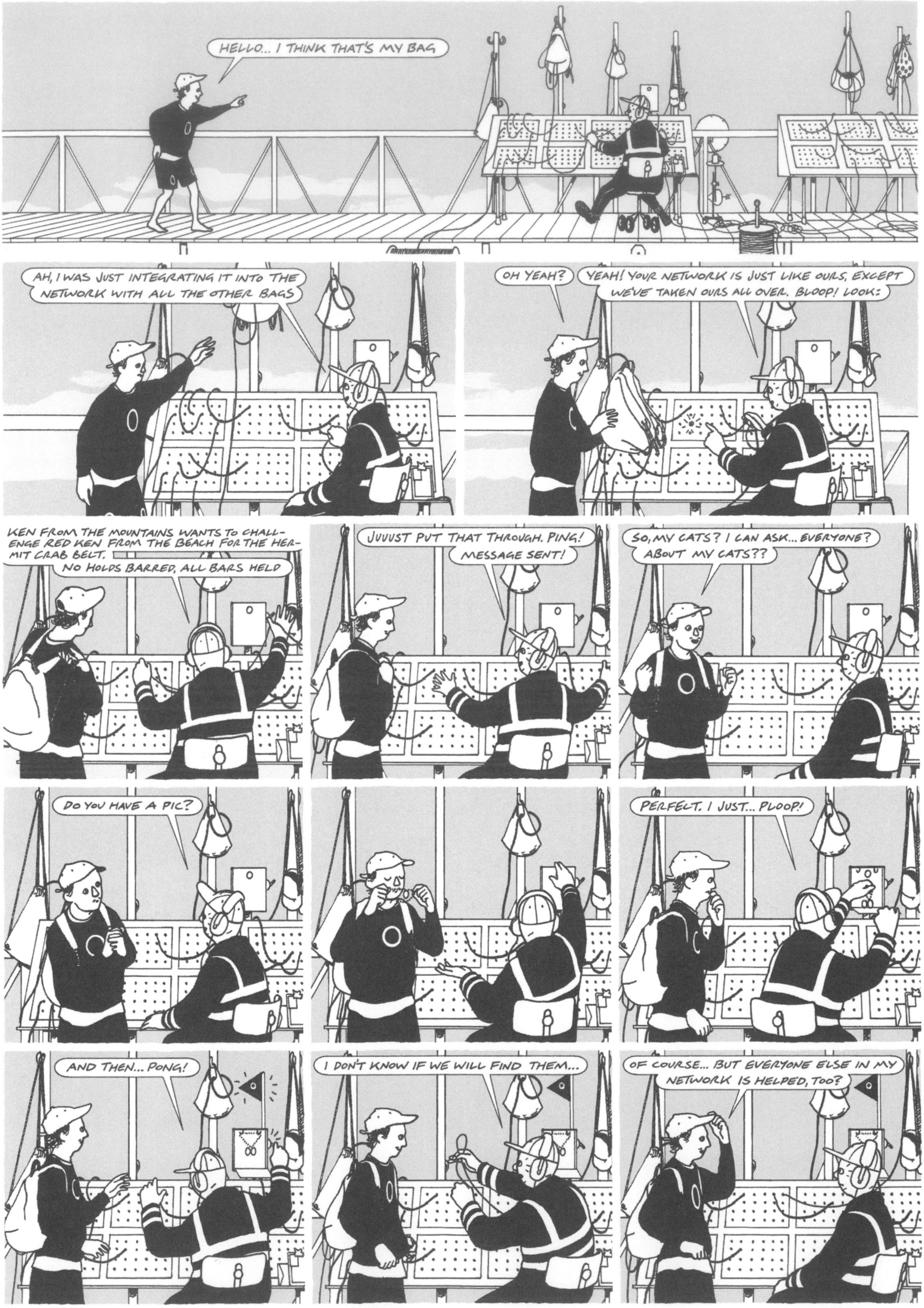
HELLO... I THINK THAT'S MY BAG
AH, I WAS JUST INTEGRATING IT INTO THE NETWORK WITH ALL THE OTHER BAGS
OH YEAH?
YEAH! YOUR NETWORK IS JUST LIKE OURS, EXCEPT WE'VE TAKEN OURS ALL OVER. BLOOP! LOOK:
KEN FROM THE MOUNTAINS WANTS TO CHALLENGE RED KEN FROM THE BEACH FOR THE HERMIT CRAB BELT.
NO HOLDS BARRED, ALL BARS HELD
JUUUST PUT THAT THROUGH. PING!
MESSAGE SENT!
SO, MY CATS? I CAN ASK... EVERYONE? ABOUT MY CATS??
DO YOU HAVE A PIC?
PERFECT. I JUST... PLOOP!
AND THEN... PONG!
I DON'T KNOW IF WE WILL FIND THEM...
OF COURSE... BUT EVERYONE ELSE IN MY NETWORK IS HELPED, TOO?

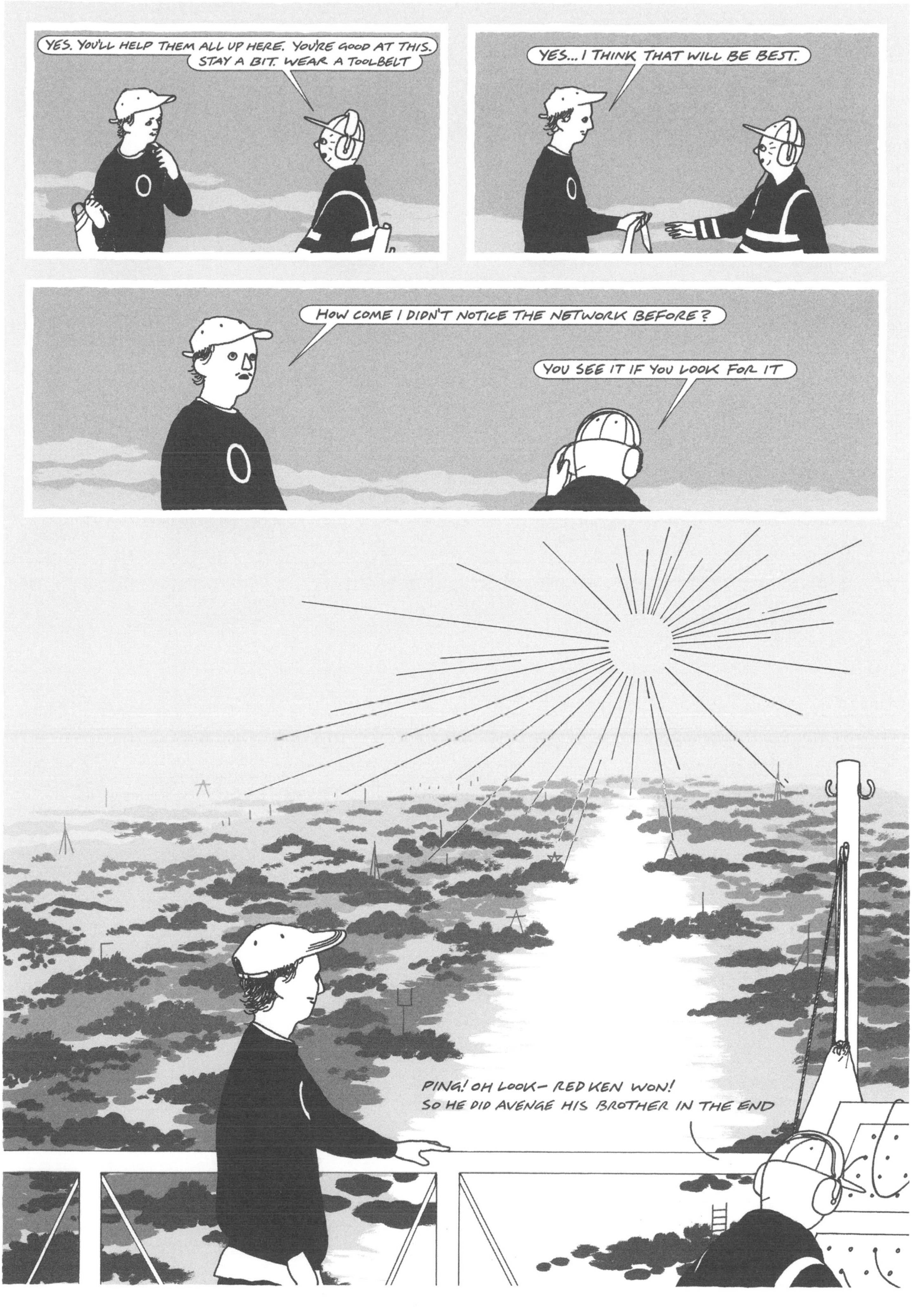
YES. YOU'LL HELP THEM ALL UP HERE. YOU'RE GOOD AT THIS.
STAY A BIT. WEAR A TOOLBELT
YES... I THINK THAT WILL BE BEST.
HOW COME I DIDN'T NOTICE THE NETWORK BEFORE?
YOU SEE IT IF YOU LOOK FOR IT
PING! OH LOOK- RED KEN WON!
SO HE DID AVENGE HIS BROTHER IN THE END

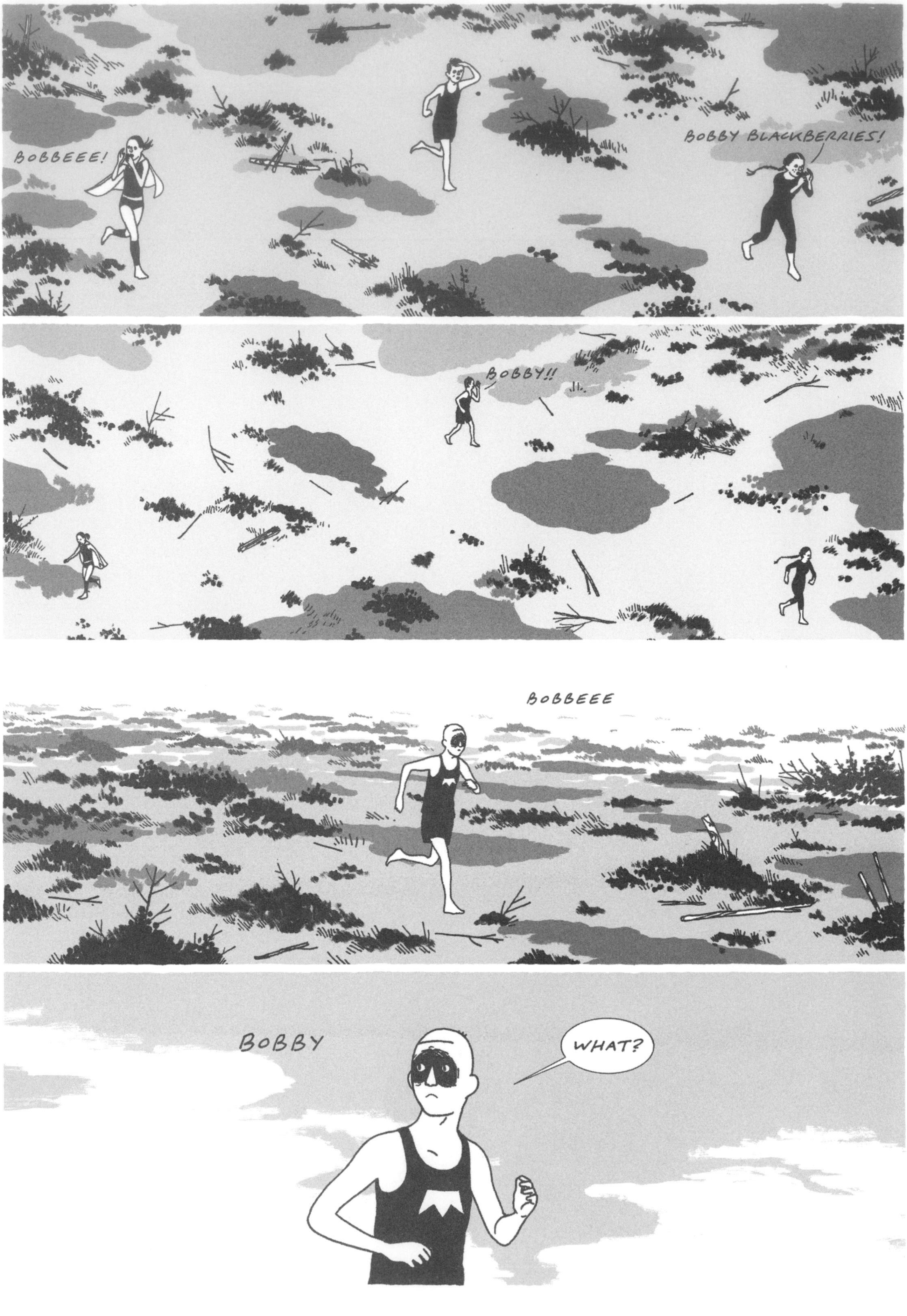
BOBBEEE!
BOBBY BLACKBERRIES!
BOBBY!!
BOBBEEE
BOBBY
WHAT?

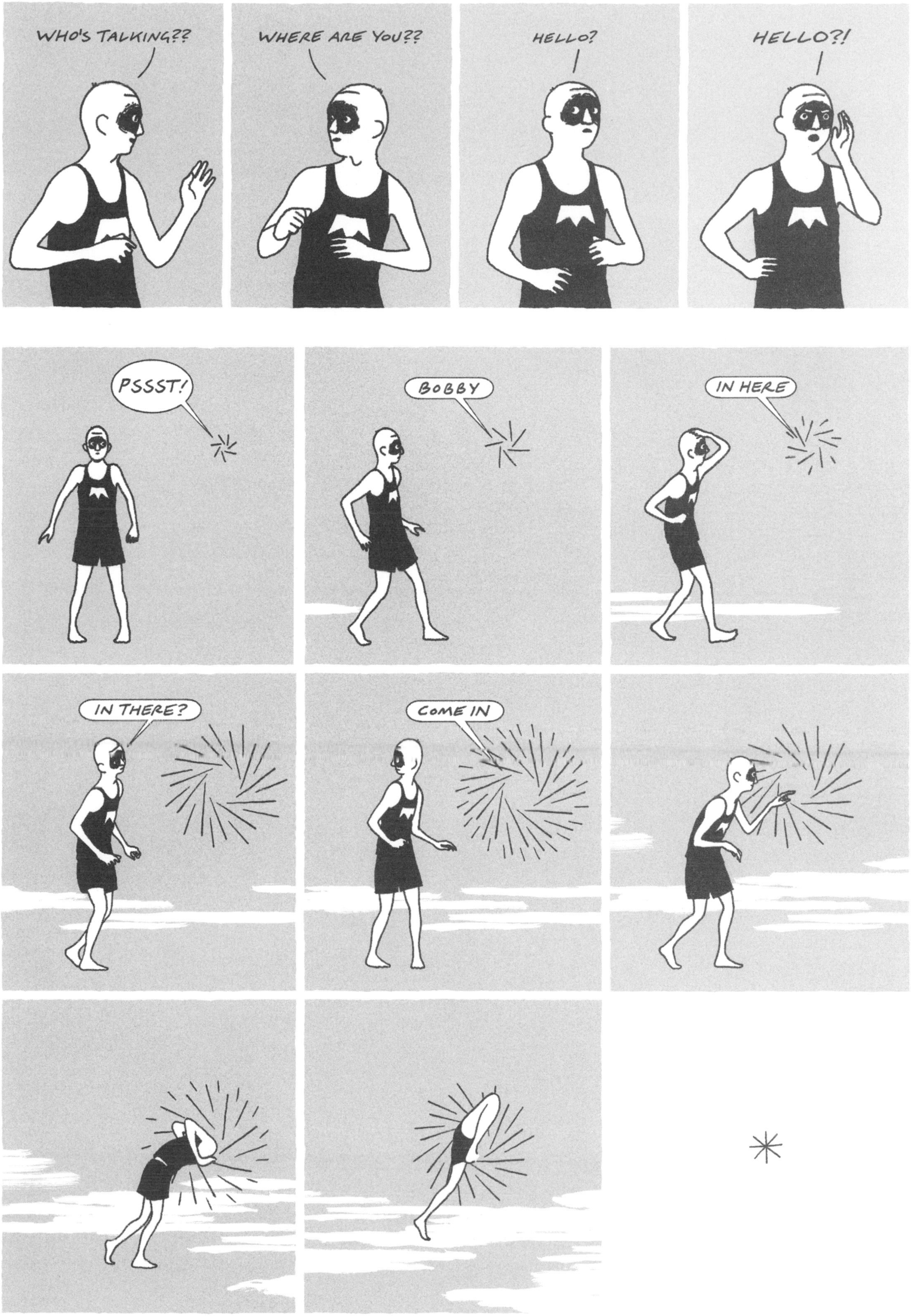
WHO'S TALKING??
WHERE ARE YOU??
HELLO?
HELLO?!
PSSST!
BOBBY
IN HERE
IN THERE?
COME IN

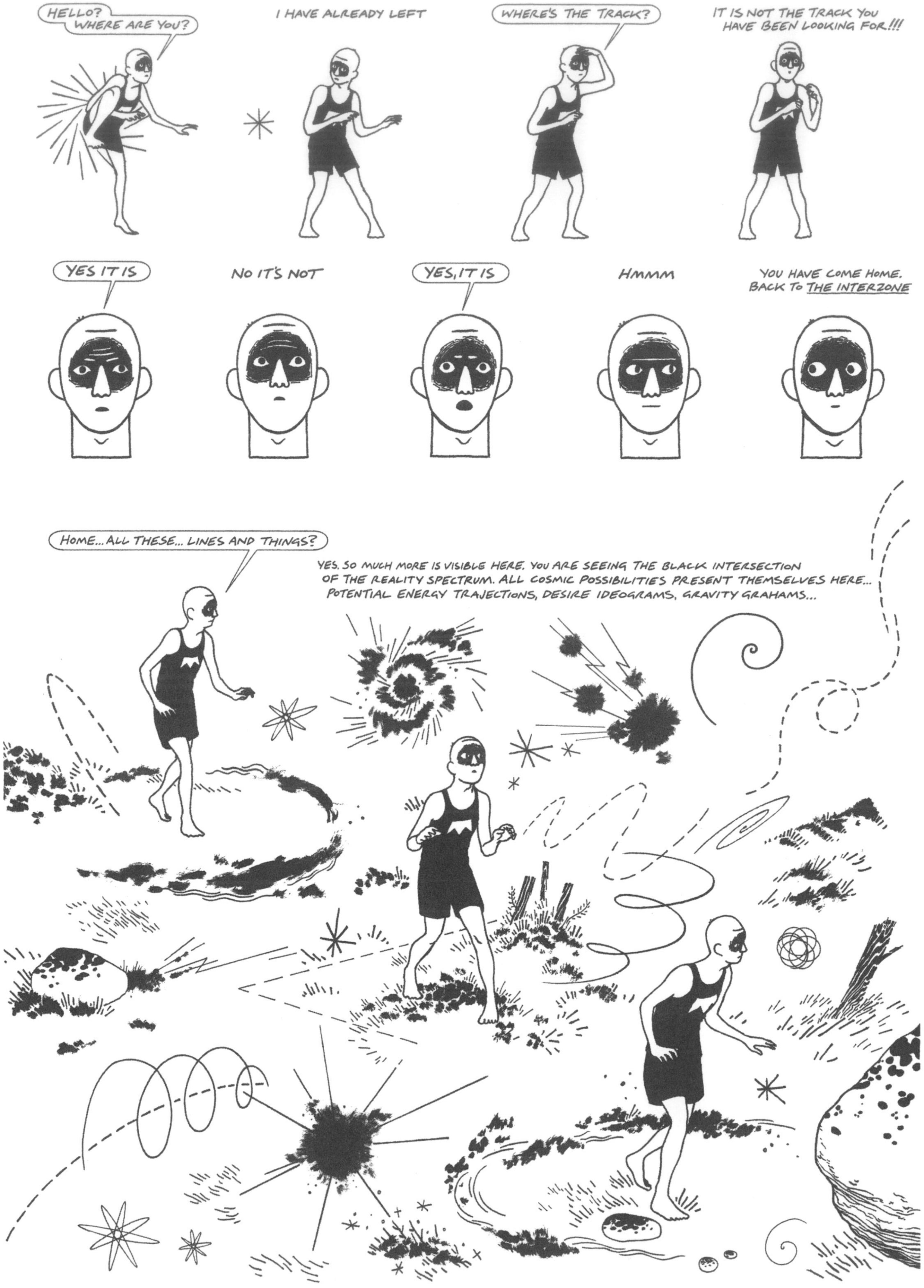
HELLO? WHERE ARE YOU?
I HAVE ALREADY LEFT
WHERE'S THE TRACK?
IT IS NOT THE TRACK YOU HAVE BEEN LOOKING FOR!!!
YES IT IS
NO IT'S NOT
YES, IT IS
HMMM
YOU HAVE COME HOME. BACK TO THE INTERZONE
HOME... ALL THESE... LINES AND THINGS?
YES. SO MUCH MORE IS VISIBLE HERE. YOU ARE SEEING THE BLACK INTERSECTION OF THE REALITY SPECTRUM. ALL COSMIC POSSIBILITIES PRESENT THEMSELVES HERE... POTENTIAL ENERGY TRAJECTIONS, DESIRE IDEOGRAMS, GRAVITY GRAHAMS...

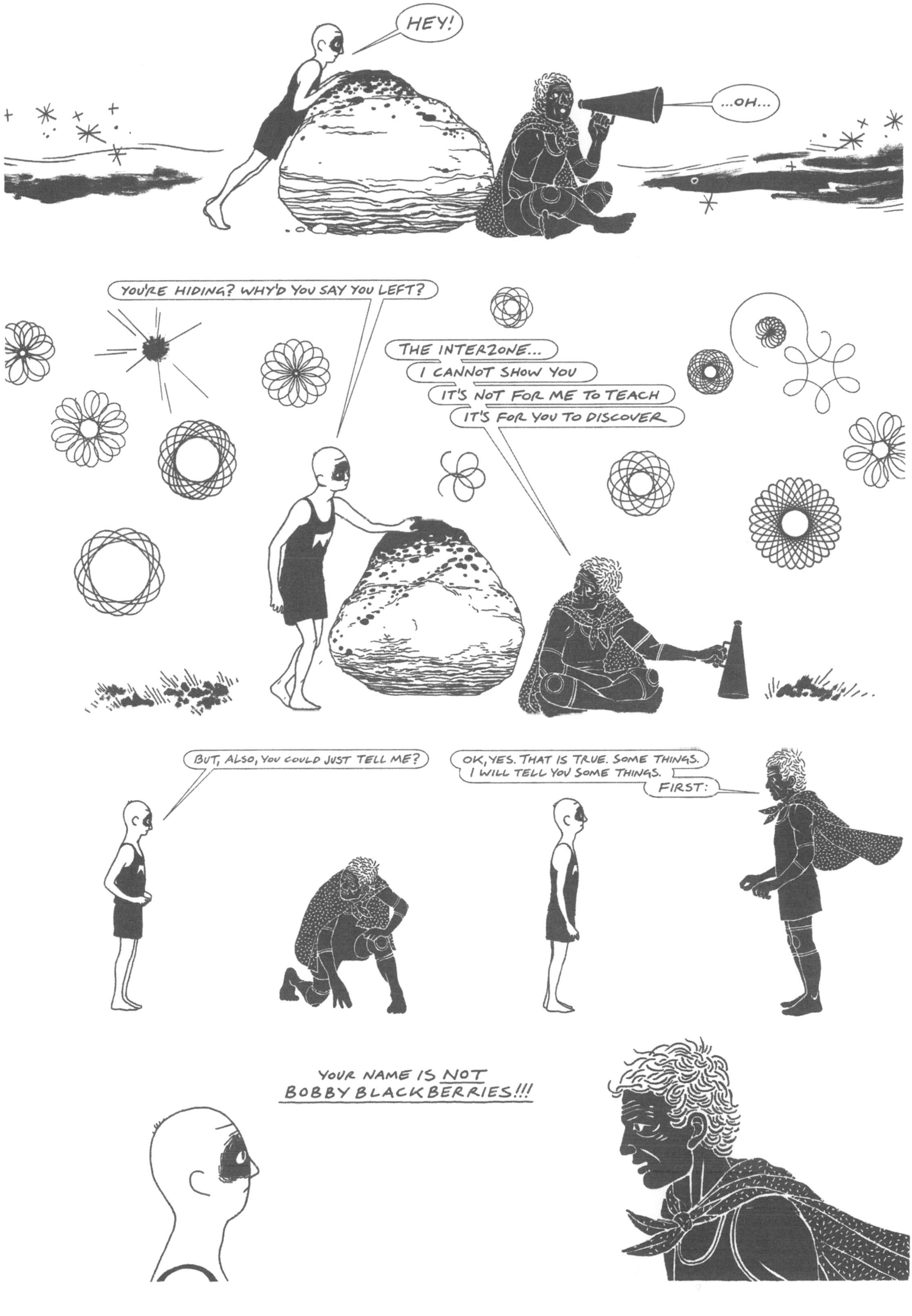

HEY!
...OH...
YOU'RE HIDING? WHY'D YOU SAY YOU LEFT?
THE INTERZONE...
I CANNOT SHOW YOU
IT'S NOT FOR ME TO TEACH
IT'S FOR YOU TO DISCOVER
BUT, ALSO, YOU COULD JUST TELL ME?
OK, YES. THAT IS TRUE. SOME THINGS. I WILL TELL YOU SOME THINGS.
FIRST:
YOUR NAME IS NOT BOBBY BLACKBERRIES!!!

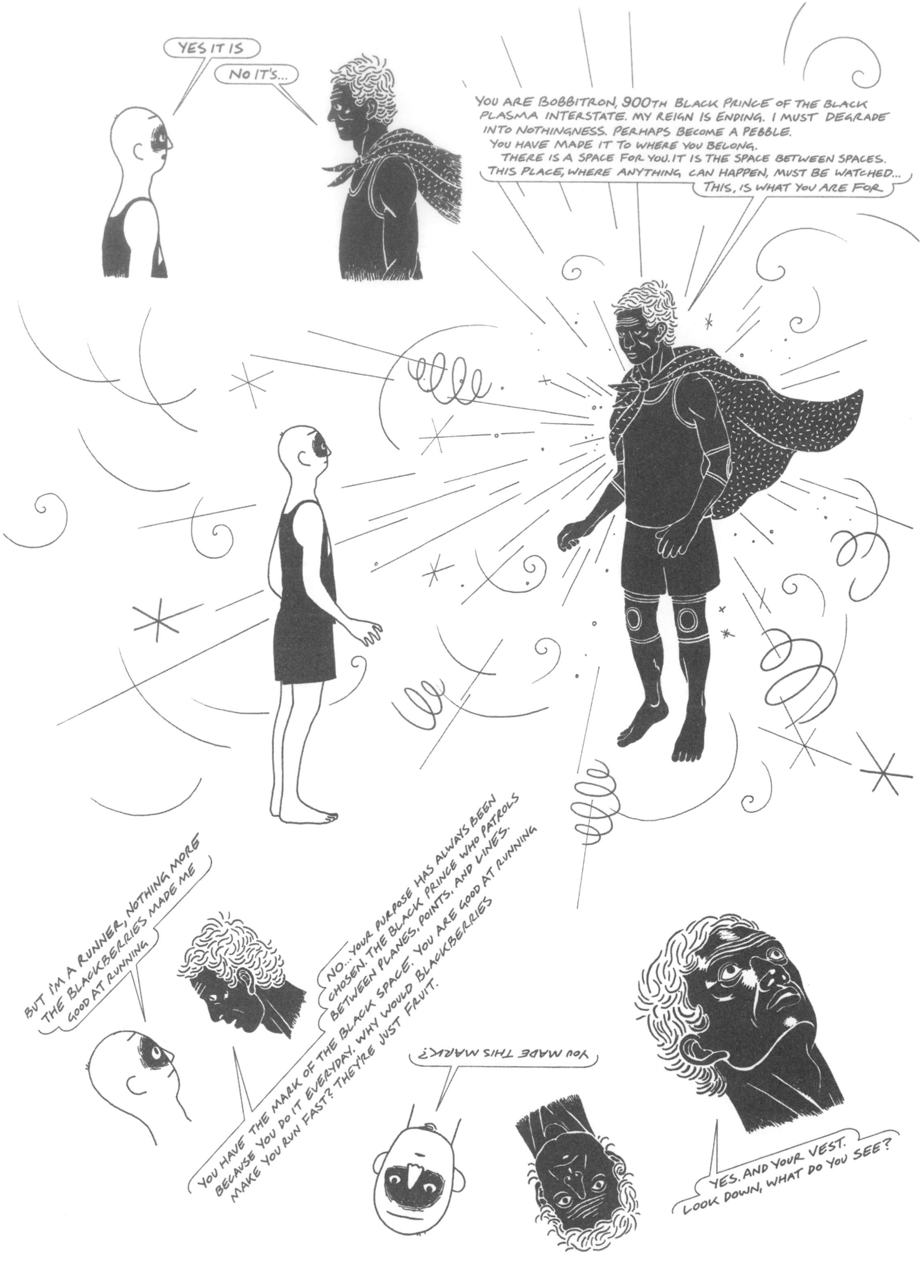

YES IT IS
NO IT'S...
YOU ARE BOBBITRON, 900TH BLACK PRINCE OF THE BLACK PLASMA INTERSTATE. MY REIGN IS ENDING. I MUST DEGRADE INTO NOTHINGNESS. PERHAPS BECOME A PEBBLE. YOU HAVE MADE IT TO WHERE YOU BELONG. THERE IS A SPACE FOR YOU. IT IS THE SPACE BETWEEN SPACES. THIS PLACE, WHERE ANYTHING CAN HAPPEN, MUST BE WATCHED...
THIS, IS WHAT YOU ARE FOR
BUT I'M A RUNNER, NOTHING MORE. THE BLACKBERRIES MADE ME GOOD AT RUNNING
NO... YOUR PURPOSE HAS ALWAYS BEEN CHOSEN. THE BLACK PRINCE WHO PATROLS BETWEEN PLANES, POINTS, AND LINES.
YOU HAVE THE MARK OF THE BLACK SPACE. YOU ARE GOOD AT RUNNING BECAUSE YOU DO IT EVERYDAY. WHY WOULD BLACKBERRIES MAKE YOU RUN FAST? THEY'RE JUST FRUIT.
YOU MADE THIS MARK?
YES. AND YOUR VEST. LOOK DOWN, WHAT DO YOU SEE?

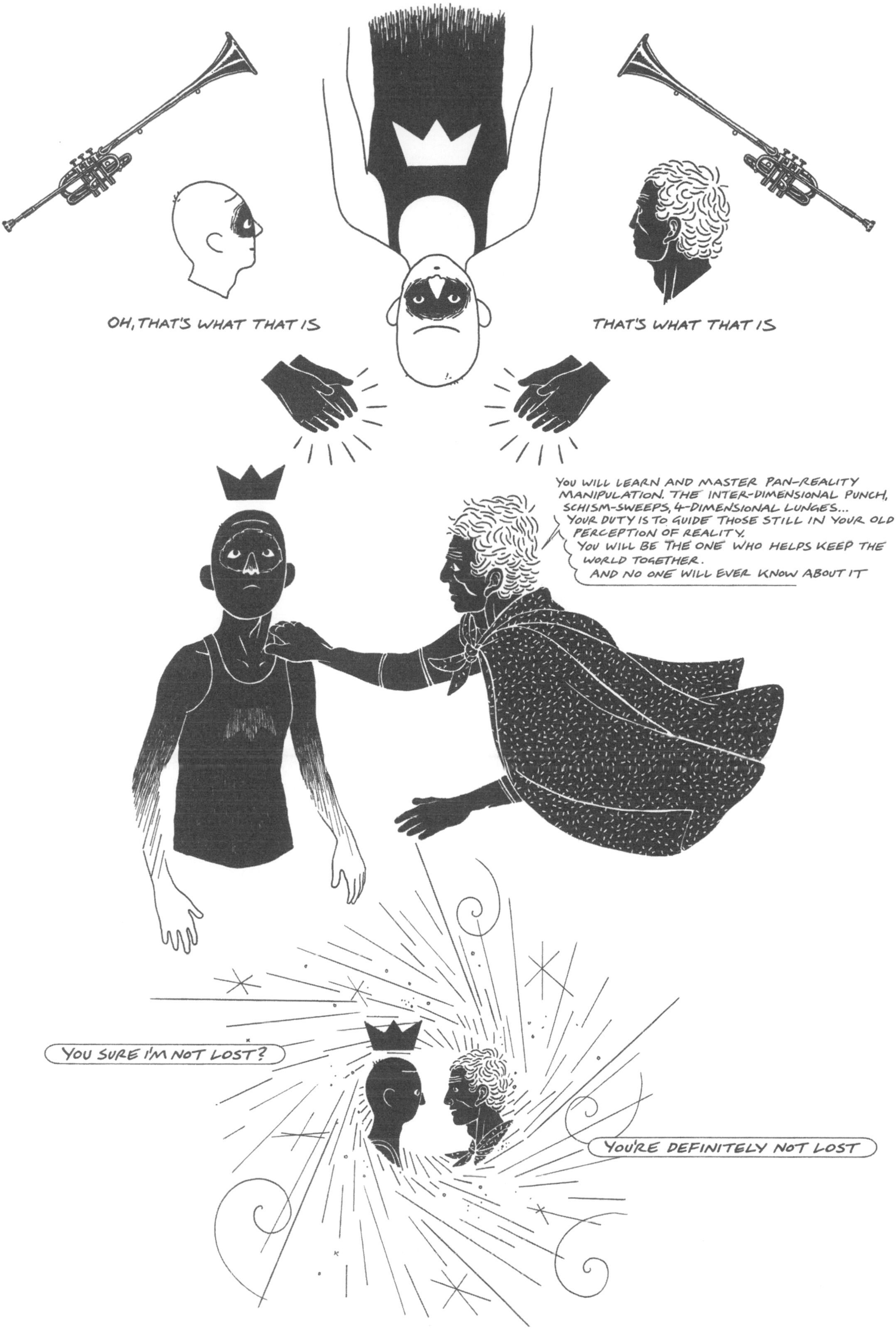
OH, THAT'S WHAT THAT IS
THAT'S WHAT THAT IS
YOU WILL LEARN AND MASTER PAN-REALITY MANIPULATION. THE INTER-DIMENSIONAL PUNCH, SCHISM-SWEEPS, 4-DIMENSIONAL LUNGES...
YOUR DUTY IS TO GUIDE THOSE STILL IN YOUR OLD PERCEPTION OF REALITY.
YOU WILL BE THE ONE WHO HELPS KEEP THE WORLD TOGETHER.
AND NO ONE WILL EVER KNOW ABOUT IT
YOU SURE I'M NOT LOST?
YOU'RE DEFINITELY NOT LOST

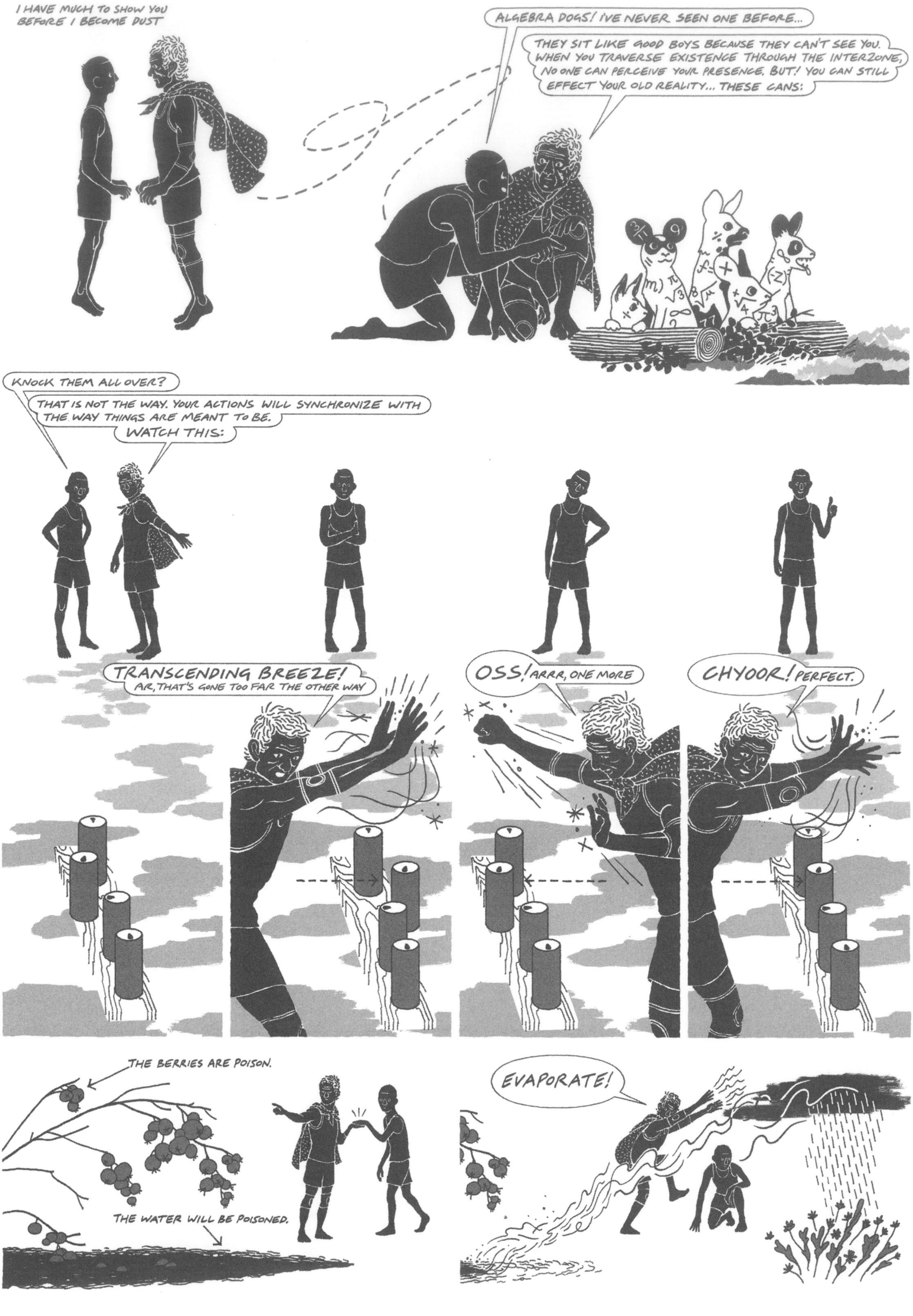
I HAVE MUCH TO SHOW YOU BEFORE I BECOME DUST
ALGEBRA DOGS! I'VE NEVER SEEN ONE BEFORE...
THEY SIT LIKE GOOD BOYS BECAUSE THEY CAN'T SEE YOU. WHEN YOU TRAVERSE EXISTENCE THROUGH THE INTERZONE, NO ONE CAN PERCEIVE YOUR PRESENCE. BUT! YOU CAN STILL EFFECT YOUR OLD REALITY... THESE CANS:
KNOCK THEM ALL OVER?
THAT IS NOT THE WAY. YOUR ACTIONS WILL SYNCHRONIZE WITH THE WAY THINGS ARE MEANT TO BE.
WATCH THIS:
TRANSCENDING BREEZE!
AR, THAT'S GONE TOO FAR THE OTHER WAY
OSS! ARRR, ONE MORE
CHYOOR! PERFECT.
THE BERRIES ARE POISON.
THE WATER WILL BE POISONED.
EVAPORATE!

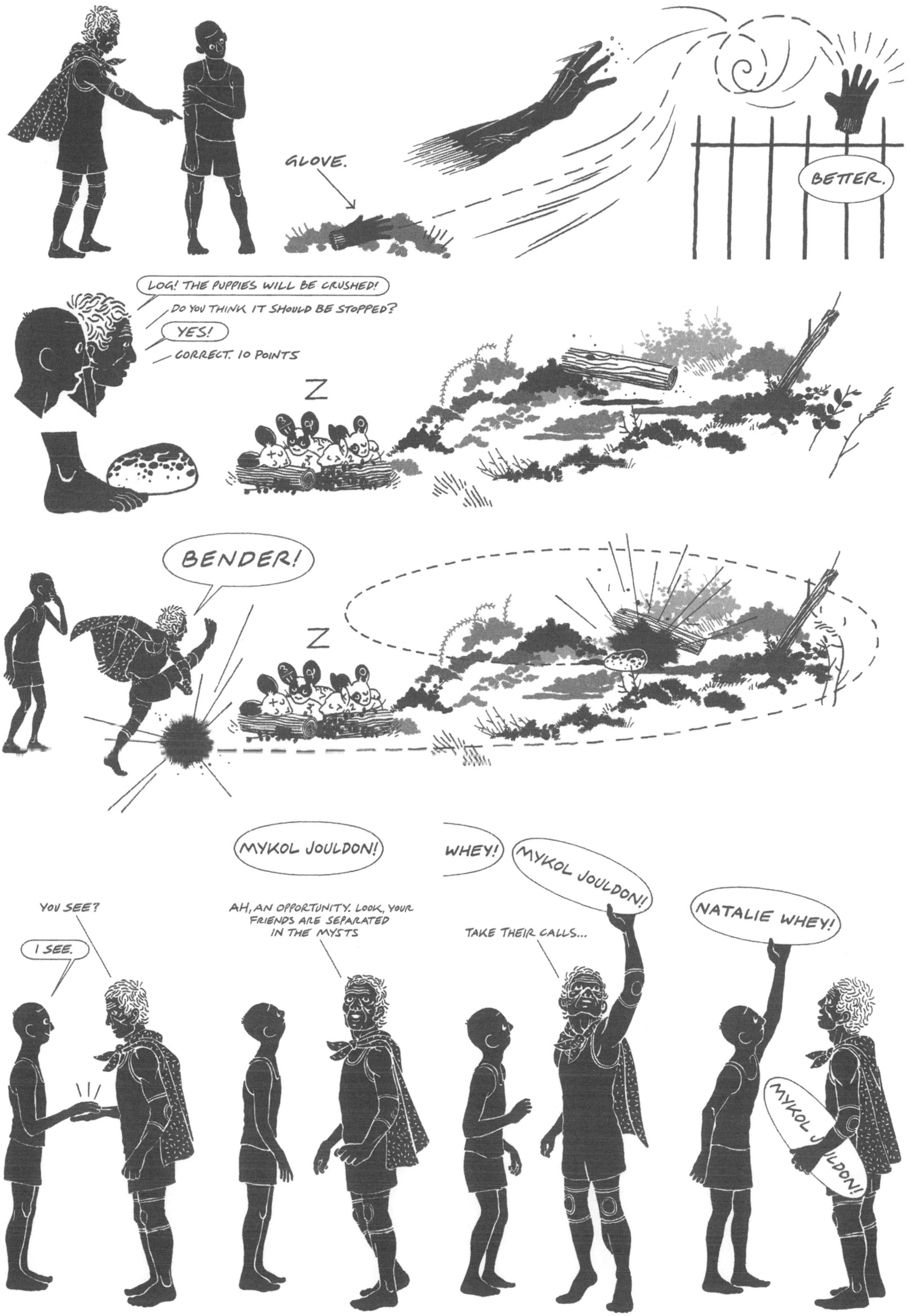
GLOVE.
BETTER.
LOG! THE PUPPIES WILL BE CRUSHED!
DO YOU THINK IT SHOULD BE STOPPED?
YES!
CORRECT. 10 POINTS
Z
BENDER!
Z
MYKOL JOULDON!
WHEY!
MYKOL JOULDON!
YOU SEE?
I SEE.
AH, AN OPPORTUNITY. LOOK, YOUR FRIENDS ARE SEPARATED IN THE MYSTS
TAKE THEIR CALLS...
NATALIE WHEY!
MYKOL JOULDON!

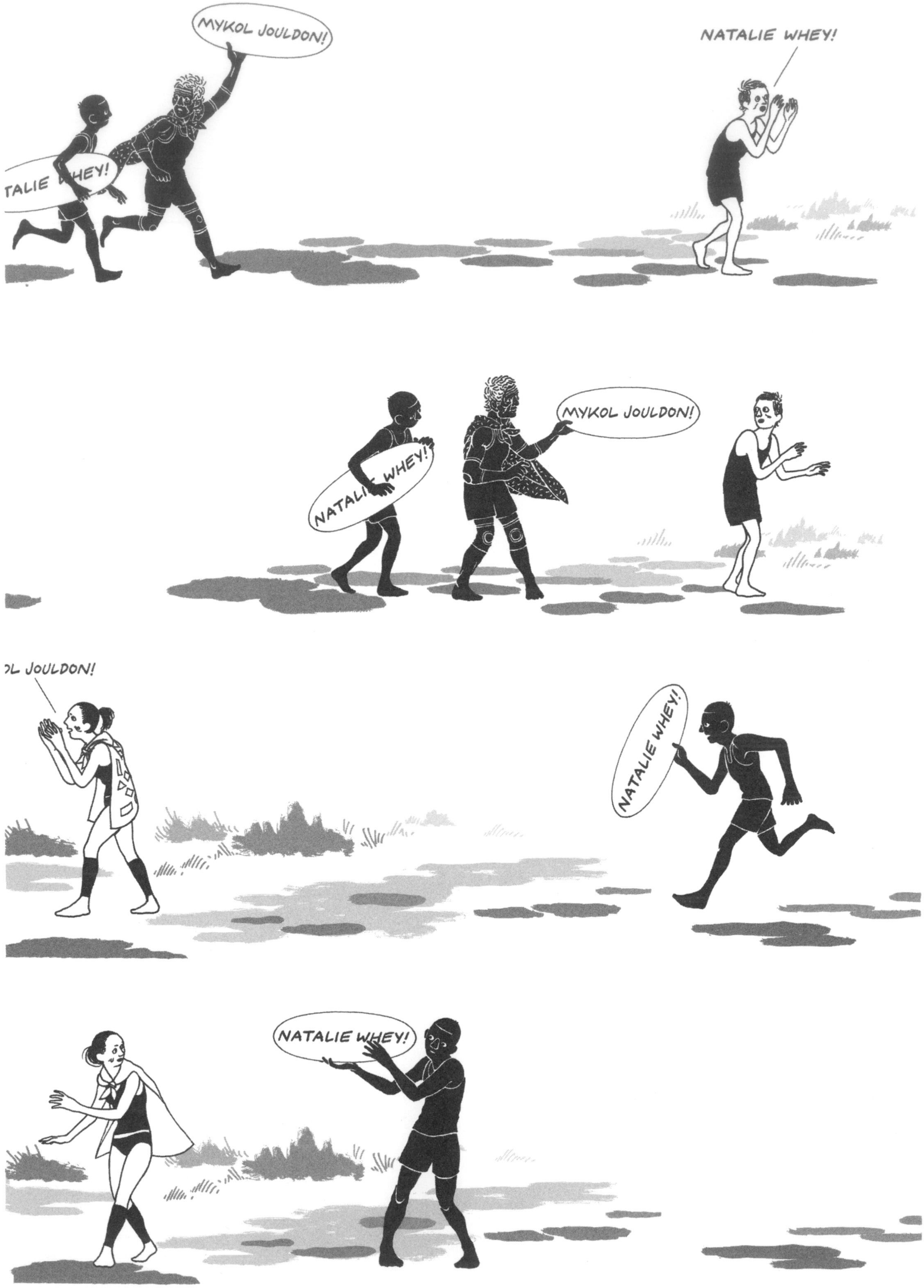
MYKOL JOULDON!
TALIE WHEY!
NATALIE WHEY!
NATALI WHEY!
MYKOL JOULDON!
OL JOULDON!
NATALIE WHEY!
NATALIE WHEY!

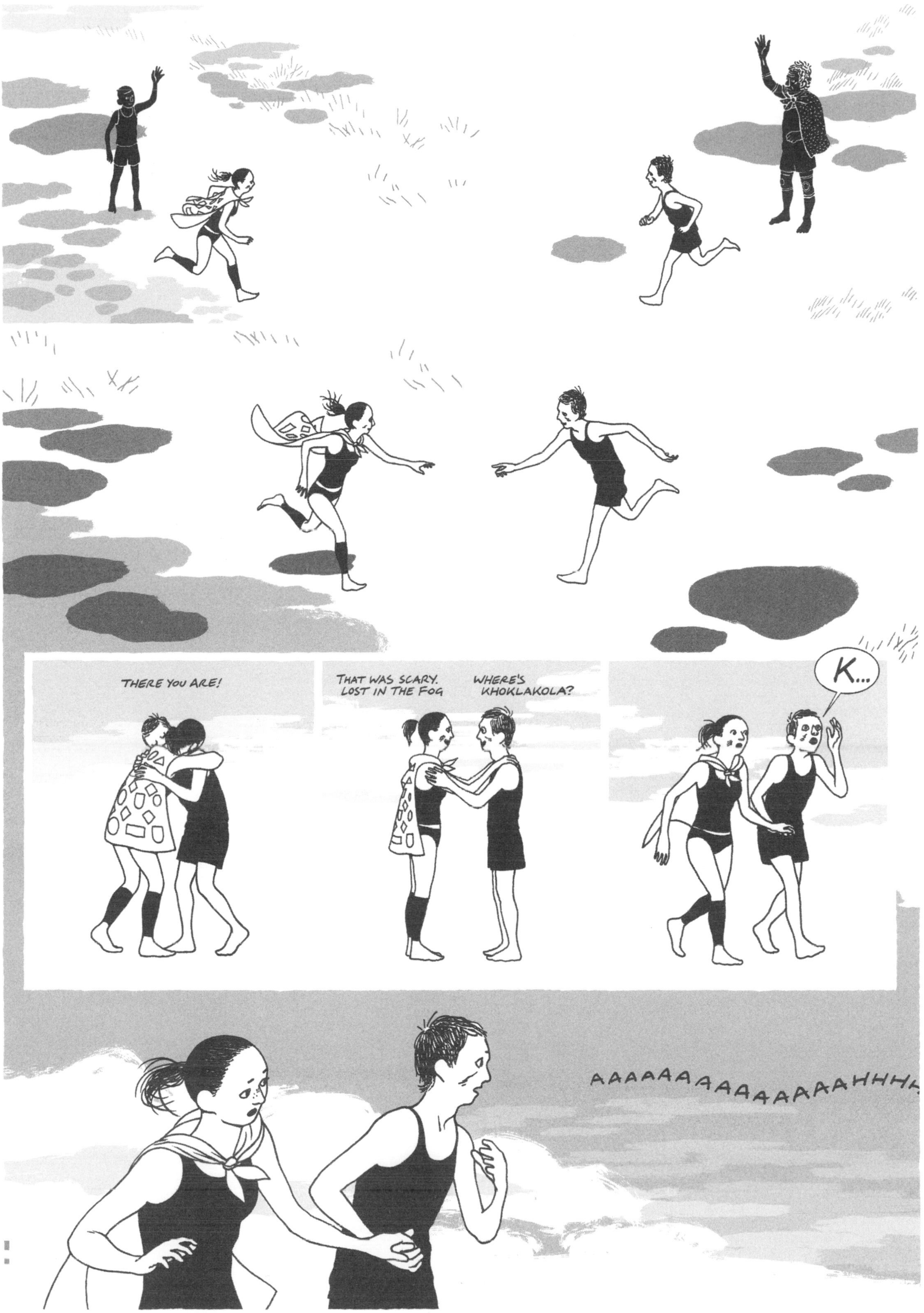

THERE YOU ARE!
THAT WAS SCARY. LOST IN THE FOG
WHERE'S KHOKLAKOLA?
K...
AAAAAAAAAAAAAAAHHHH

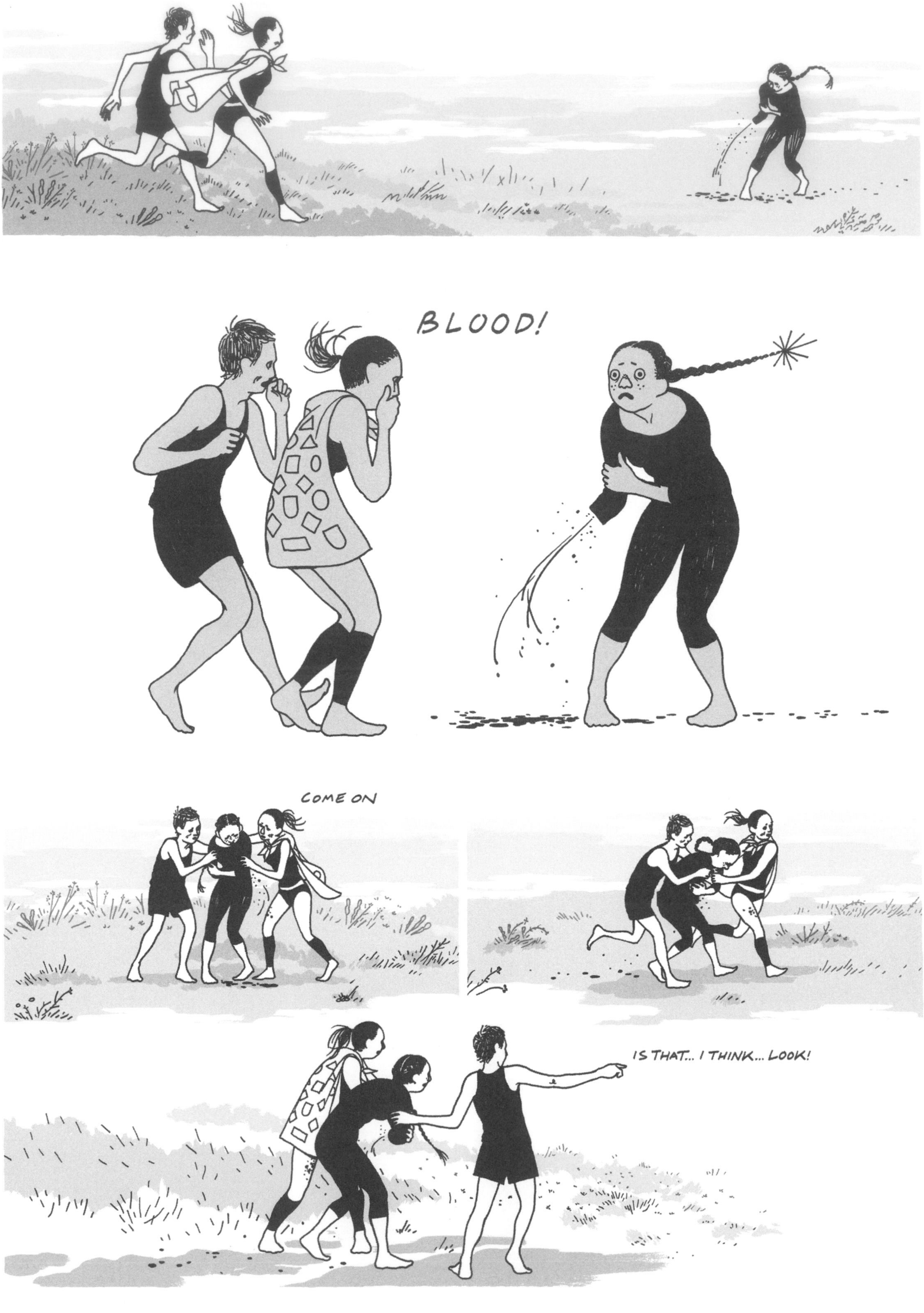
BLOOD!
COME ON
IS THAT... I THINK... LOOK!

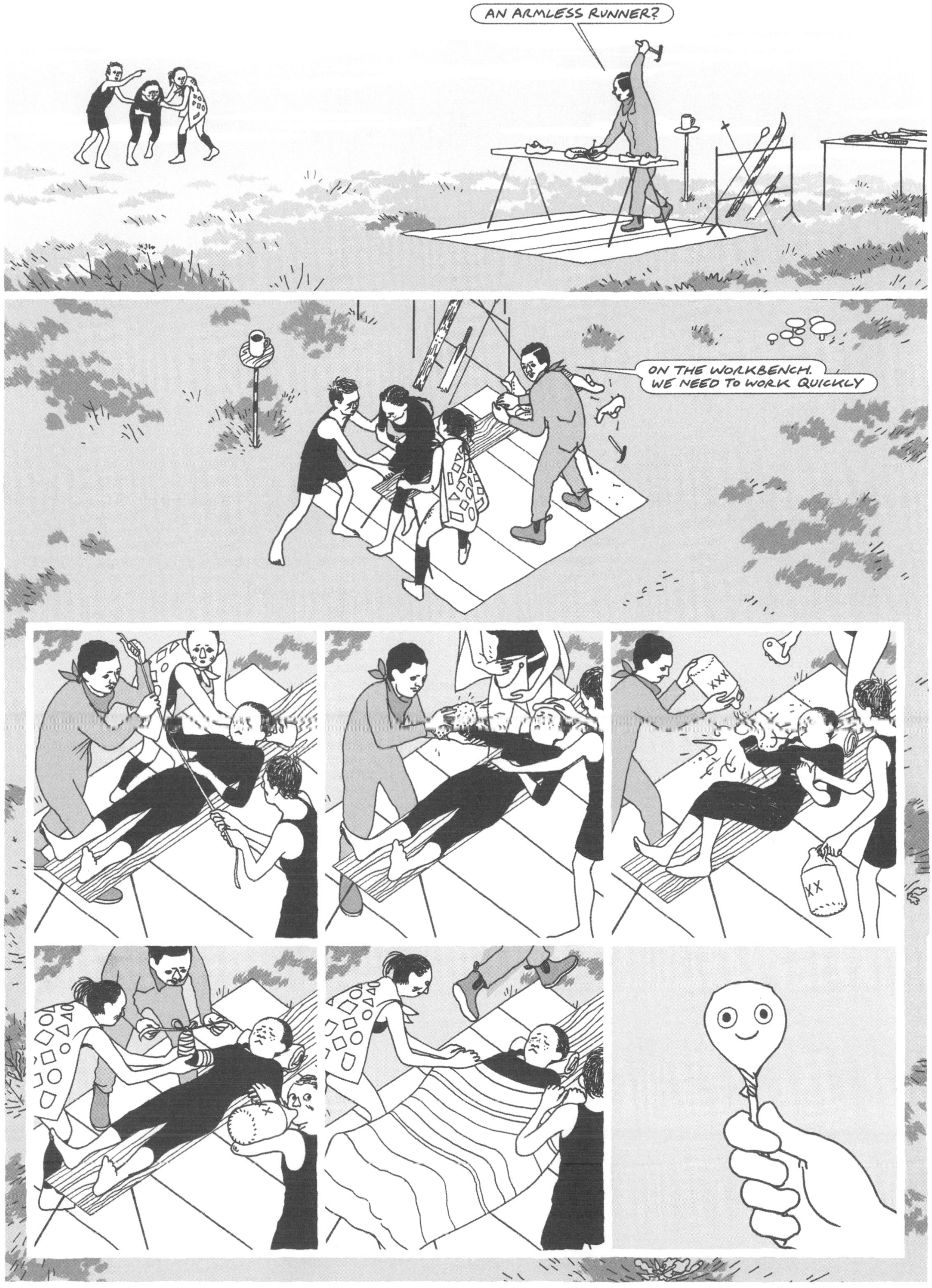
AN ARMLESS RUNNER?
ON THE WORKBENCH.
WE NEED TO WORK QUICKLY

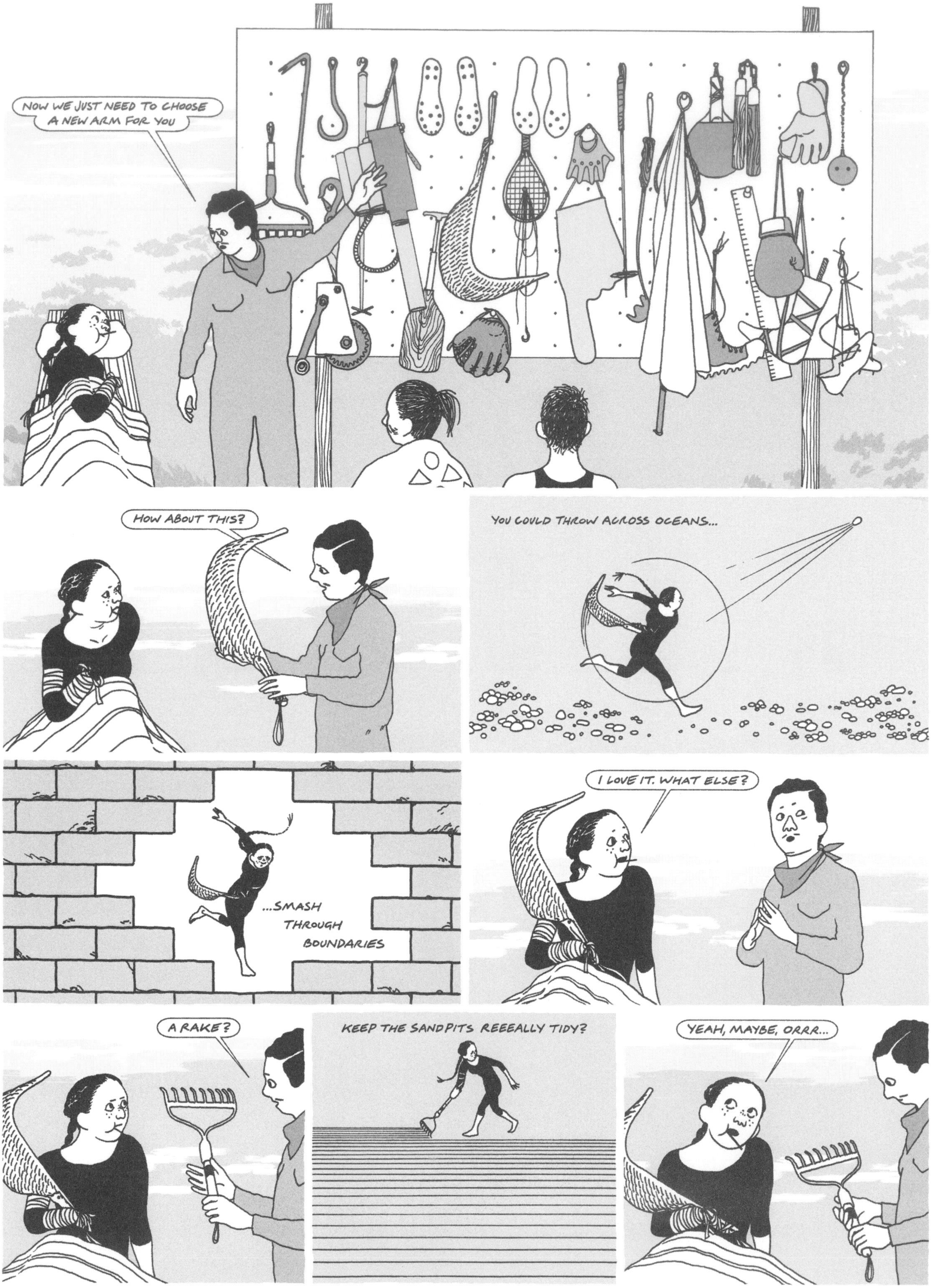
NOW WE JUST NEED TO CHOOSE A NEW ARM FOR YOU
HOW ABOUT THIS?
YOU COULD THROW ACROSS OCEANS...
...SMASH THROUGH BOUNDARIES
I LOVE IT. WHAT ELSE?
A RAKE?
KEEP THE SANDPITS REEEALLY TIDY?
YEAH, MAYBE, ORRR...

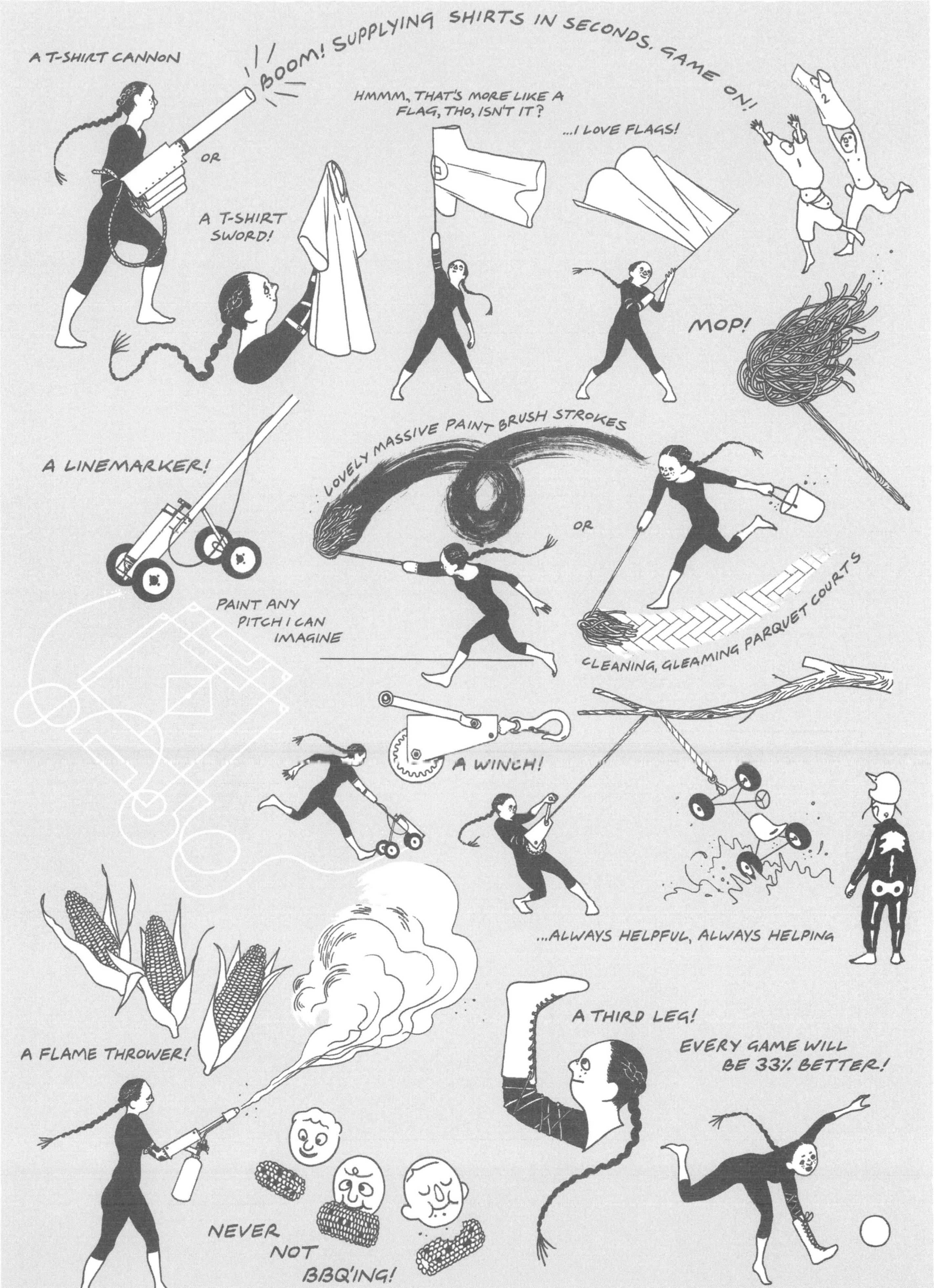
A T-SHIRT CANNON
BOOM! SUPPLYING SHIRTS IN SECONDS. GAME ON!
OR
A T-SHIRT SWORD!
HMMM.. THAT'S MORE LIKE A FLAG, THO, ISN'T IT?
...I LOVE FLAGS!
MOP!
A LINEMARKER!
LOVELY MASSIVE PAINT BRUSH STROKES
OR
PAINT ANY PITCH I CAN IMAGINE
CLEANING, GLEAMING PARQUET COURTS
A WINCH!
...ALWAYS HELPFUL, ALWAYS HELPING
A THIRD LEG!
EVERY GAME WILL BE 33% BETTER!
A FLAME THROWER!
NEVER NOT BBQ'ING!

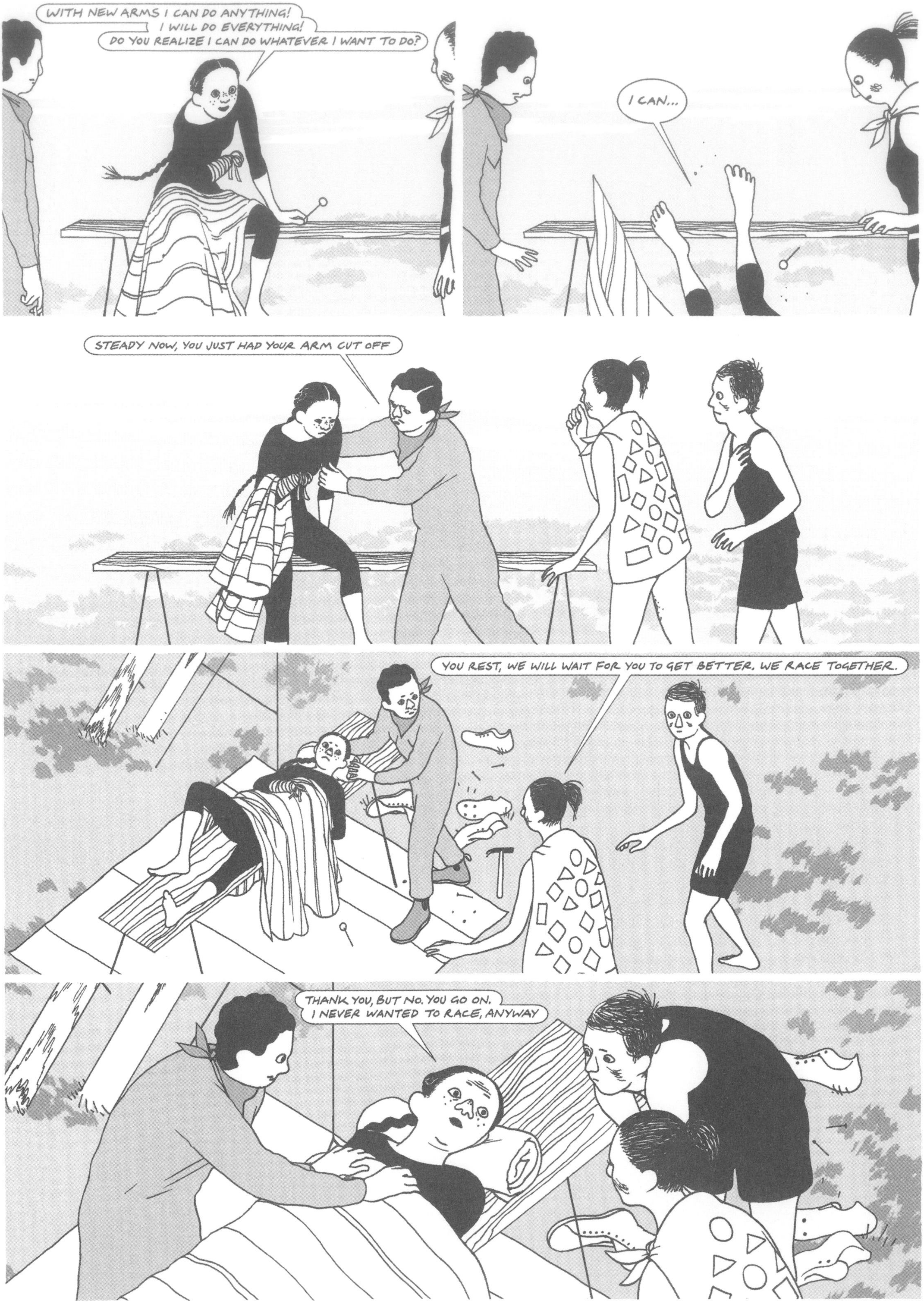
WITH NEW ARMS I CAN DO ANYTHING!
I WILL DO EVERYTHING!
DO YOU REALIZE I CAN DO WHATEVER I WANT TO DO?
I CAN...
STEADY NOW, YOU JUST HAD YOUR ARM CUT OFF
YOU REST, WE WILL WAIT FOR YOU TO GET BETTER. WE RACE TOGETHER.
THANK YOU, BUT NO. YOU GO ON.
I NEVER WANTED TO RACE, ANYWAY

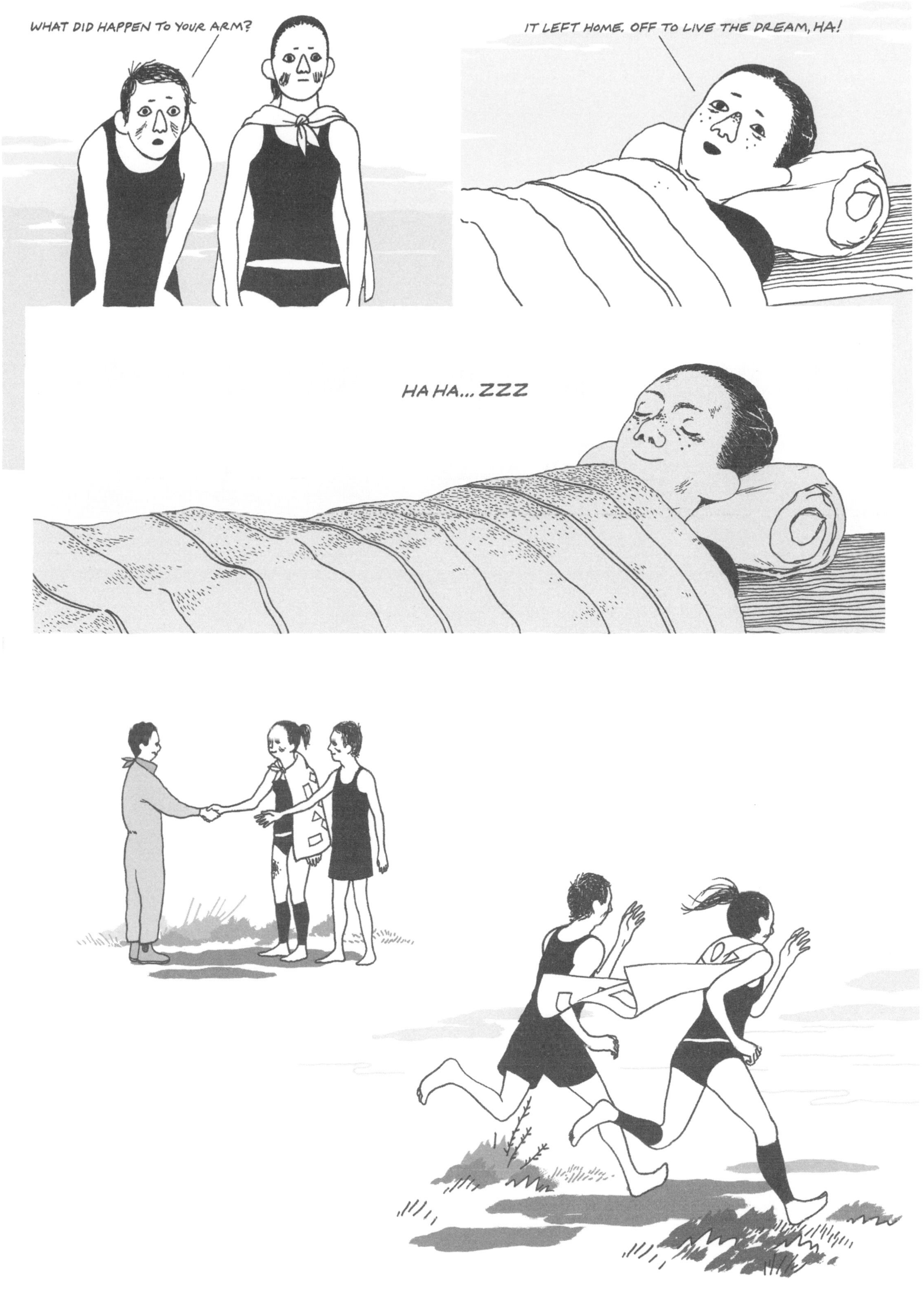
WHAT DID HAPPEN TO YOUR ARM?
IT LEFT HOME. OFF TO LIVE THE DREAM, HA!
HA HA... ZZZ

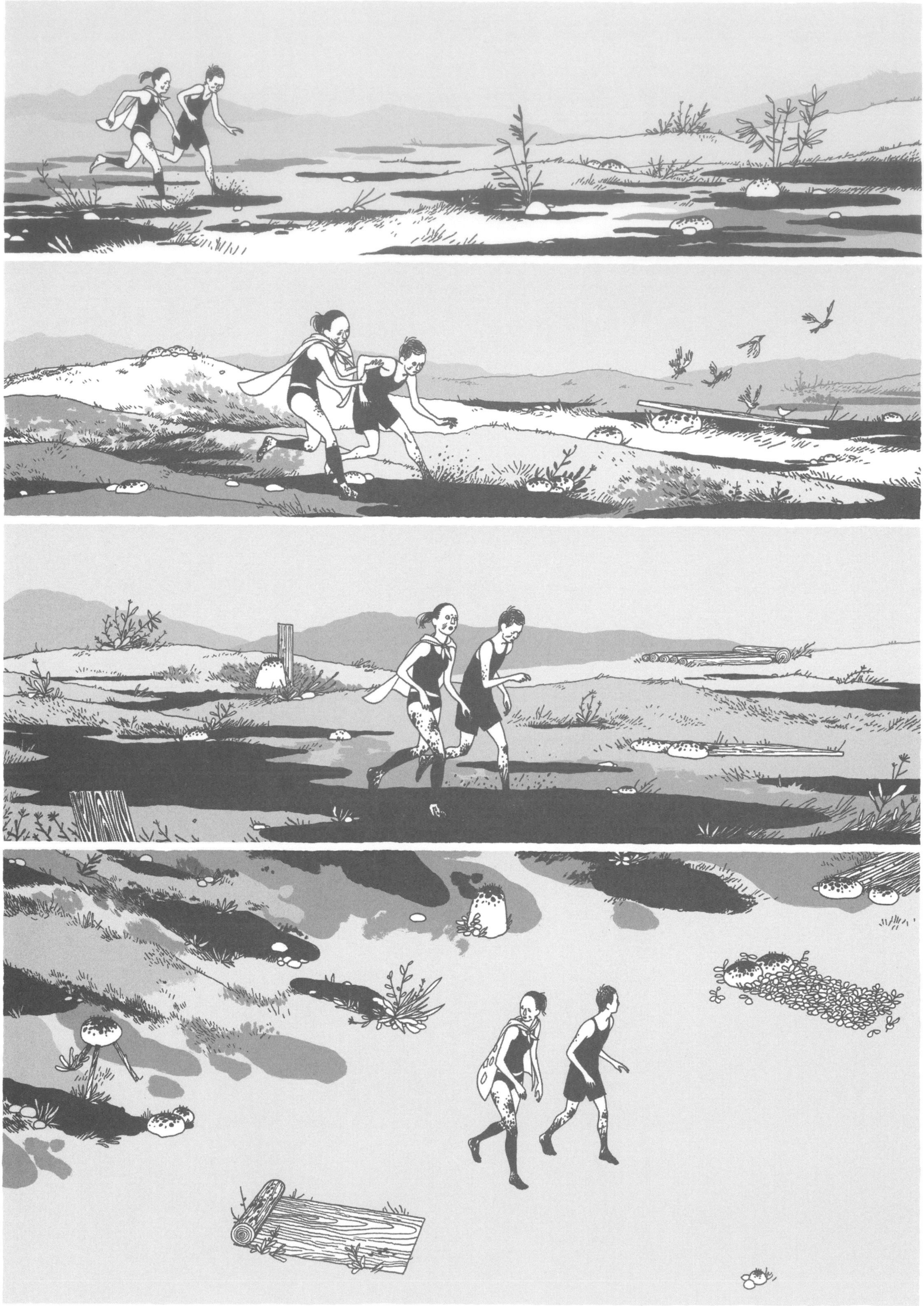

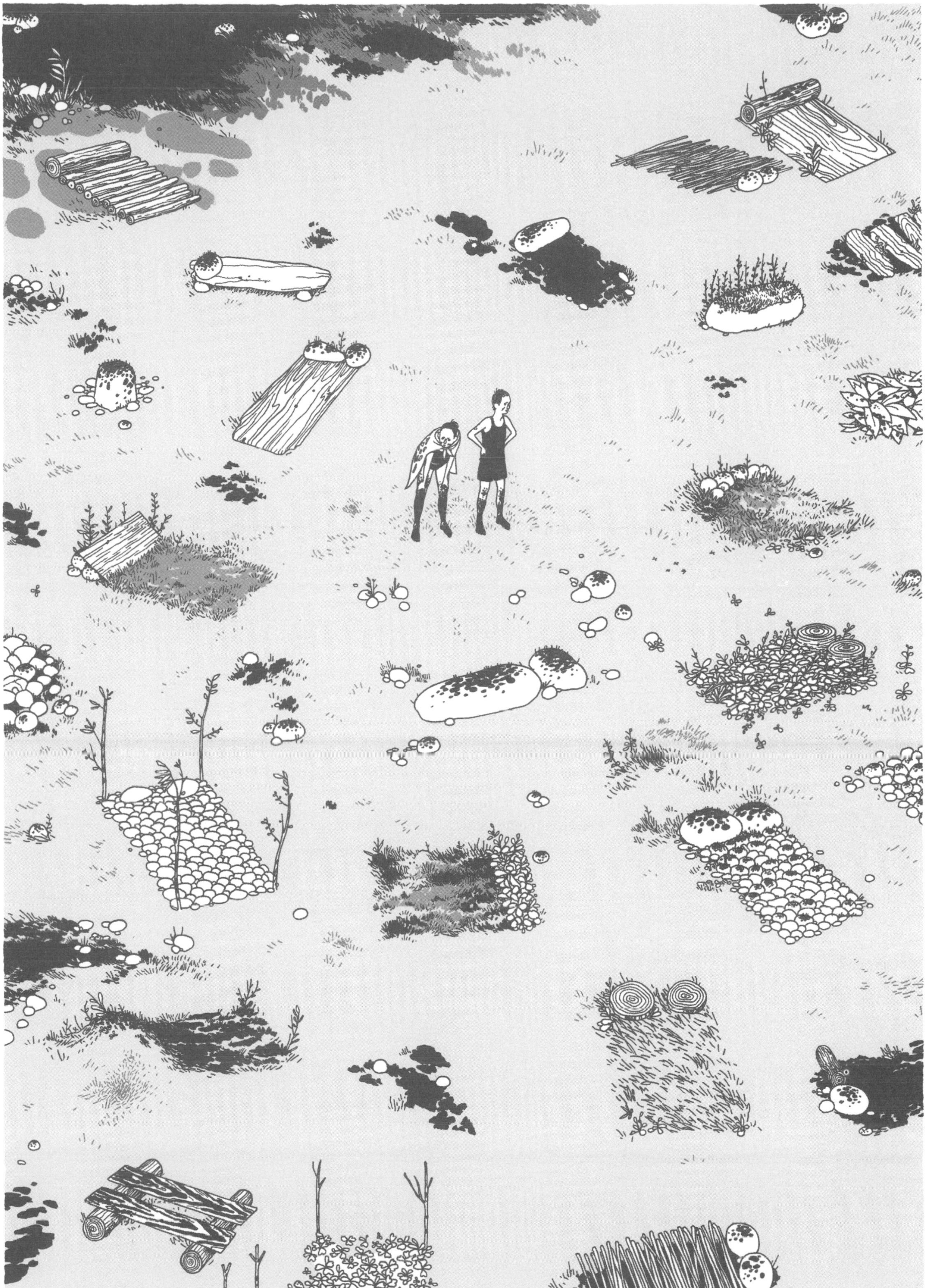

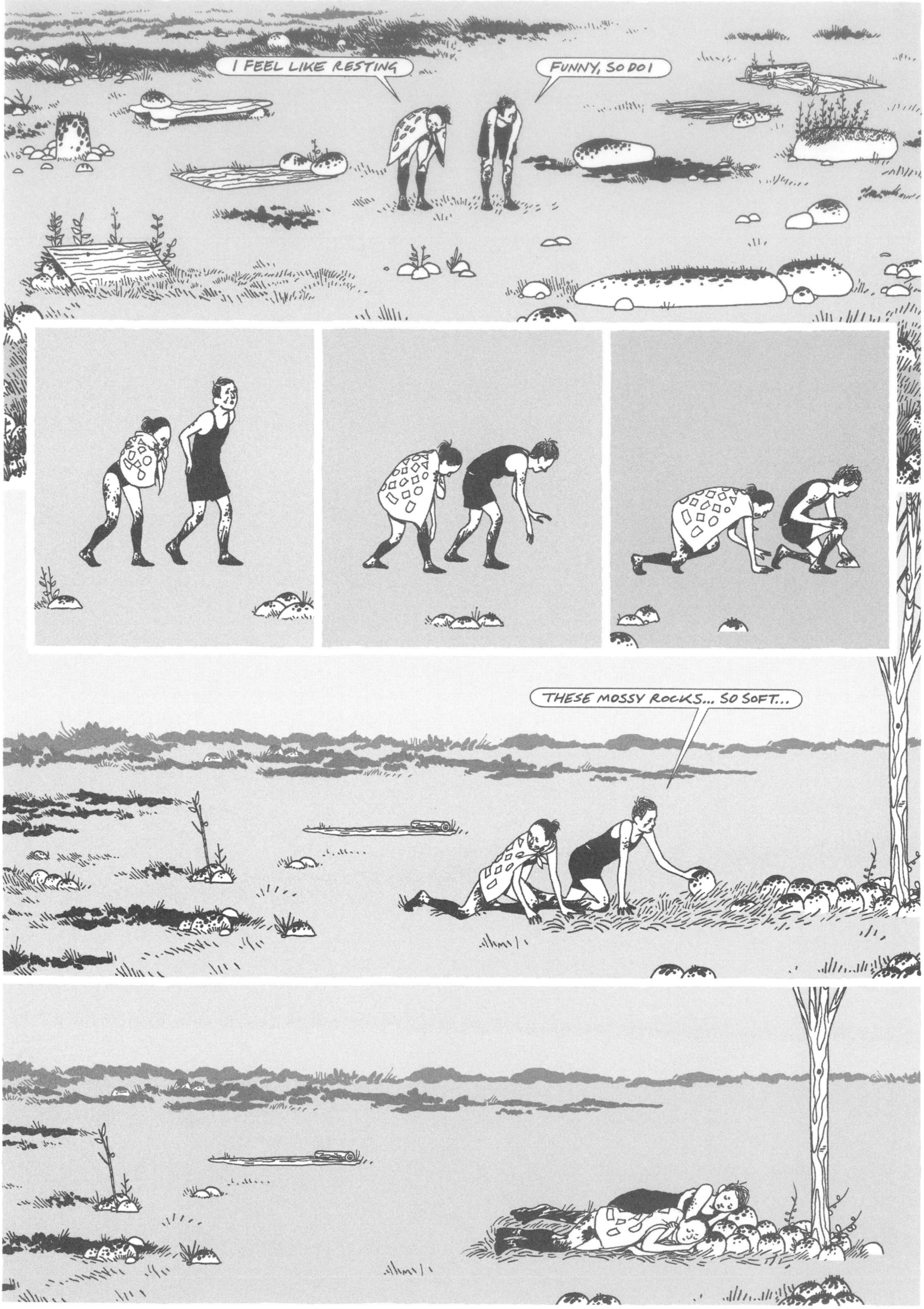
I FEEL LIKE RESTING
FUNNY, SO DO I
THESE MOSSY ROCKS... SO SOFT...

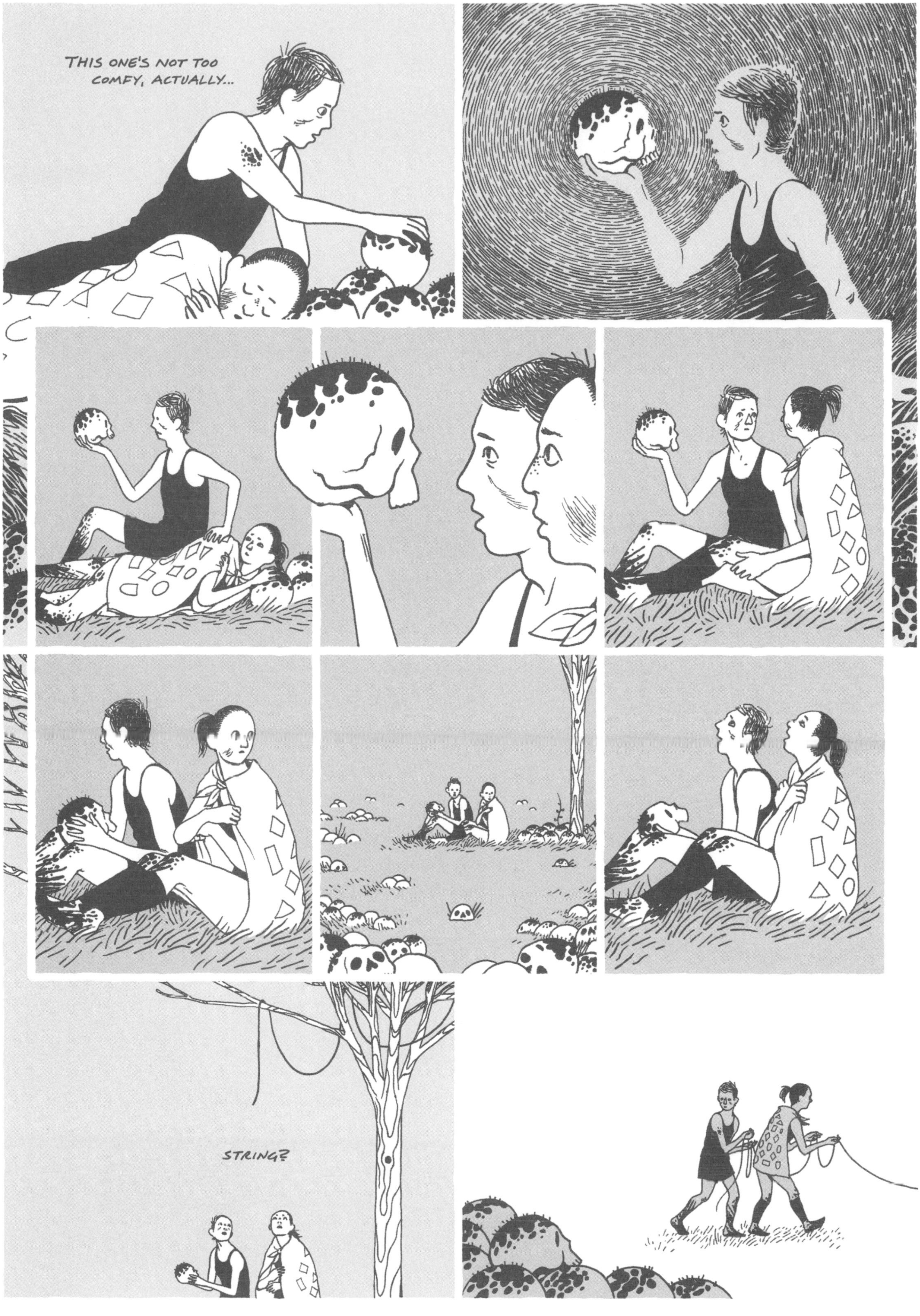
THIS ONE'S NOT TOO COMFY, ACTUALLY...
STRING?

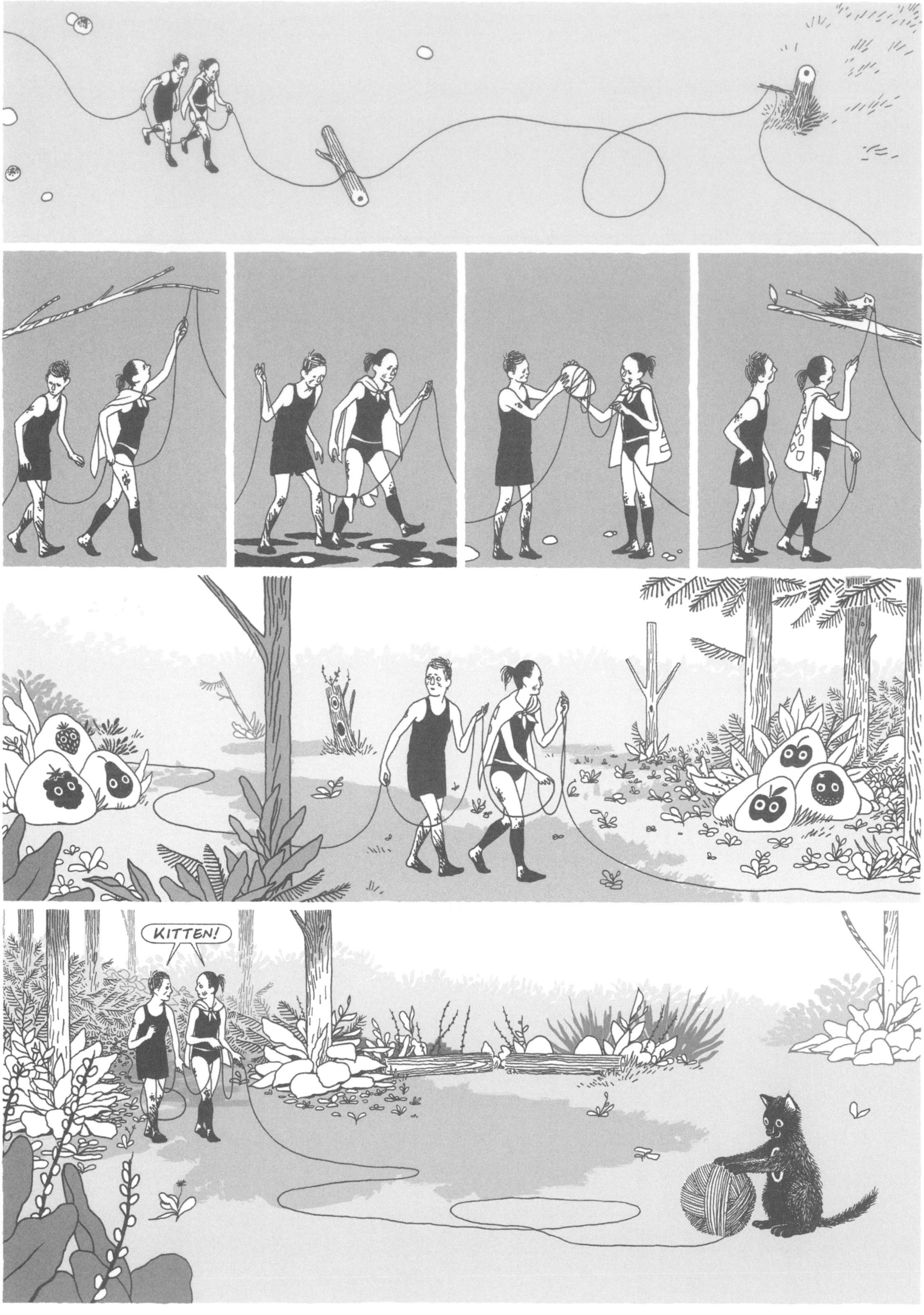
KITTEN!

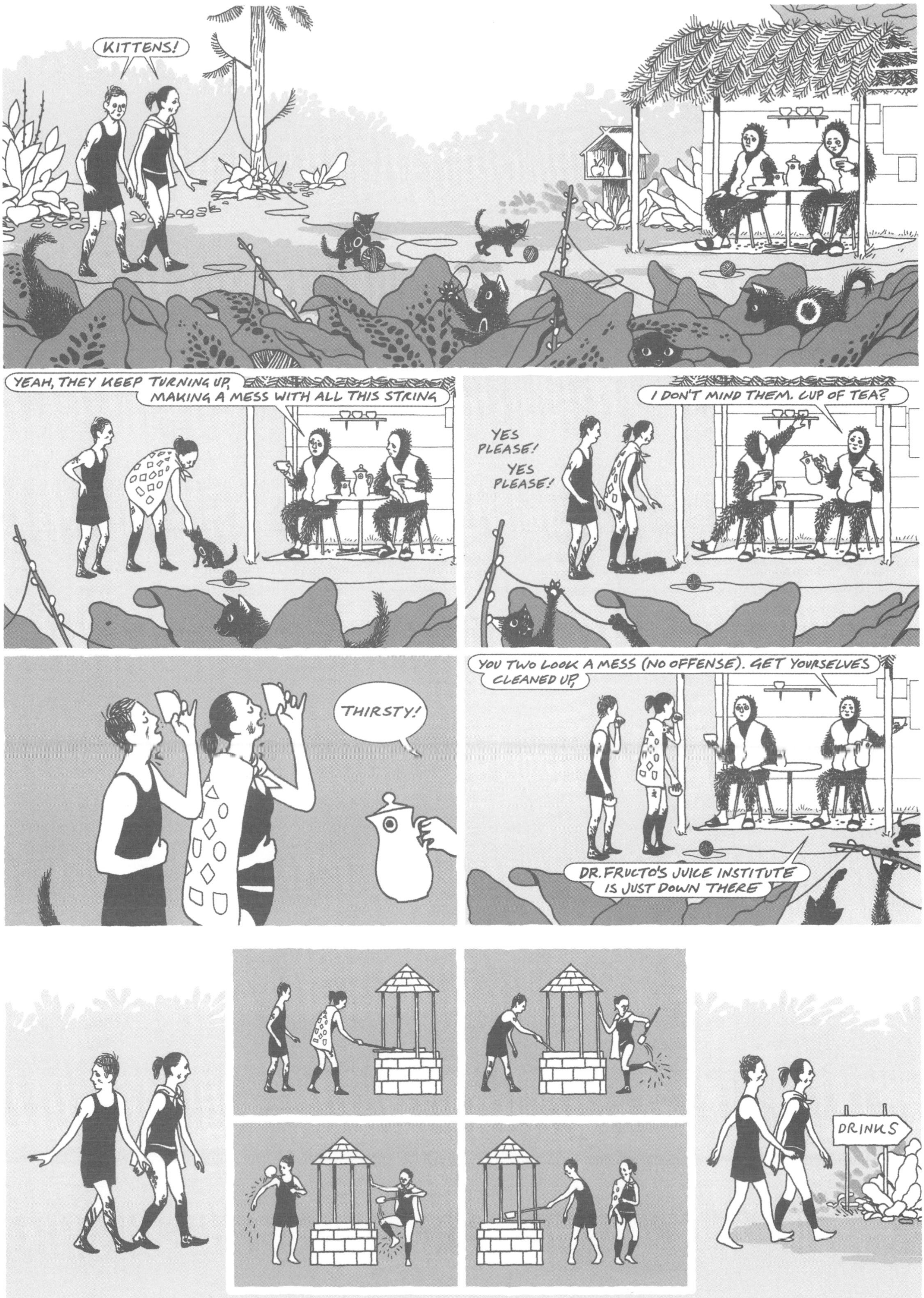
KITTENS!
YEAH, THEY KEEP TURNING UP, MAKING A MESS WITH ALL THIS STRING
I DON'T MIND THEM. CUP OF TEA?
YES PLEASE!
YES PLEASE!
THIRSTY!
YOU TWO LOOK A MESS (NO OFFENSE). GET YOURSELVES CLEANED UP,
DR. FRUCTO'S JUICE INSTITUTE IS JUST DOWN THERE
DRINKS

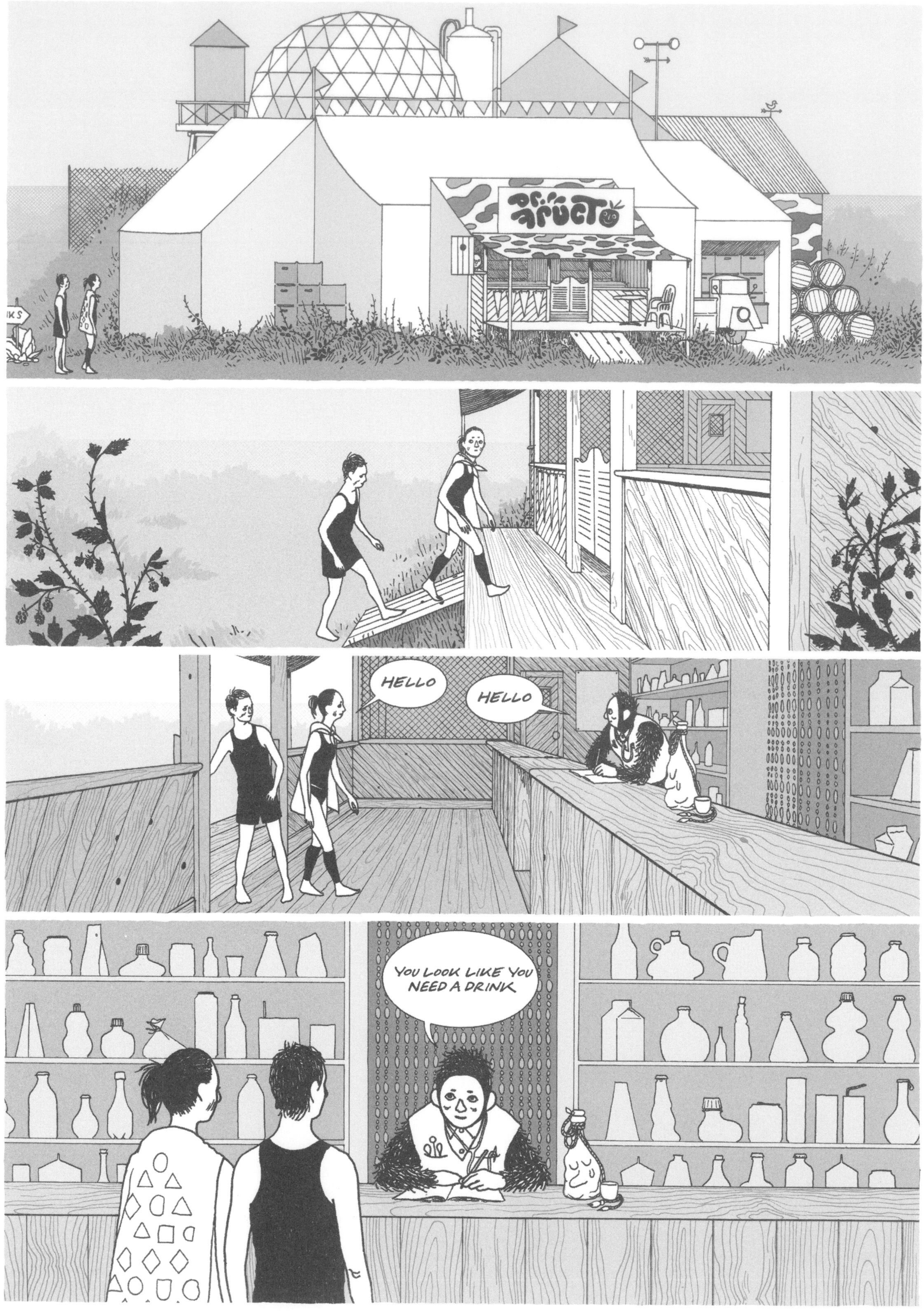
HELLO
HELLO
YOU LOOK LIKE YOU NEED A DRINK

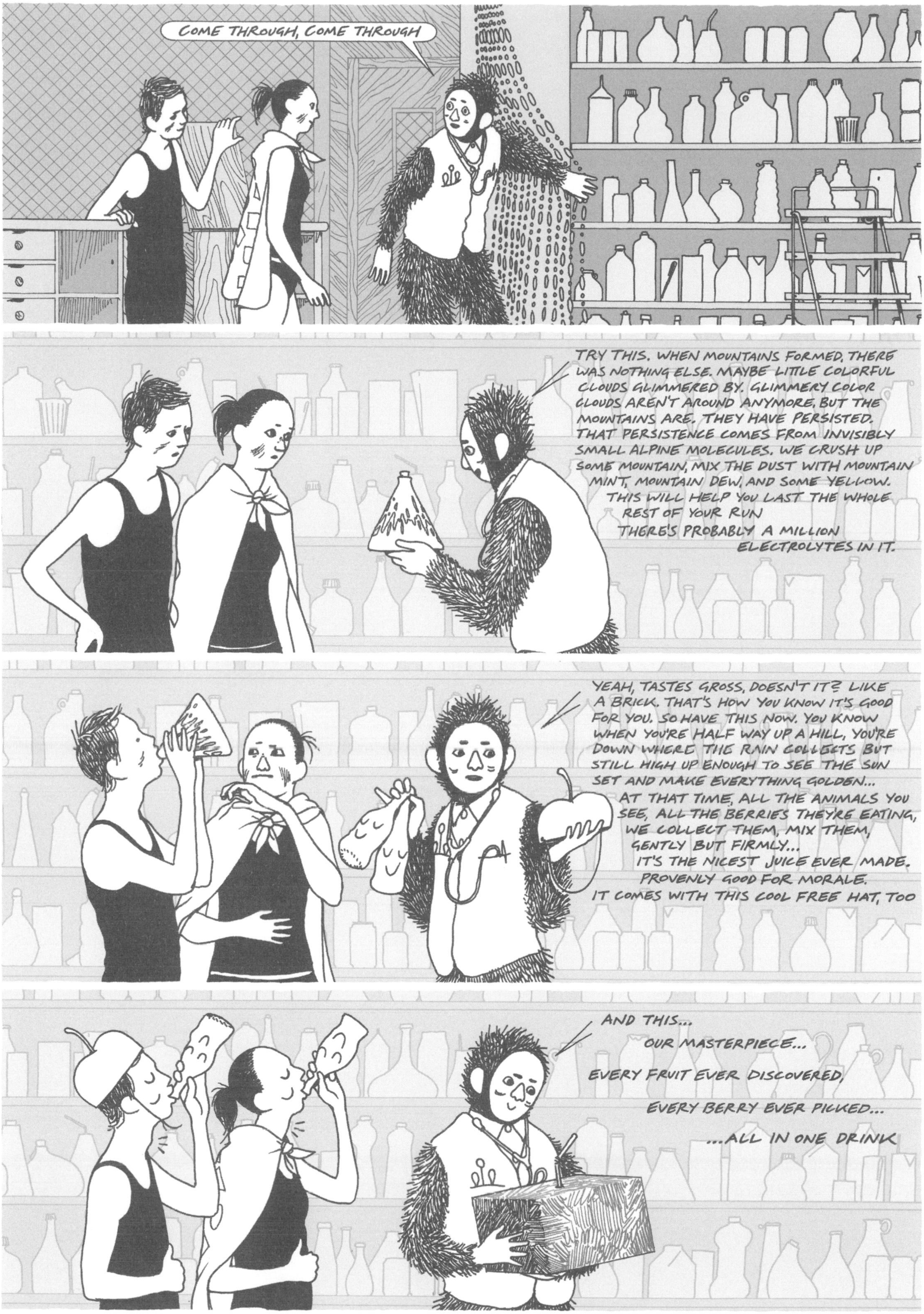
COME THROUGH, COME THROUGH
TRY THIS. WHEN MOUNTAINS FORMED, THERE WAS NOTHING ELSE. MAYBE LITTLE COLORFUL CLOUDS GLIMMERED BY. GLIMMERY COLOR CLOUDS AREN'T AROUND ANYMORE, BUT THE MOUNTAINS ARE. THEY HAVE PERSISTED. THAT PERSISTENCE COMES FROM INVISIBLY SMALL ALPINE MOLECULES. WE CRUSH UP SOME MOUNTAIN, MIX THE DUST WITH MOUNTAIN MINT, MOUNTAIN DEW, AND SOME YELLOW. THIS WILL HELP YOU LAST THE WHOLE REST OF YOUR RUN
THERE'S PROBABLY A MILLION ELECTROLYTES IN IT.
YEAH, TASTES GROSS, DOESN'T IT? LIKE A BRICK. THAT'S HOW YOU KNOW IT'S GOOD FOR YOU. SO HAVE THIS NOW. YOU KNOW WHEN YOU'RE HALF WAY UP A HILL, YOU'RE DOWN WHERE THE RAIN COLLECTS BUT STILL HIGH UP ENOUGH TO SEE THE SUN SET AND MAKE EVERYTHING GOLDEN...
AT THAT TIME, ALL THE ANIMALS YOU SEE, ALL THE BERRIES THEY'RE EATING, WE COLLECT THEM, MIX THEM, GENTLY BUT FIRMLY...
IT'S THE NICEST JUICE EVER MADE.
PROVENLY GOOD FOR MORALE.
IT COMES WITH THIS COOL FREE HAT, TOO
AND THIS...
OUR MASTERPIECE...
EVERY FRUIT EVER DISCOVERED,
EVERY BERRY EVER PICKED...
...ALL IN ONE DRINK

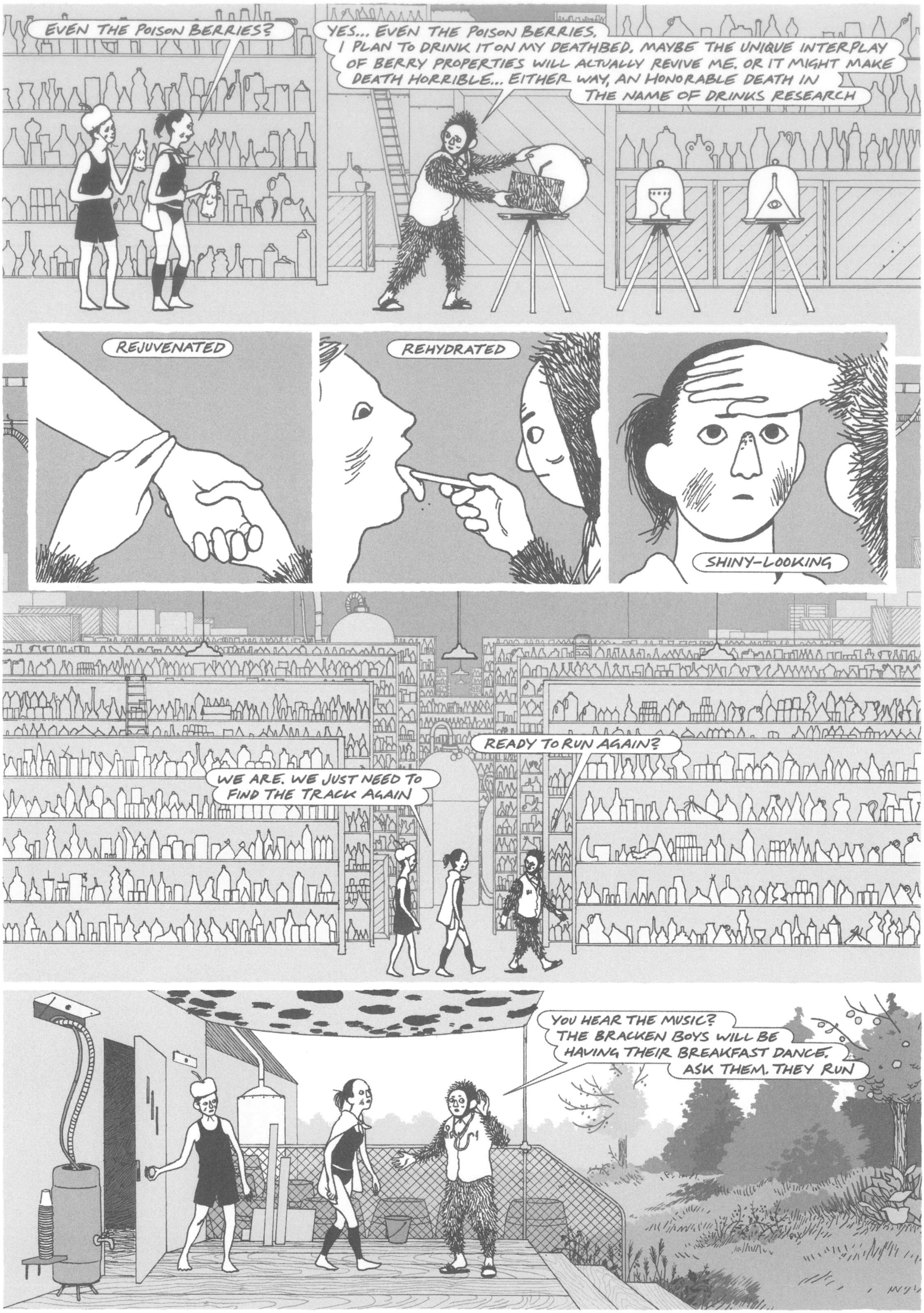
EVEN THE POISON BERRIES?
YES... EVEN THE POISON BERRIES. I PLAN TO DRINK IT ON MY DEATHBED. MAYBE THE UNIQUE INTERPLAY OF BERRY PROPERTIES WILL ACTUALLY REVIVE ME. OR IT MIGHT MAKE DEATH HORRIBLE... EITHER WAY, AN HONORABLE DEATH IN THE NAME OF DRINKS RESEARCH
REJUVENATED
REHYDRATED
SHINY-LOOKING
READY TO RUN AGAIN?
WE ARE. WE JUST NEED TO FIND THE TRACK AGAIN
YOU HEAR THE MUSIC? THE BRACKEN BOYS WILL BE HAVING THEIR BREAKFAST DANCE. ASK THEM. THEY RUN

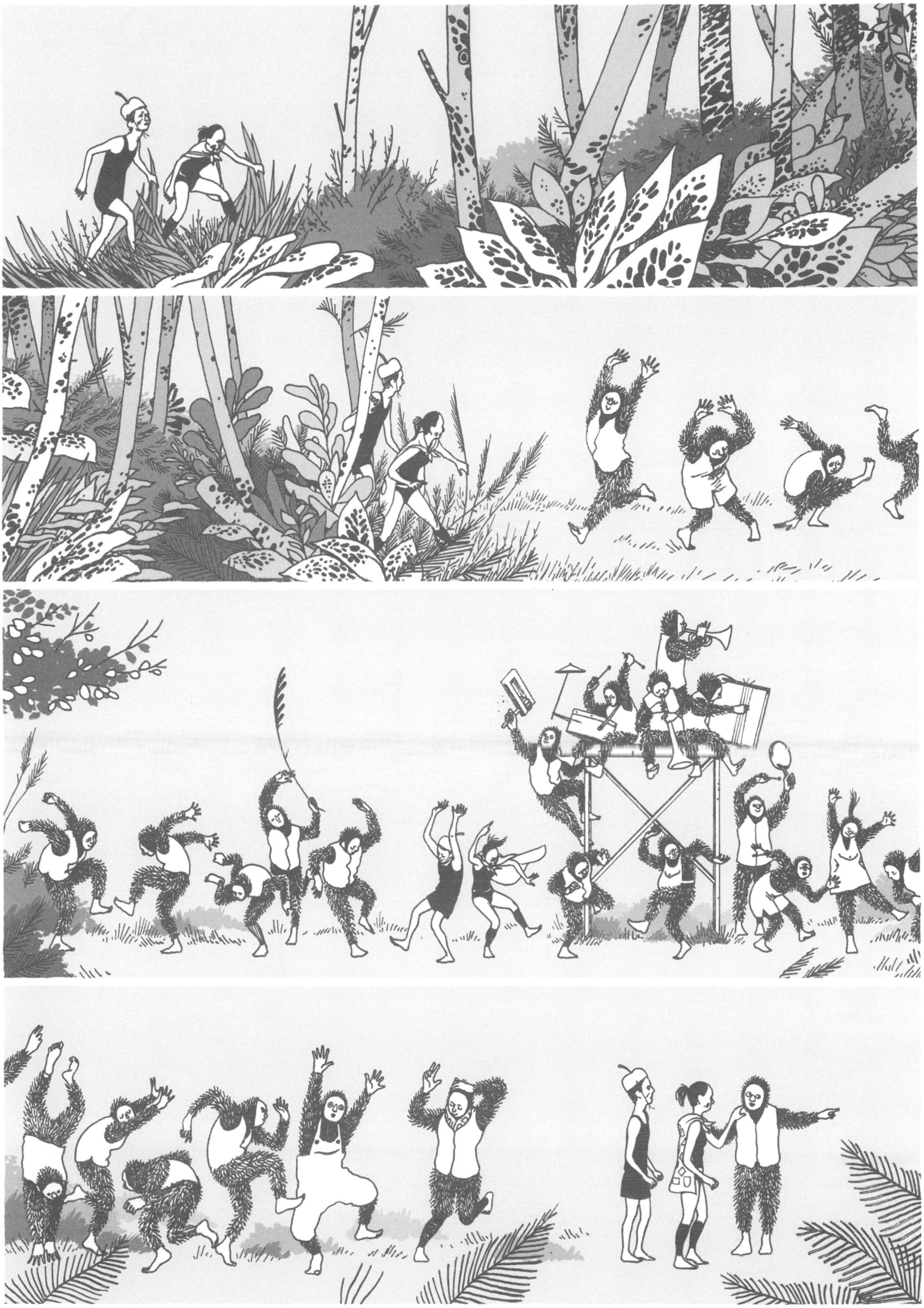

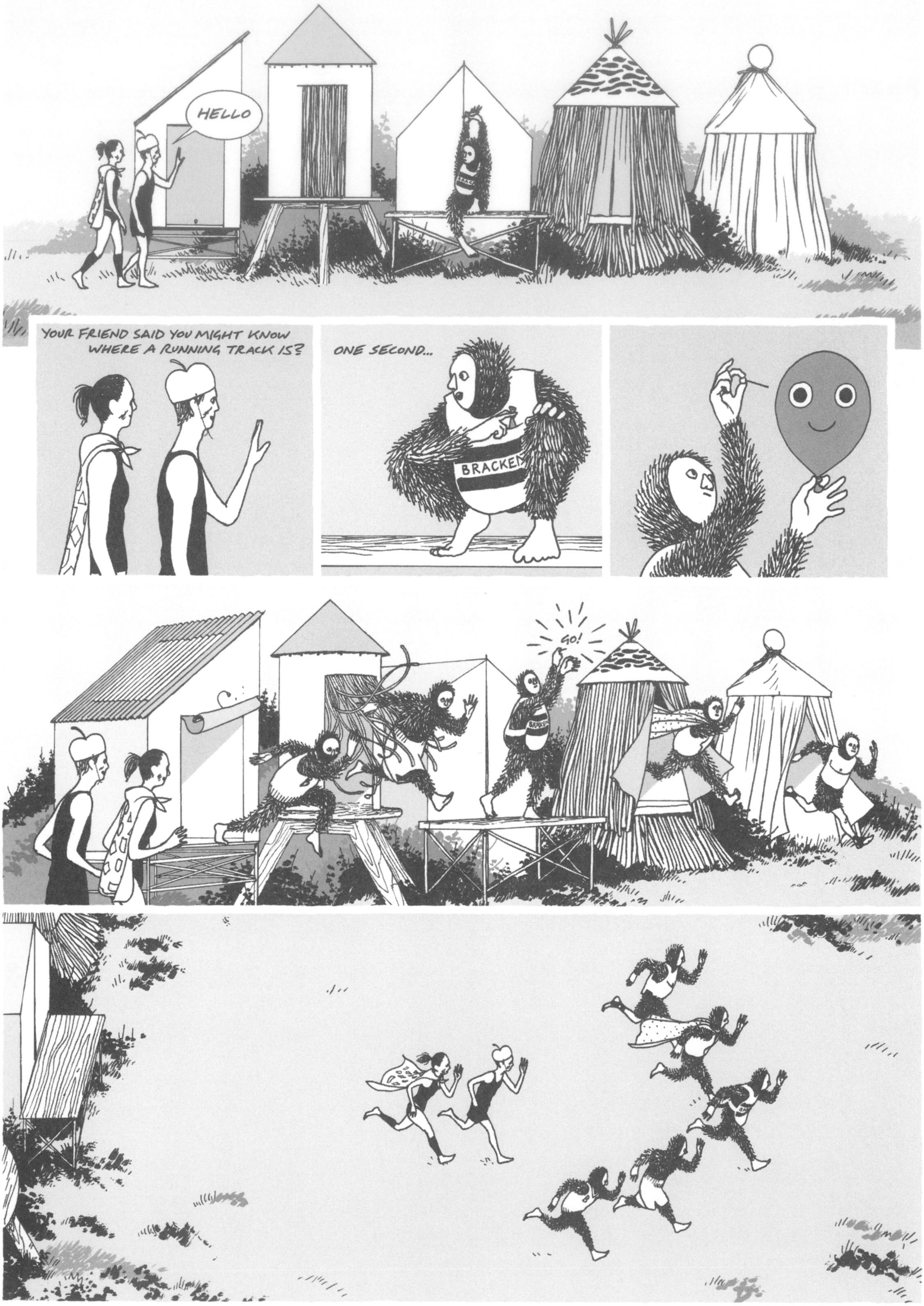
HELLO
YOUR FRIEND SAID YOU MIGHT KNOW WHERE A RUNNING TRACK IS?
ONE SECOND...
BRACKEN
GO!

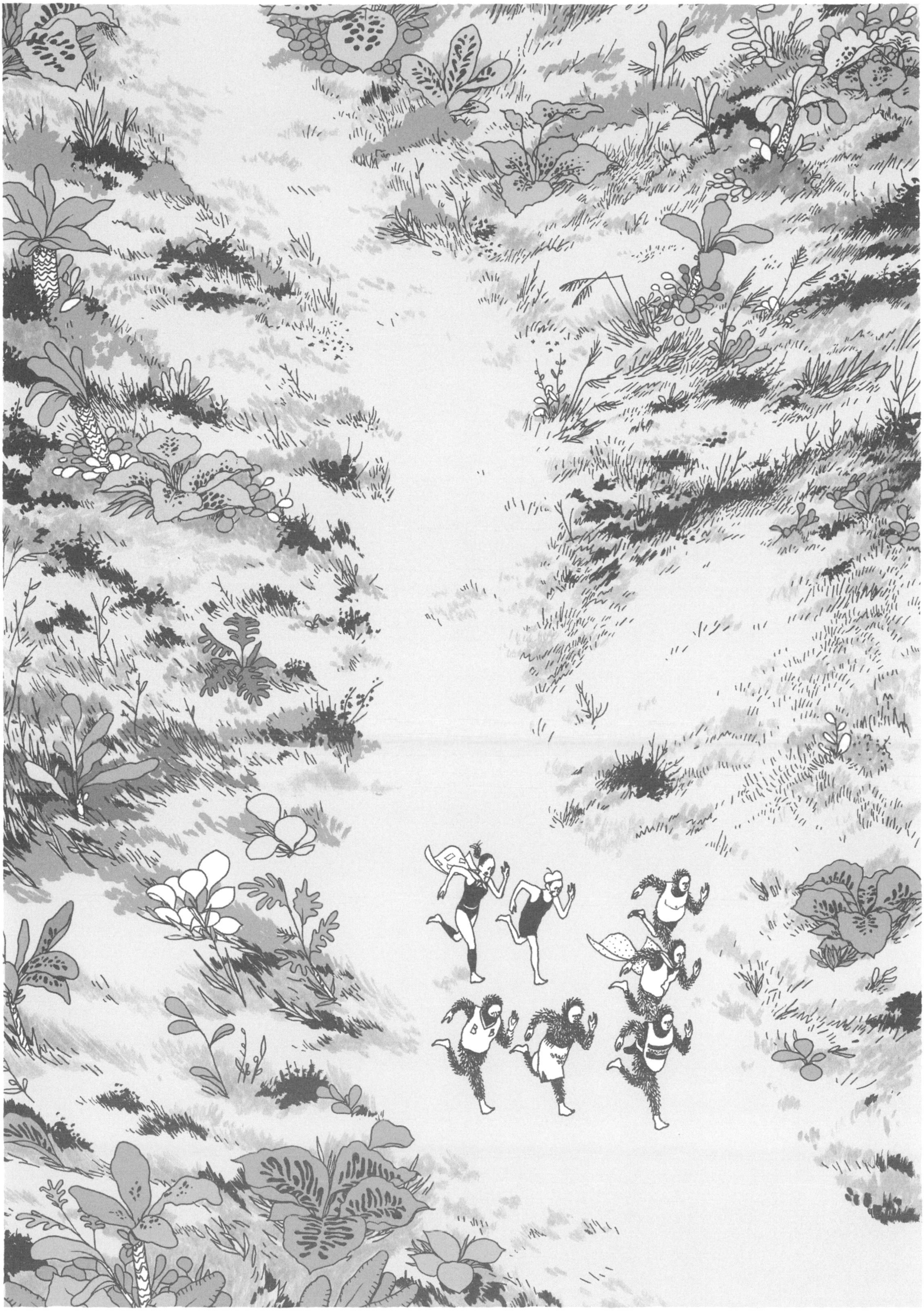

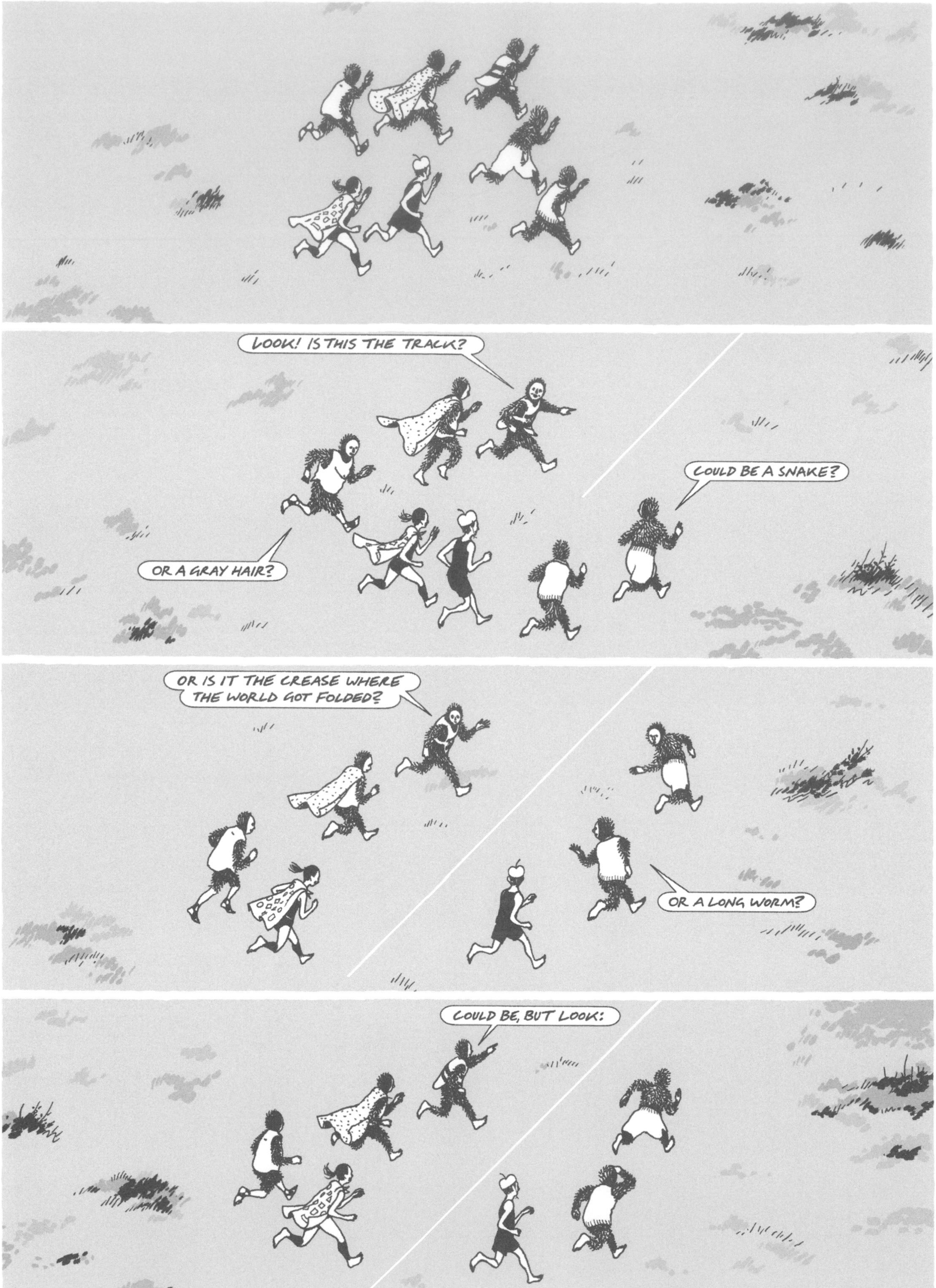
LOOK! IS THIS THE TRACK?
COULD BE A SNAKE?
OR A GRAY HAIR?
OR IS IT THE CREASE WHERE THE WORLD GOT FOLDED?
OR A LONG WORM?
COULD BE, BUT LOOK:

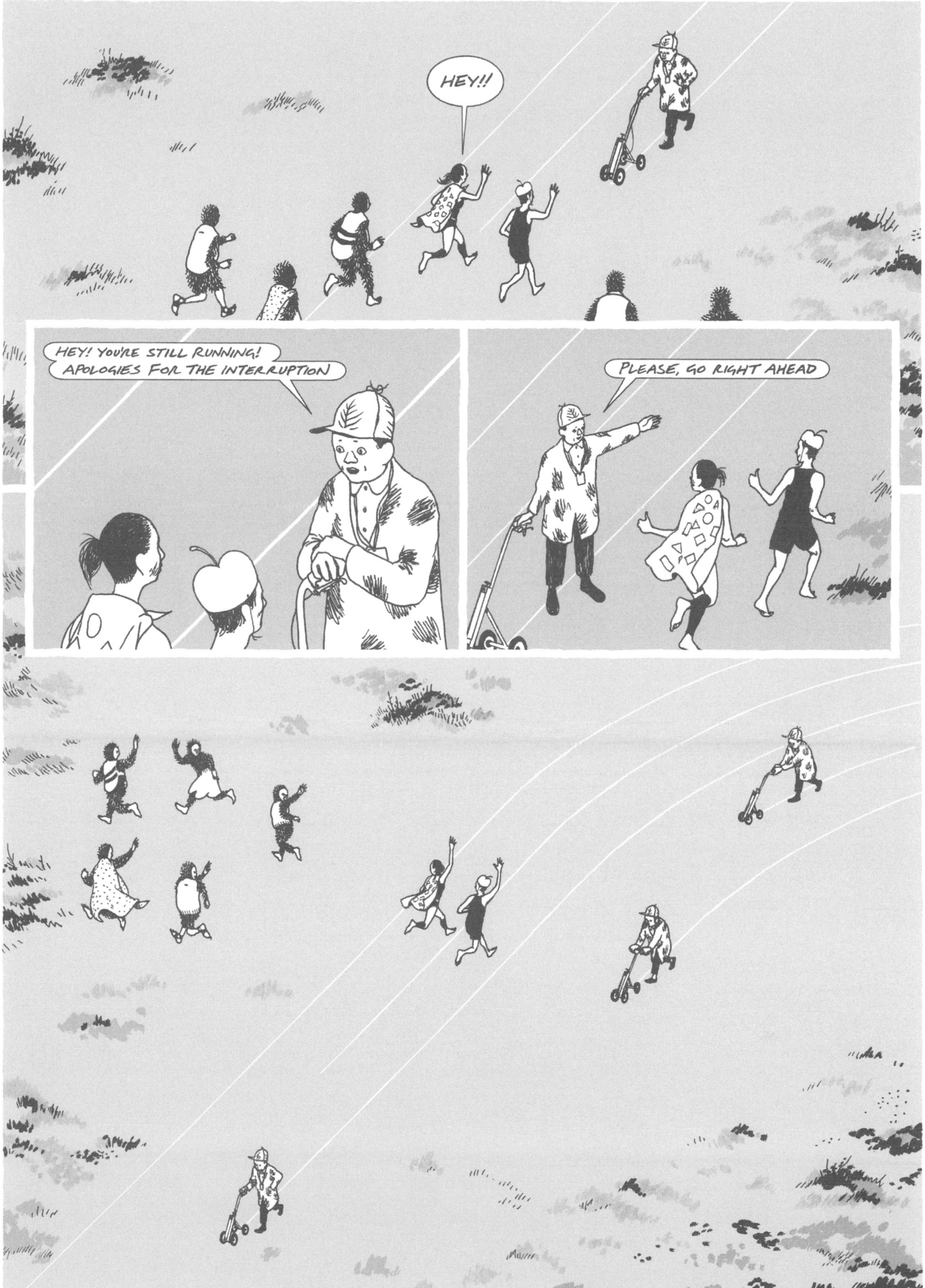
HEY!!
HEY! YOU'RE STILL RUNNING! APOLOGIES FOR THE INTERRUPTION
PLEASE, GO RIGHT AHEAD

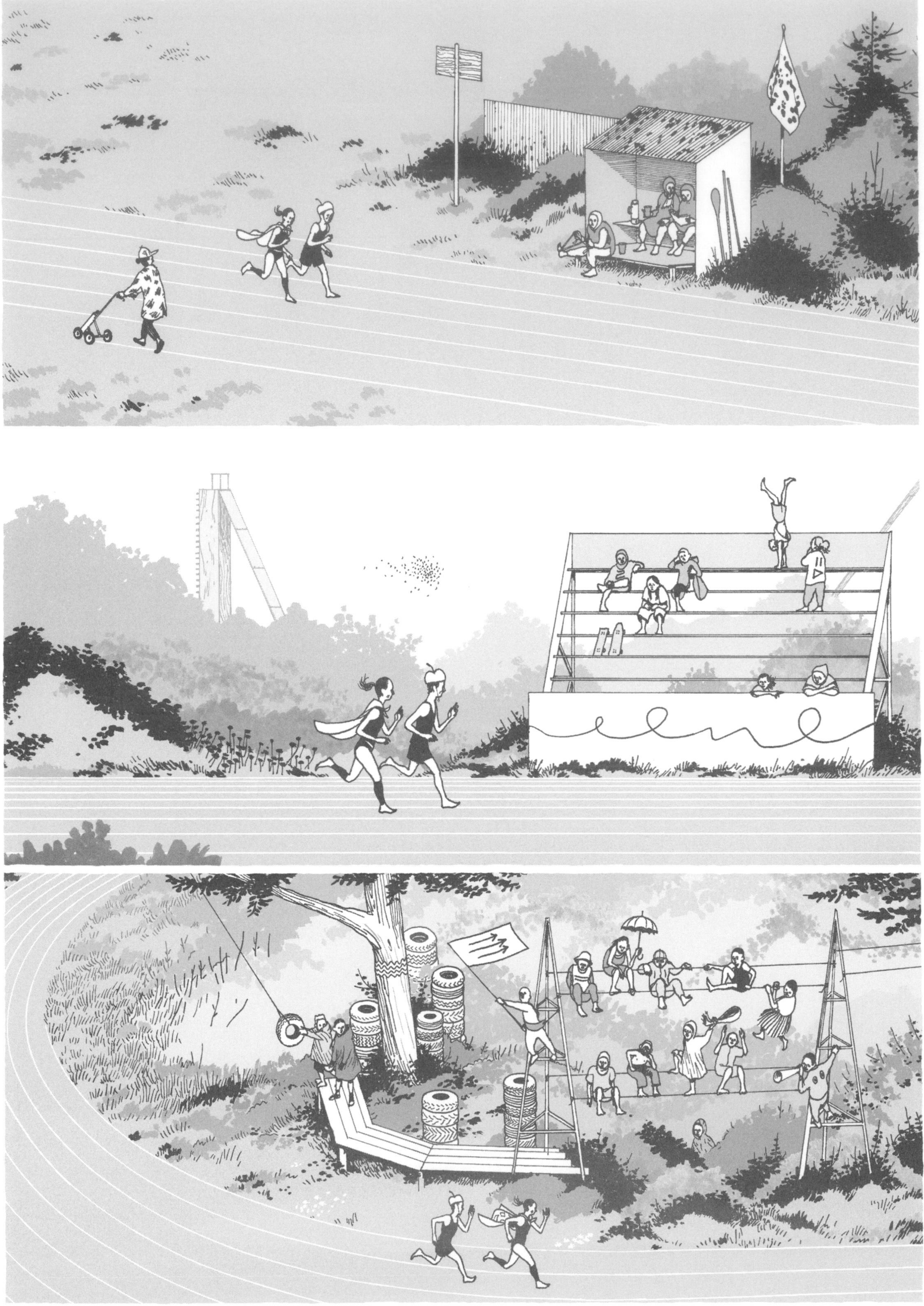

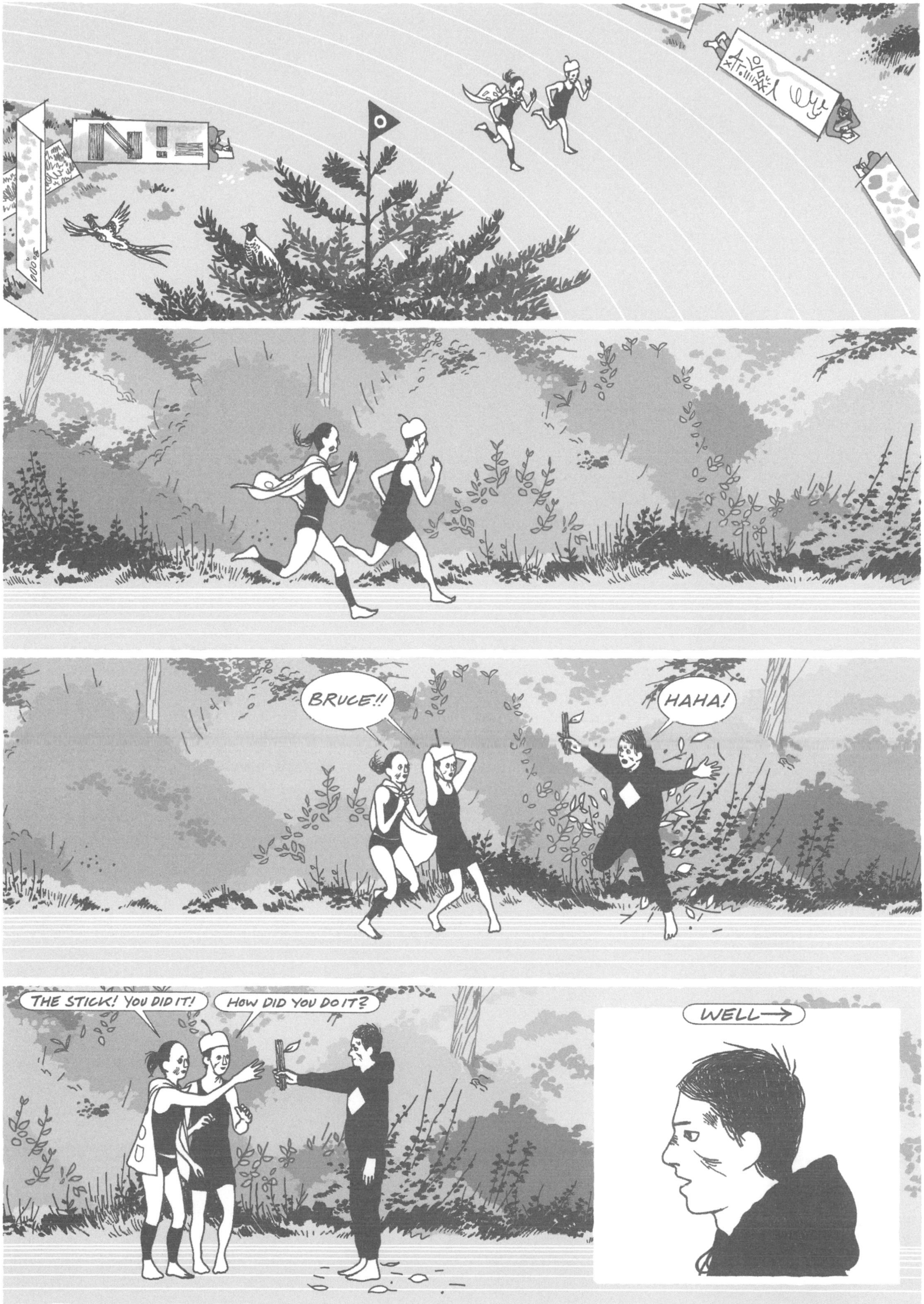
BRUCE!!
HAHA!
THE STICK! YOU DID IT!
HOW DID YOU DO IT?
WELL→

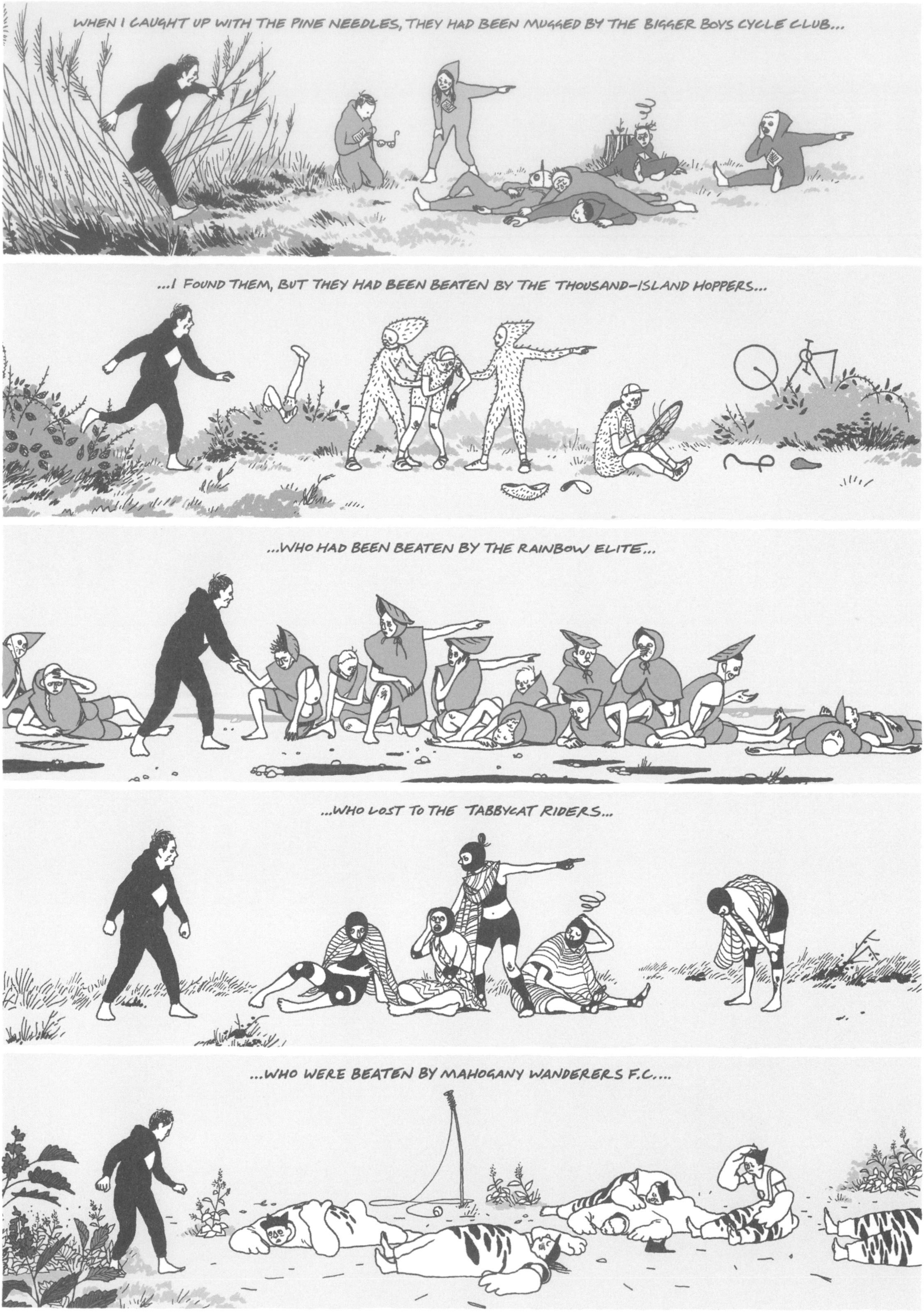
WHEN I CAUGHT UP WITH THE PINE NEEDLES, THEY HAD BEEN MUGGED BY THE BIGGER BOYS CYCLE CLUB...
...I FOUND THEM, BUT THEY HAD BEEN BEATEN BY THE THOUSAND-ISLAND HOPPERS...
...WHO HAD BEEN BEATEN BY THE RAINBOW ELITE...
...WHO LOST TO THE TABBYCAT RIDERS...
...WHO WERE BEATEN BY MAHOGANY WANDERERS F.C....

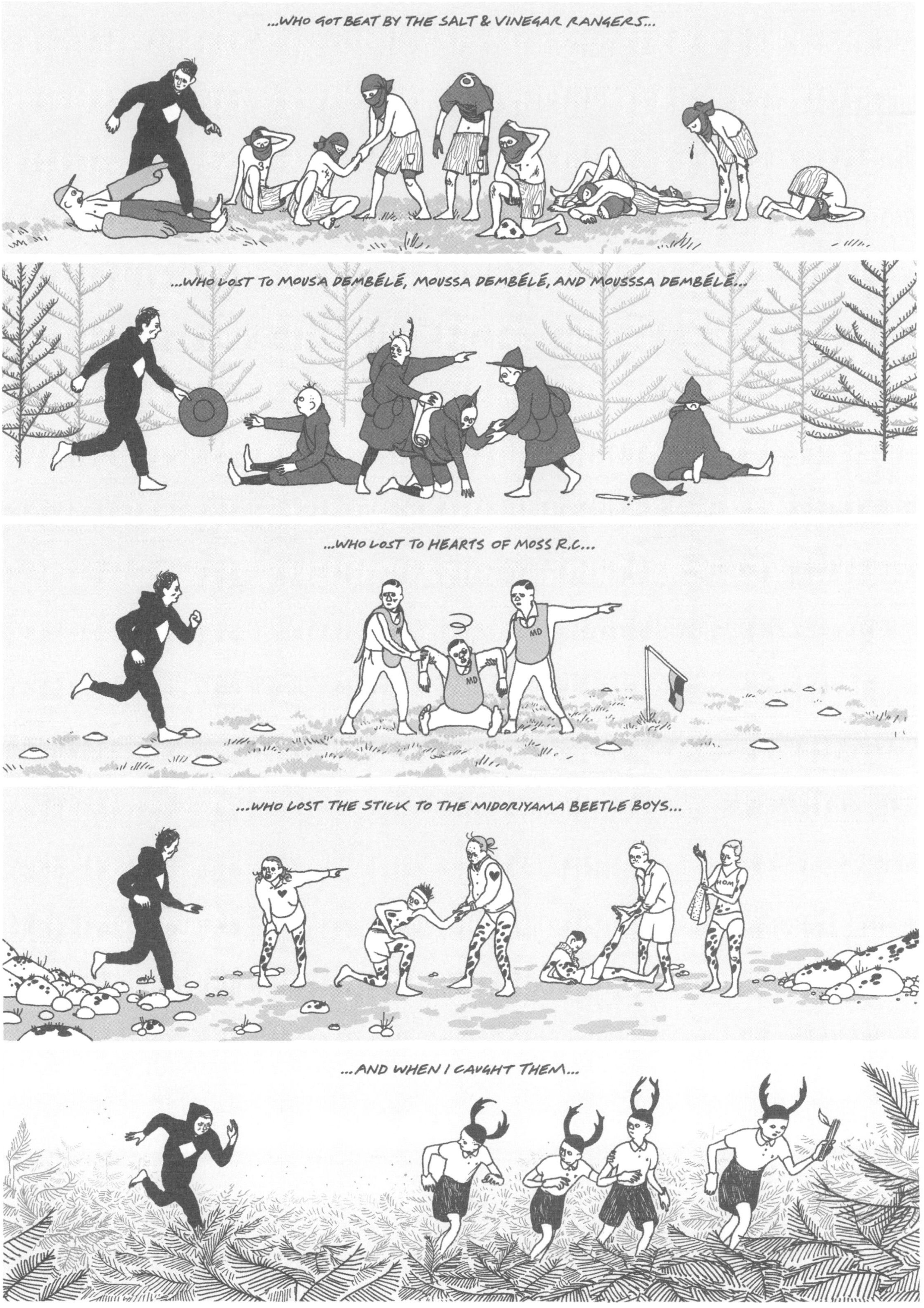
...WHO GOT BEAT BY THE SALT & VINEGAR RANGERS...
...WHO LOST TO MOUSA DEMBÉLÉ, MOUSSA DEMBÉLÉ, AND MOUSSSA DEMBÉLÉ...
...WHO LOST TO HEARTS OF MOSS R.C...
MD
MD
...WHO LOST THE STICK TO THE MIDORIYAMA BEETLE BOYS...
HOM
...AND WHEN I CAUGHT THEM...

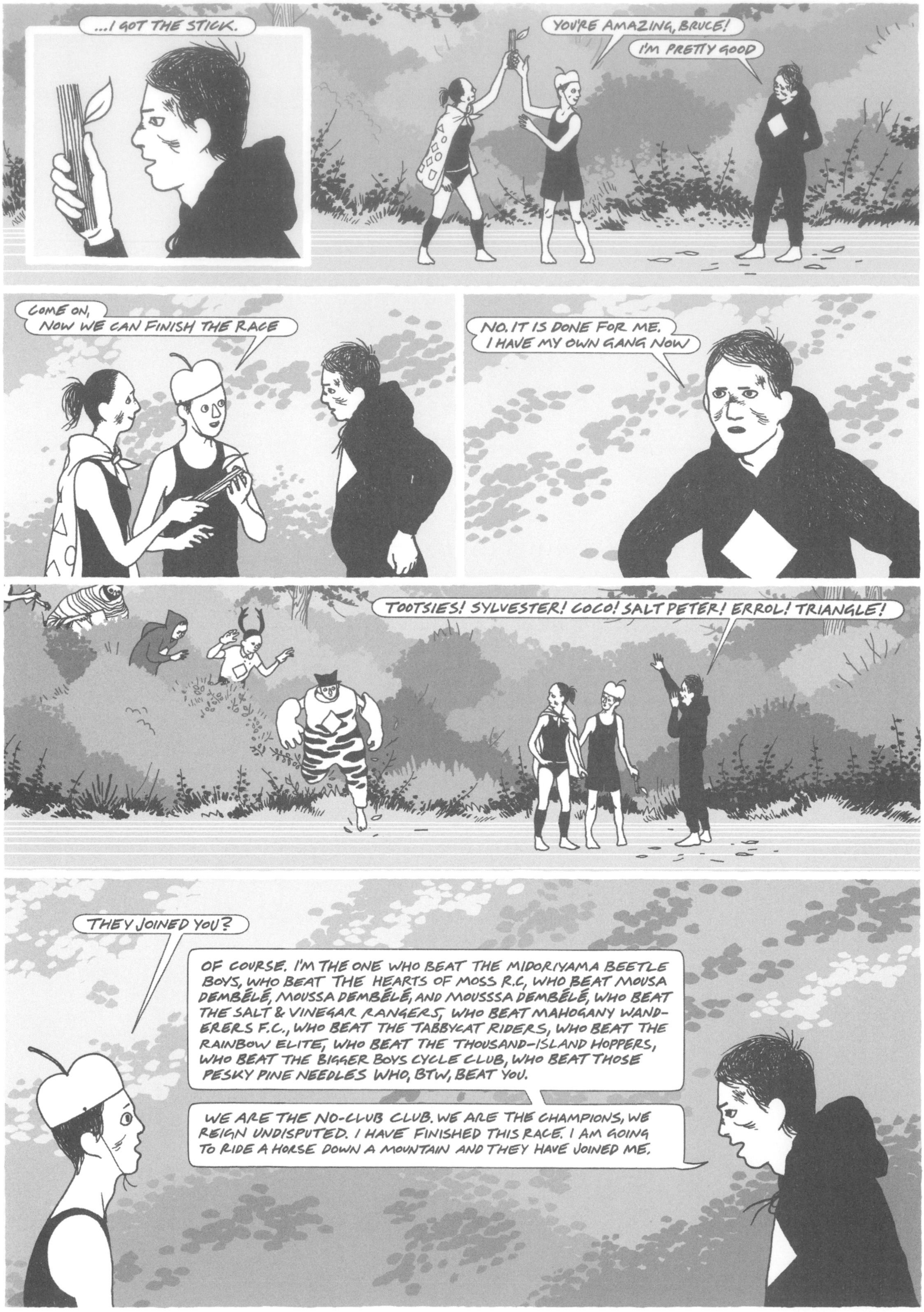
...I GOT THE STICK.
YOU'RE AMAZING, BRUCE!
I'M PRETTY GOOD
COME ON, NOW WE CAN FINISH THE RACE
NO. IT IS DONE FOR ME. I HAVE MY OWN GANG NOW
TOOTSIES! SYLVESTER! COCO! SALT PETER! ERROL! TRIANGLE!
THEY JOINED YOU?
OF COURSE. I'M THE ONE WHO BEAT THE MIDORIYAMA BEETLE BOYS, WHO BEAT THE HEARTS OF MOSS R.C, WHO BEAT MOUSA DEMBÉLÉ, MOUSSA DEMBÉLÉ, AND MOUSSSA DEMBÉLÉ, WHO BEAT THE SALT & VINEGAR RANGERS, WHO BEAT MAHOGANY WANDERERS F.C., WHO BEAT THE TABBYCAT RIDERS, WHO BEAT THE RAINBOW ELITE, WHO BEAT THE THOUSAND-ISLAND HOPPERS, WHO BEAT THE BIGGER BOYS CYCLE CLUB, WHO BEAT THOSE PESKY PINE NEEDLES WHO, BTW, BEAT YOU.
WE ARE THE NO-CLUB CLUB. WE ARE THE CHAMPIONS, WE REIGN UNDISPUTED. I HAVE FINISHED THIS RACE. I AM GOING TO RIDE A HORSE DOWN A MOUNTAIN AND THEY HAVE JOINED ME.

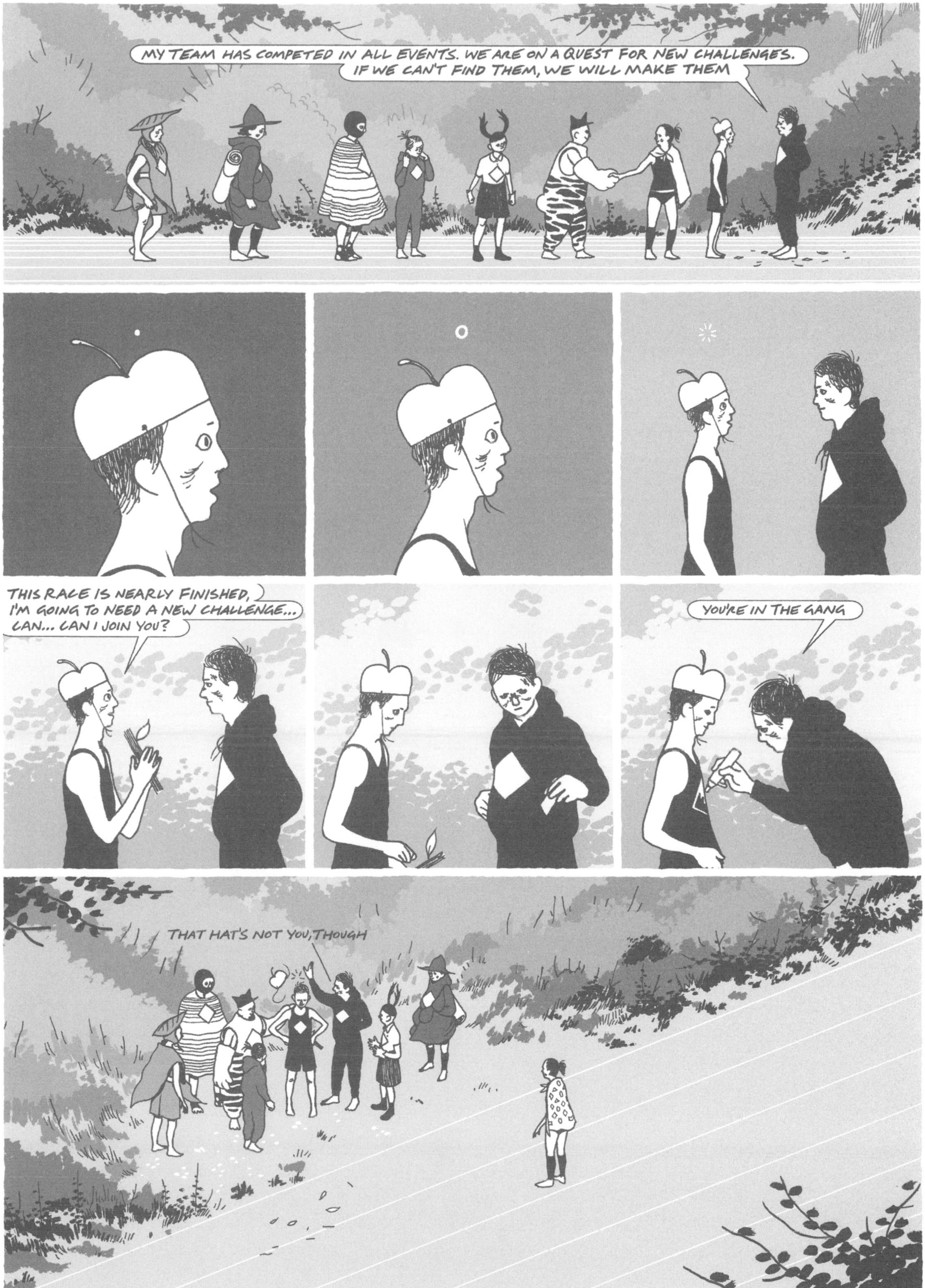
MY TEAM HAS COMPETED IN ALL EVENTS. WE ARE ON A QUEST FOR NEW CHALLENGES. IF WE CAN'T FIND THEM, WE WILL MAKE THEM
THIS RACE IS NEARLY FINISHED, I'M GOING TO NEED A NEW CHALLENGE... CAN... CAN I JOIN YOU?
YOU'RE IN THE GANG
THAT HAT'S NOT YOU, THOUGH

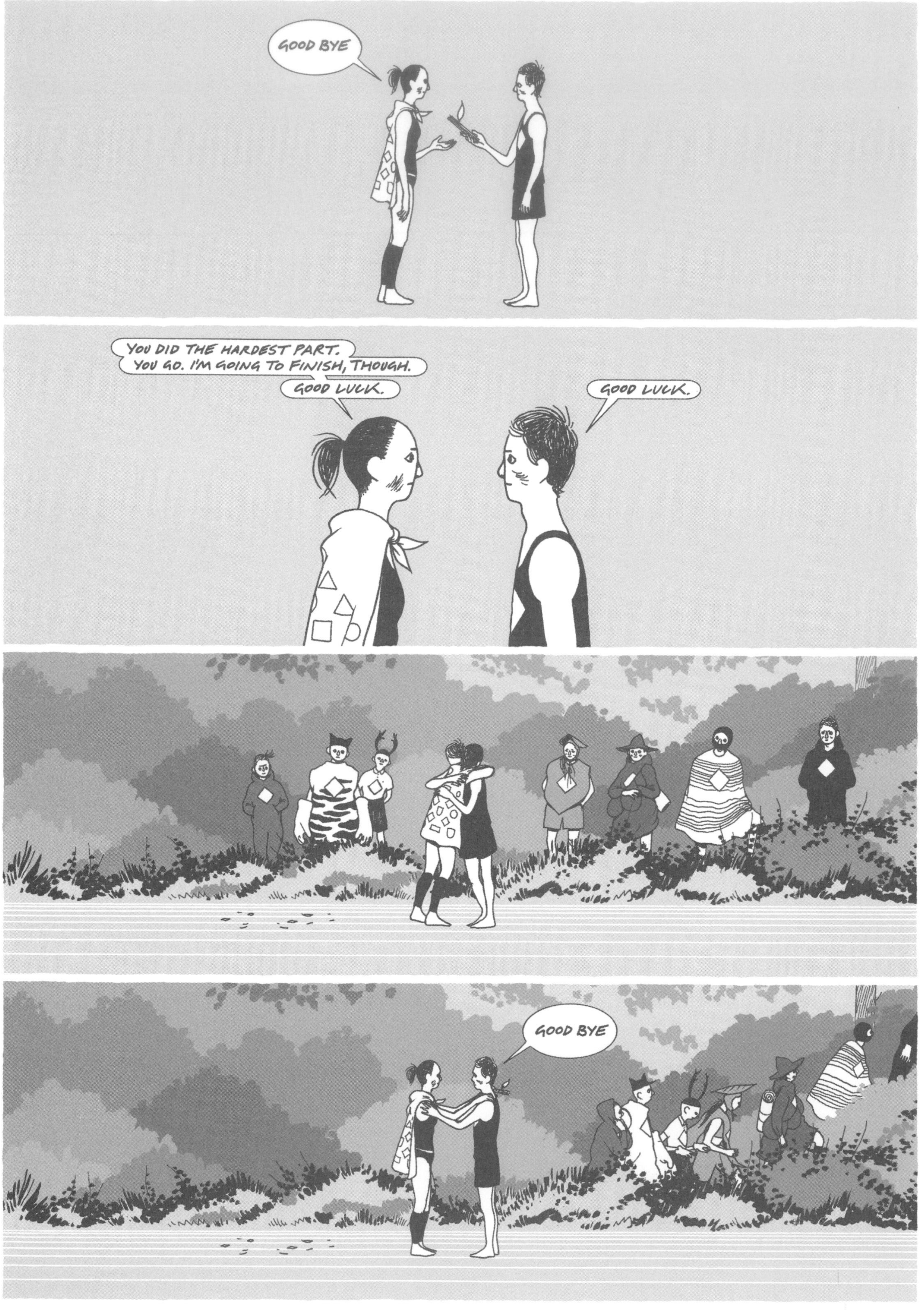
GOOD BYE
YOU DID THE HARDEST PART.
YOU GO. I'M GOING TO FINISH, THOUGH.
GOOD LUCK.
GOOD LUCK.
GOOD BYE

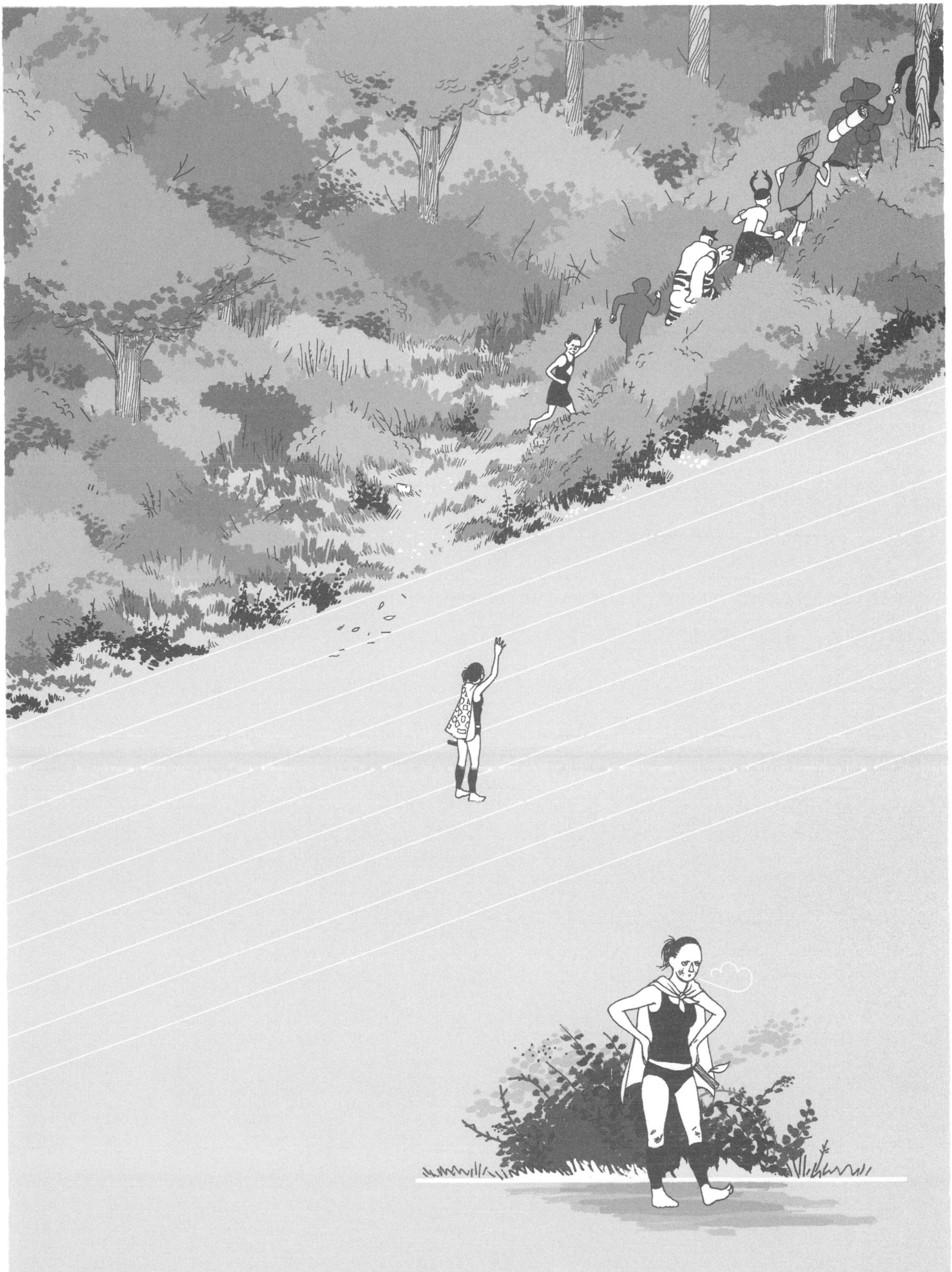

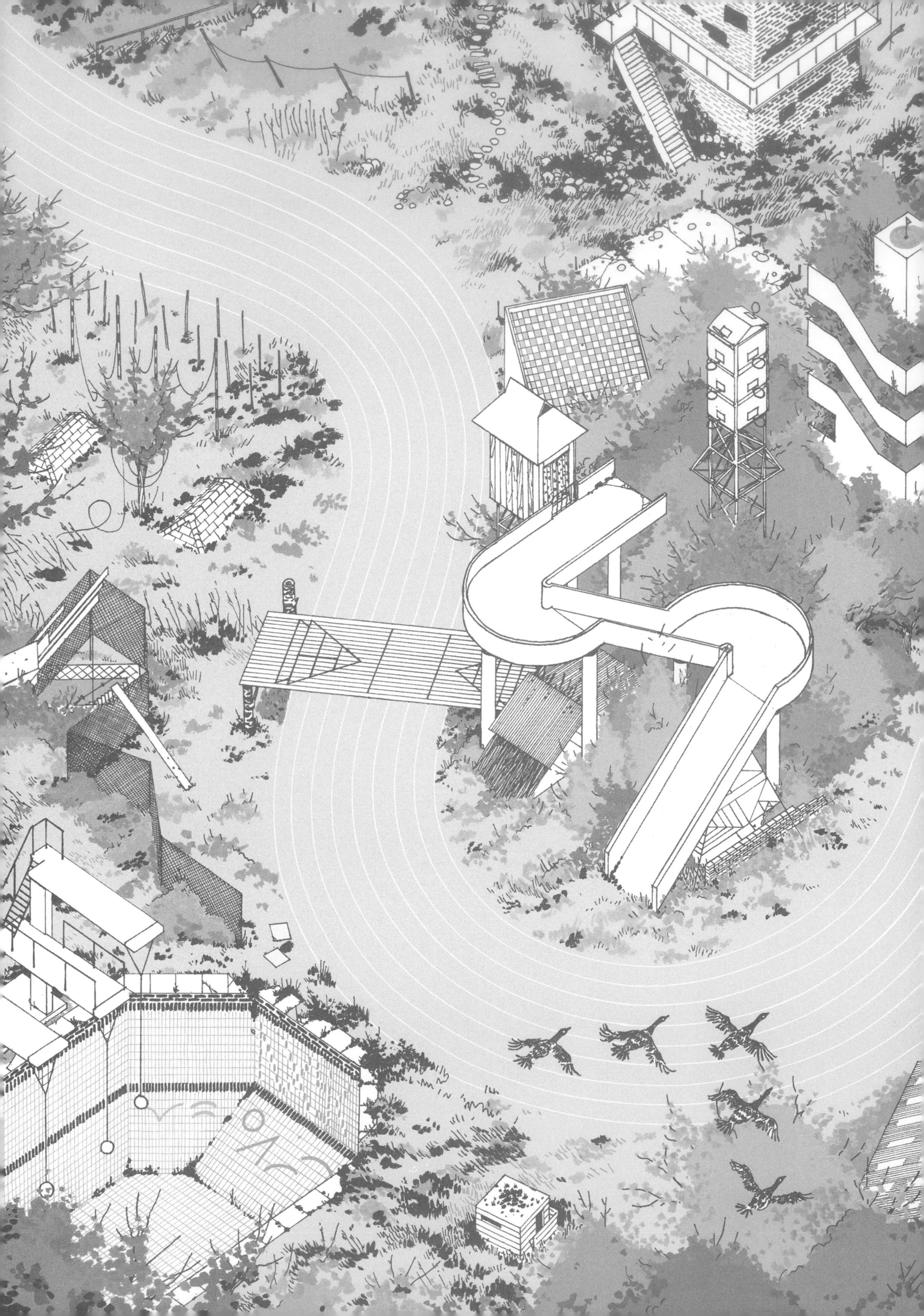

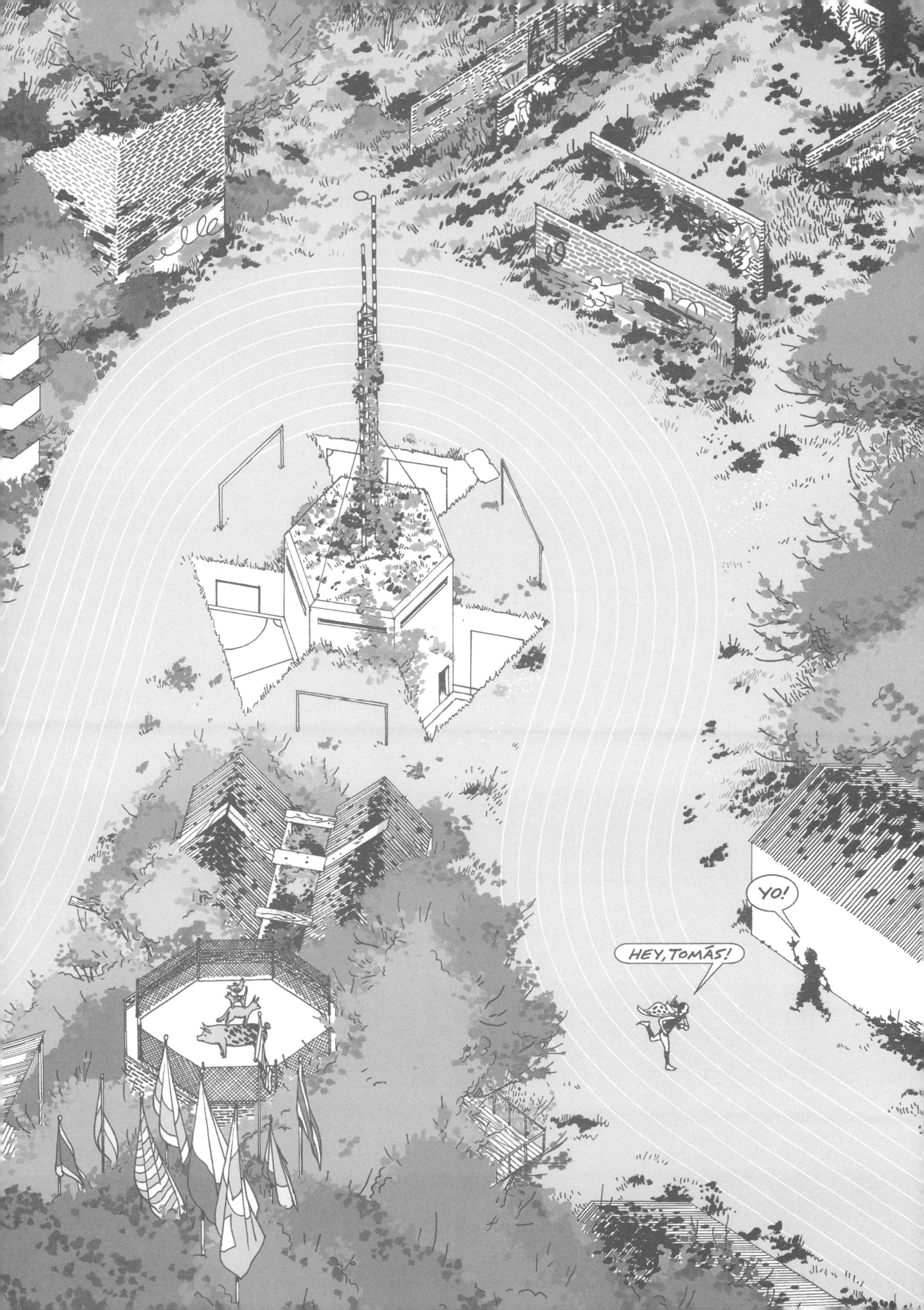
YO!
HEY, TOMÁS!

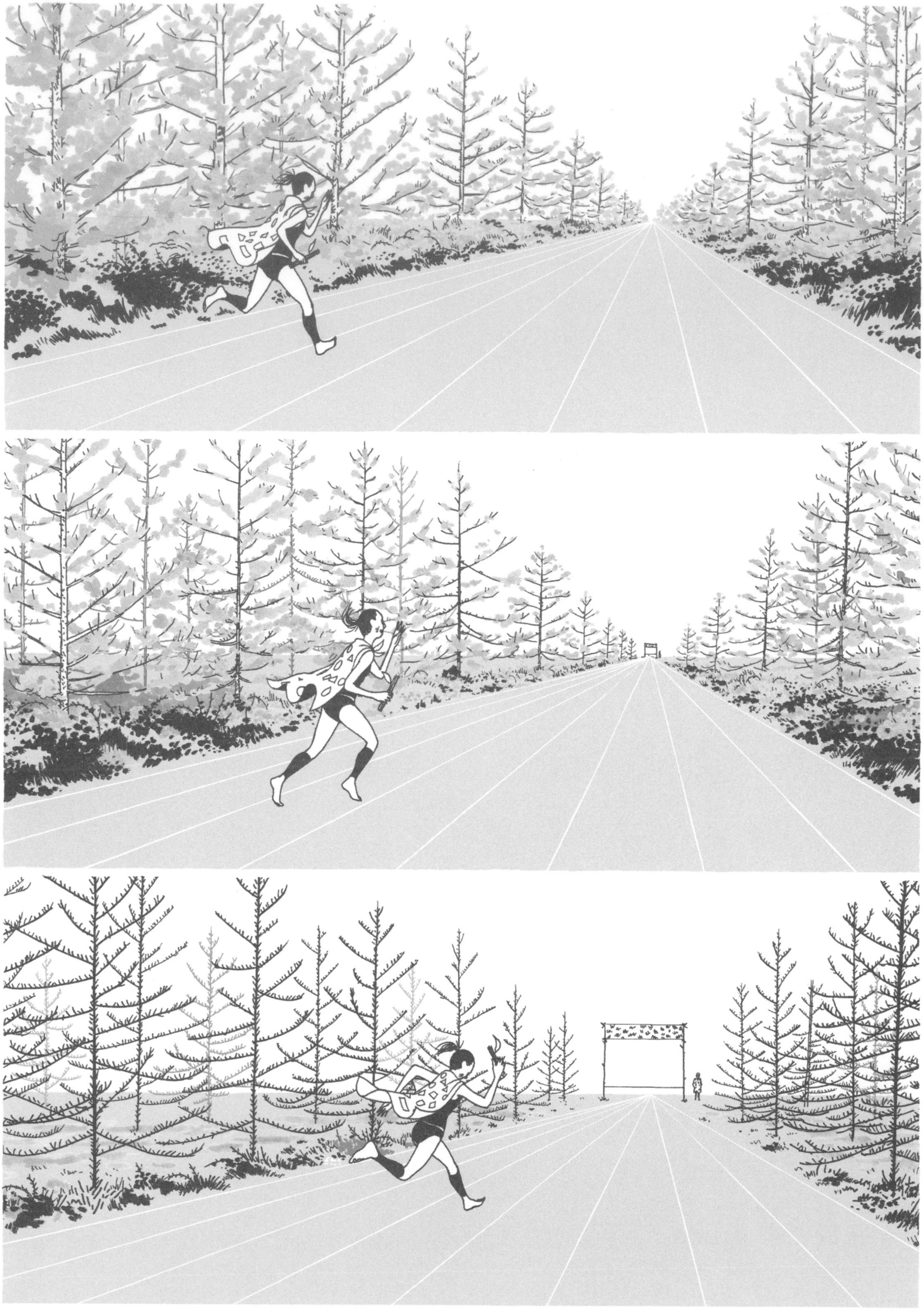

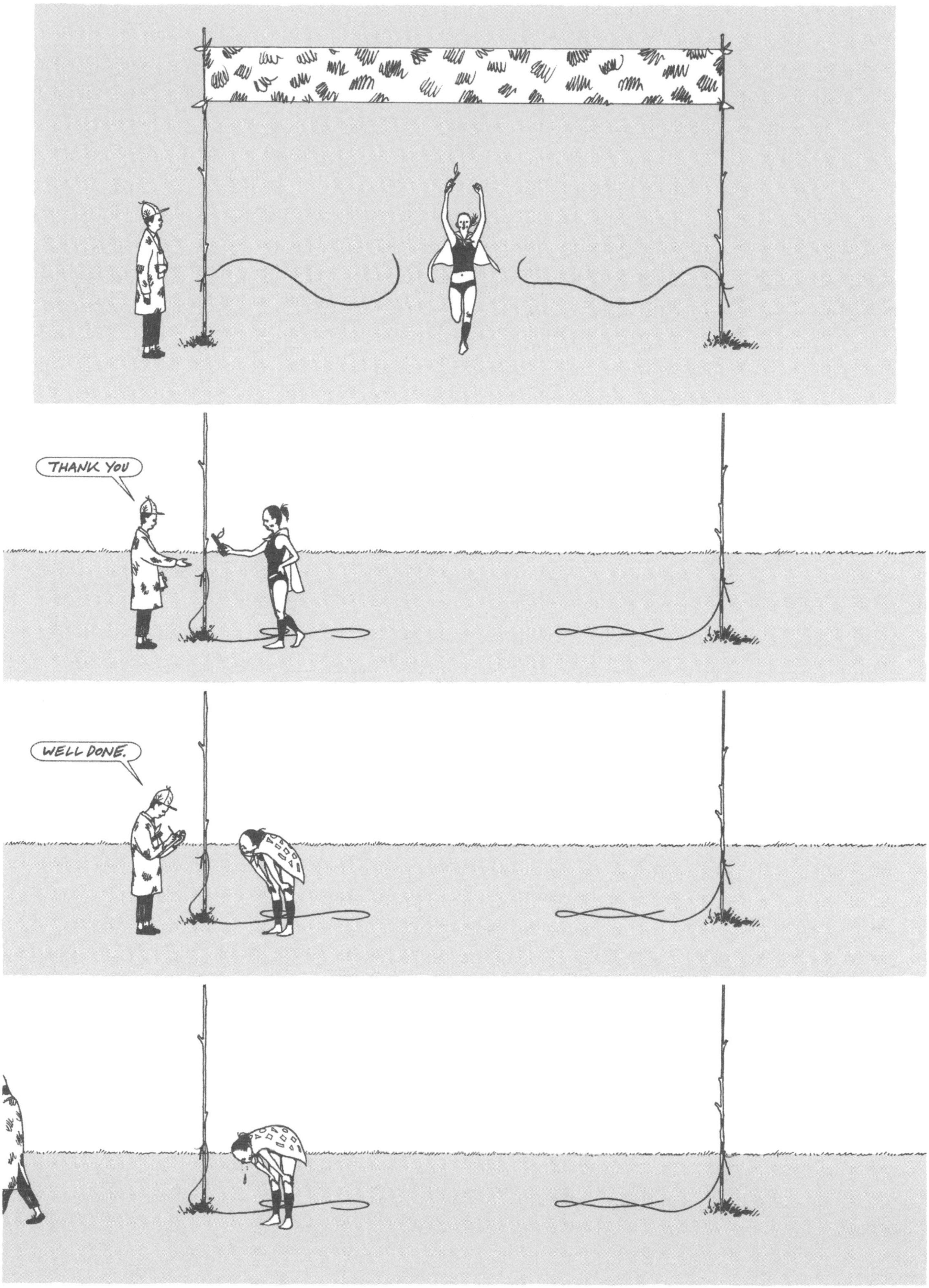
THANK YOU
WELL DONE.

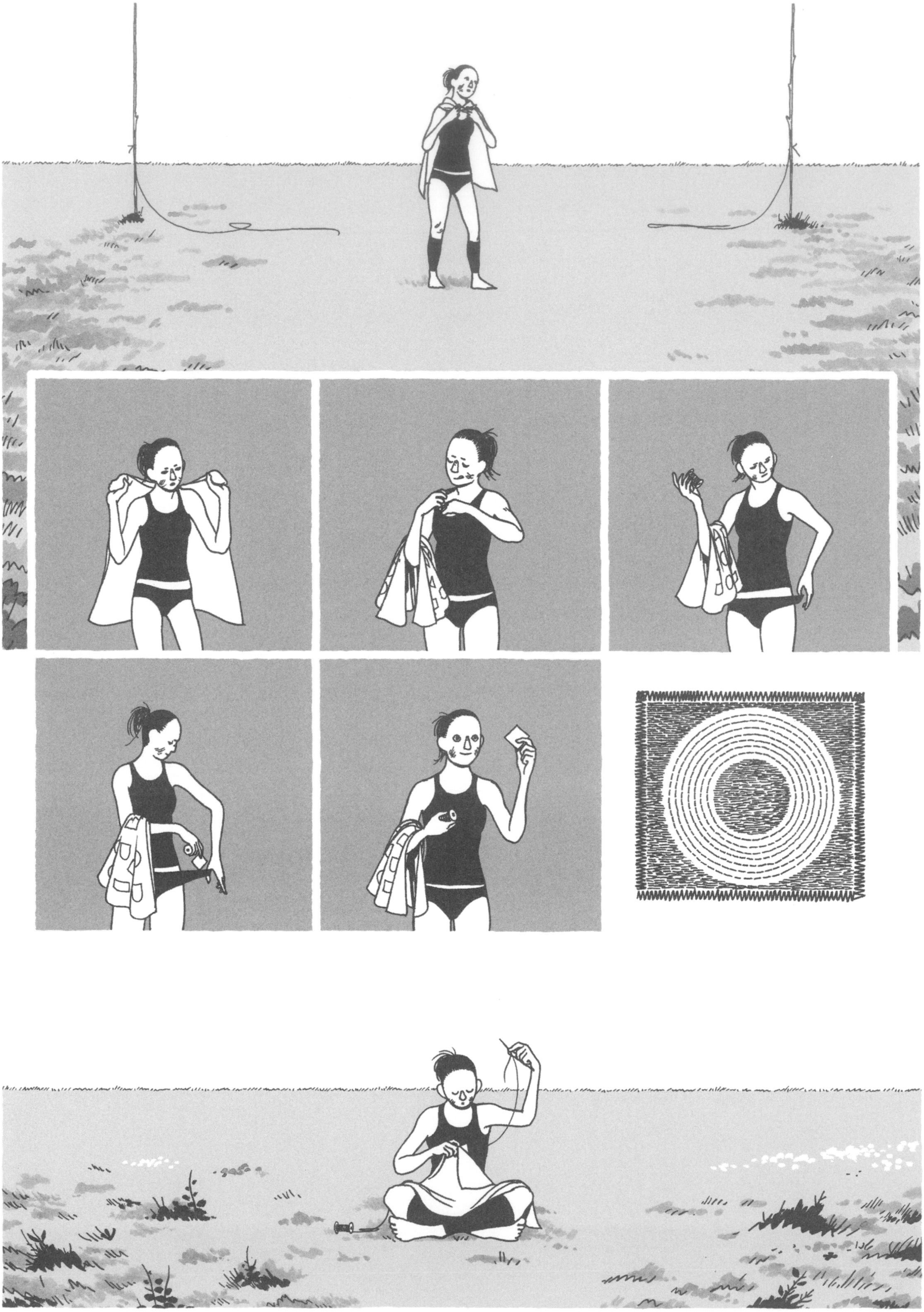

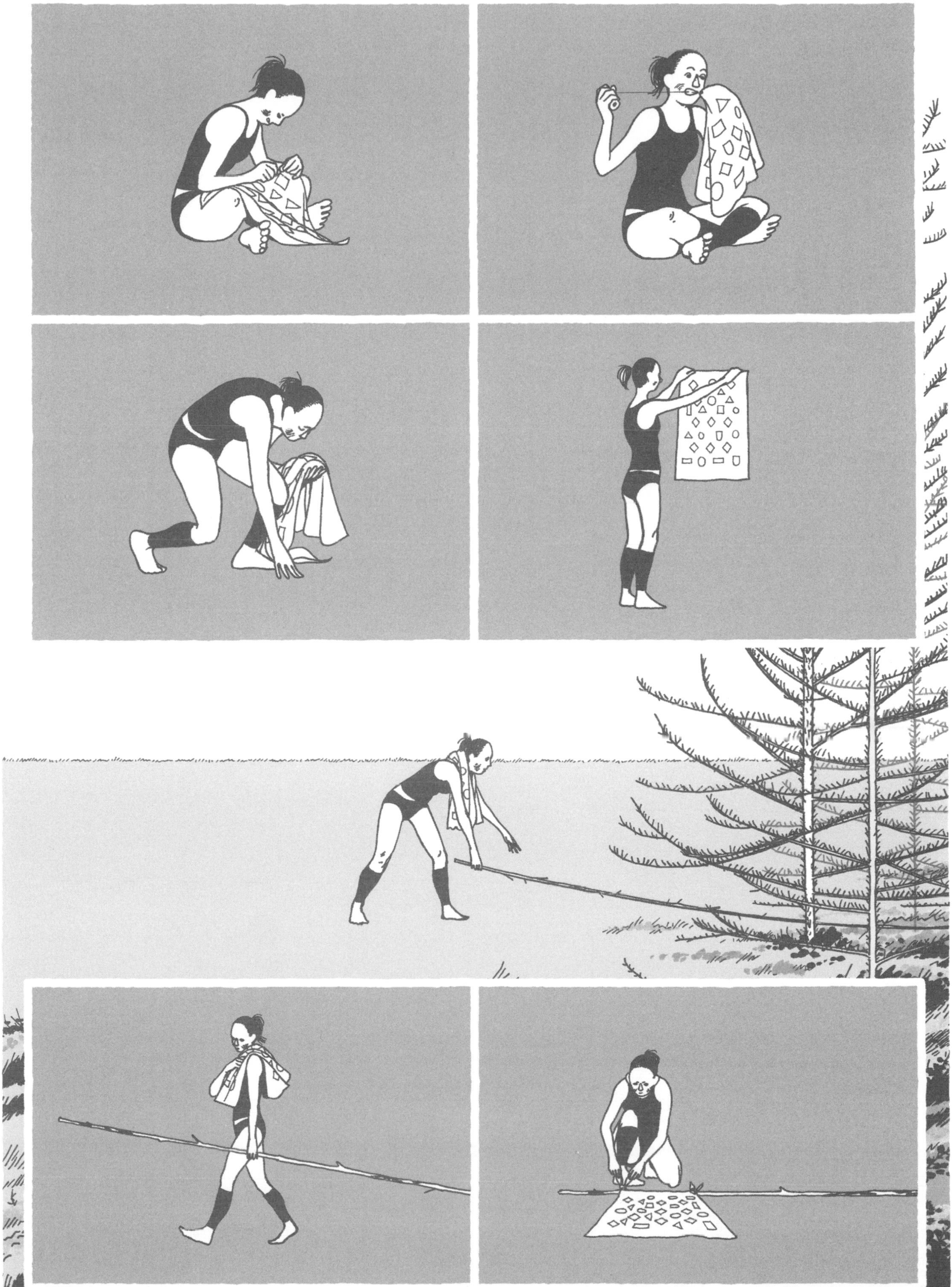

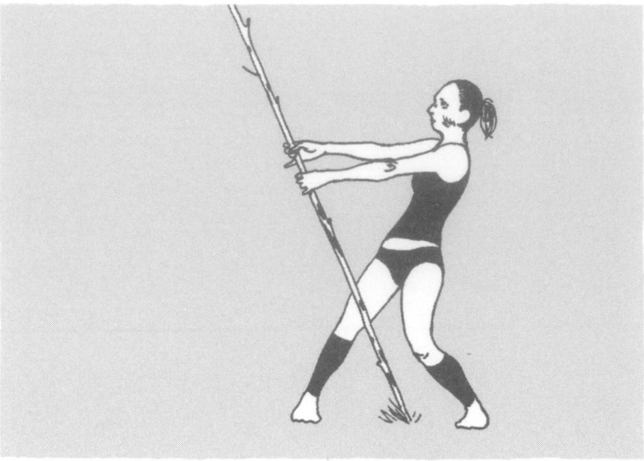

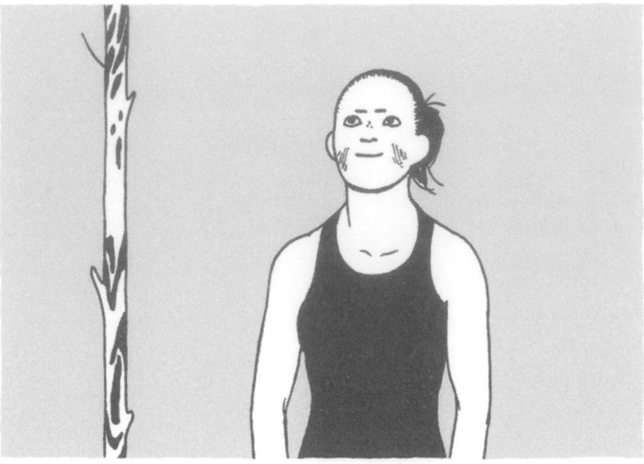

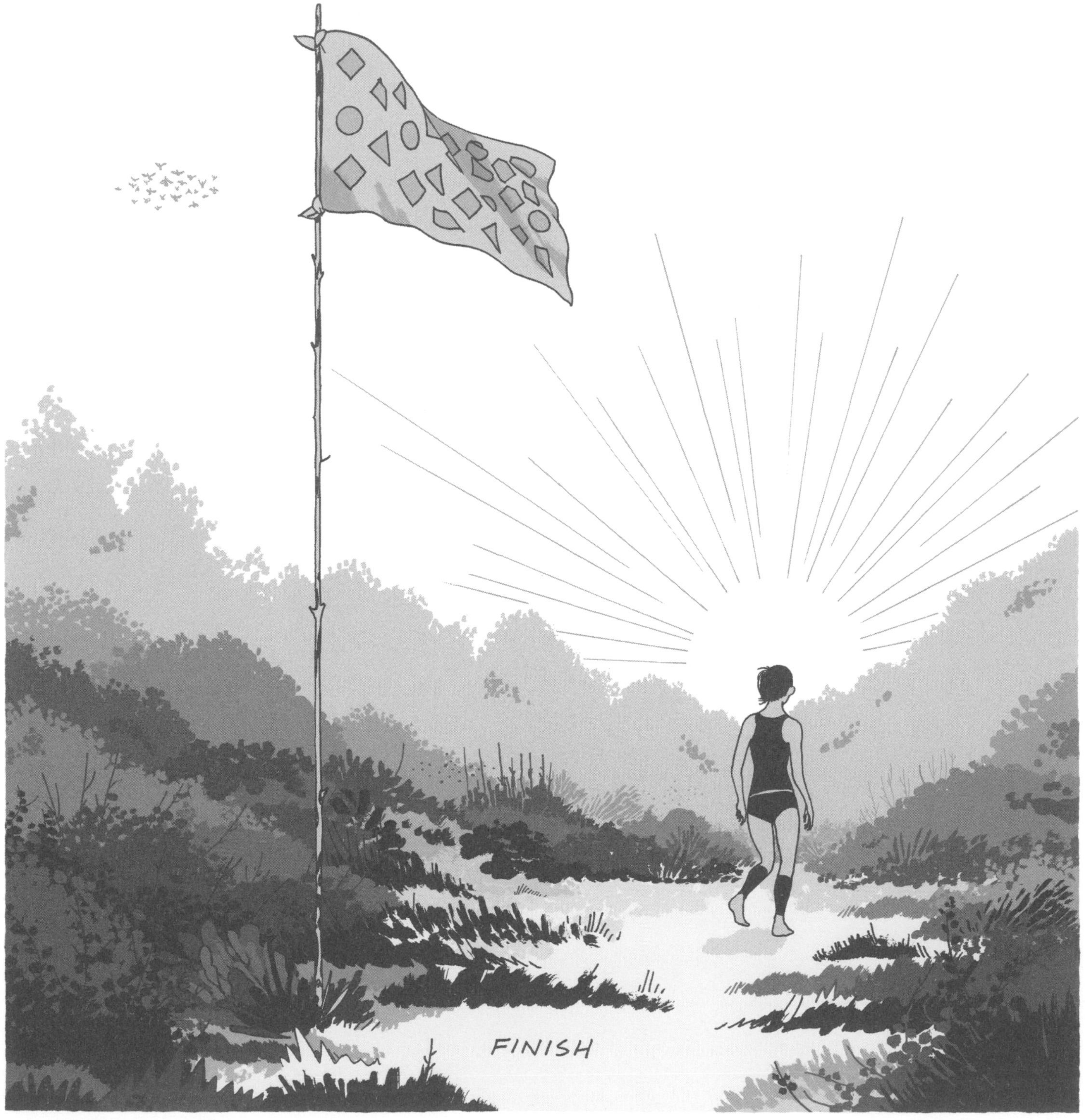
FINISH

ABOUT THE AUTHOR:

HENRY MCCAUSLAND: BORN 1981, SCORPIO.
ARTIST, ILLUSTRATOR & COMICS AUTHOR
LIVING AND WORKING IN LONDON, UK, EUROPE